DISORDERED PERSONALITIES
A PRIMER

RAPID PSYCHLER PRESS

David J. Robinson BA, MD, FRCPC

Diplomate of the American Board
of Psychiatry and Neurology

Lecturer, Department of Psychiatry
University of Western Ontario, London, Ontario, Canada

Staff Psychiatrist, Department of Psychiatry
St. Joseph's Hospital, London, Ontario, Canada

RAPID PSYCHLER PRESS
P.O. BOX 8117
LONDON, ONTARIO, CANADA
N6G 2B0

fax 519-657-9753
email psychler@odyssey.on.ca
website http://www.odyssey.on.ca/psychler

ISBN 0-9680324-0-0
PRINTED IN CANADA
COPYRIGHT, 1996, RAPID PSYCHLER PRESS
FIRST EDITION

DEDICATED TO MY TEACHERS
JOHN WIENER MD, FRCPC
RIMA STYRA MD, FRCPC
GERARD LIPPERT MD, FRCPC
ALLAN TENNEN MD, FRCPC
HAROLD MERSKEY DM, FRCPC
PAUL STEINBERG MD, FRCPC
JOHN MOUNT MD, FRCPC

AND TO MY COLLABORATOR
BRIAN CHAPMAN

Foreword

A comedian once said that he didn't want people to just laugh and listen, or even laugh and learn, but rather laugh and *change*. He had a point. As I look back over my academic career, the good teachers I had all shared two qualities: a comprehensive, organized knowledge of the subject and a sense of humor. My goal was to include both of these qualities in writing this book.

In recent years there has been an explosion of medical information. What has not progressed as far, are ways to manage this information. Simply keeping up with new developments could constitute a full-time job, leaving little time for treating patients. This book was written to provide a comprehensive primer on personality disorders that is both readable, and fun to read. I intended DISORDERED PERSONALITIES to help remedy the overload of information.

I heard a clinician once say, "the last time I saw a textbook case was in a textbook." He, too, had a point. This book bridges the gap between theory and practice. In order to accomplish this, I added a considerable amount of humor to create vivid mental images. Each personality was given a caricature, name, occupation, pet and favorite song. Fictitious behavior at the therapist's office was also provided to add a real-world quality to the diagnostic criteria.

These sections are in no way based on actual patients, nor are they meant to make fun of psychiatric problems. Quite the opposite. By including humor in this book, I hope to increase the reader's interest, understanding and facility in dealing with difficult personalities.

The phenomena described in this book do not just occur on psychiatry wards. Similarly, people with these diagnoses do not just appear in psychiatrist's offices. Professionals from any branch of medicine, nursing, psychology, social work or occupational therapy involving contact with patients will benefit from having an approach to dealing with different personality styles. Patients in all settings have transference reactions, regress in certain situations, resist treatment and use ego defenses.

Still, not everyone with a personality disorder is a "patient." We all live and work with strong personalities and difficult people. The principles in this book can help foster an understanding of such people. From understanding comes tolerance and empathy.

Humor and medicine have a long tradition. Freud, himself, had a good sense of humor and wrote a book about jokes. Laughter benefits both our physiology and psyche. The healing powers of humor are becoming increasingly integrated with other forms of treatment. A growing literature describes and promotes the use of humor in situations ranging from terminal illness to psychotherapy. Humor is a crucial factor in helping people deal with stress in daily situations. With all this going for it, why not include humor in education as well?

I am certain there will be detractors to the approach I have taken in this book. Every attempt to do something different draws criticism. Although sophomoric humor was used in places, it was done with the goal of making a more memorable and effective presentation. While there may be objection to the means, I do not believe fault can be found with the goal, or the degree to which this goal is achieved.

If someone has a more effective way of enhancing learning than by including humor, please contact me.

I hope this book provides you with clinically relevant material and a few laughs. Feedback, comments, stray thoughts, suggestions for improvements and future projects are very welcome.

Dave Robinson

London, Ontario, Canada
March, 1996

IF YOU ENJOY THIS BOOK AND ARE INTERESTED IN OTHER RAPID PSYCHLER PUBLICATIONS AND MERCHANDISE, PLEASE SEE P. 286.

NOTE:
Throughout this book, I have used the term "patient" to refer to people who are suffering and seek help. To me, the terms "consumer" or "consumer-survivor" reflect an unfortunate trend that is pejorative towards mental health care; labeling as if it were a trade or business, instead of a profession. These terms are also ambiguous, as it is not clear what is being "consumed" or "survived."

DISORDERED PERSONALITIES

ACKNOWLEDGMENTS

First and foremost, I am deeply indebted to **Brian Chapman** for guiding the format of this book, and providing the excellent artwork. Brian has an incredible knack for turning my partly-baked ideas into drawings that include both the essentials and his renowned sense of humor. This project could not have been completed without his advice, patience, unfailing support and skill.

Sherry Ripa from LITHOSOURCE coordinated the printing of this book. Her contagious enthusiasm and expert opinion added to every aspect of this publication. I look forward to a long association with her.

A big thank you to **Dr. John Mount** and **Dr. Paul Steinberg** for reviewing this book and offering their valuable feedback.

Dr. John Craven gave me some very needed encouragement, publishing tips and advice on administrative matters.

I am especially indebted to **Mary-Ann McLean** for her patience, understanding and support throughout the writing of the book.

Nikkie Cordy and **Tom Norry** enthusiastically reviewed early versions of each chapter and suggested improvements.

I would like to thank my editor **Sandy Oswick** for his diligence, vigilance and expertise.

I am also indebted to the following individuals for their help:

Dr. Alan Schmetzer, Indiana University School of Medicine
Dr. Quentin Rae-Grant, University of Western Ontario
Dr. Sandra Northcott, University of Western Ontario
Dr. Emmanuel Persad, University of Western Ontario
Dr. Alistair Munro, Halifax, Nova Scotia
Dr. Harold Merskey, University of Western Ontario

Assistance with the media examples was provided by **Noel Gallagher** of the LONDON FREE PRESS and **Dean Avola** (thanks bro').

I also want to thank the Rapid Psychler Press staff: **Nicole Vanderkerff, Mary-Ann McLean, Monty, Lil** and **Dr. Donna Robinson**. **Brad Groshok** and **Susan McFarland** from ODYSSEY NETWORK INC. for providing computer assistance and maintaining the website.

Finally, a thank you to the many medical students and psychiatry residents from the University of Western Ontario who shared their views and and suggested improvements for this book.

Outline of this book

The introductory chapters cover essential diagnostic and theoretical topics required for an understanding of the material in later chapters.

Introduction: Diagnostic Principles
Why Study Personality Disorders ?

What is a Personality?

What is a Personality Disorder?

How Do I Diagnose a Personality Disorder?
History of the DSM classification system
General Diagnostic Criteria for a Personality Disorder
An Integrated Classification System
Diagnostic Tidbits
Personality Change Due to A General Medical Condition
What is the ICD-10?

How can Psychological Testing Help Make a Diagnosis?
Objective Tests
Projective Tests

Introduction: Theoretical Principles
Overview
Temperament, Life Cycle Theories

What is Ego Psychology?
Ego Defenses in Personality Disorders

What's Happened Since Freud?
What is Attachment Theory?
Causation of Psychological Symptoms
What is Object Relations Theory?

Basic Psychodynamic Principles
Transference, Countertransference, Resistance

What is Cognitive Therapy?
Cognitive Techniques

What is Group Therapy?

In 1992, I was completing my psychiatry residency and wading through the information required for my exams. To help sort through this maze of material, I created a list of everyday criteria with which to recognize personality disorders. This was published as an article in the JOURNAL OF POLYMORPHOUS PERVERSITY*. Each chapter begins with an expanded version of this original article.

The personality disorder chapters contain the following sections:

TITLE PAGE AND BIOGRAPHICAL INFORMATION
CARICATURE - scene from therapist's office; the object on the table and the picture behind the patient change to reflect the personality discussed in the chapter

BIOGRAPHICAL INFORMATION - Name, Occupation, Appearance, Relationship with Animals, Favourite Song

AT THE THERAPIST'S OFFICE - Before Session, Waiting Room Reading, During Session, Fantasies Involve . . ., Relationship with Therapist, Behavior During Session, Takes to Therapy. . .

DIAGNOSTIC SHORTHAND - symbolic representation

MNEMONIC - summarizes the essentials of the diagnostic criteria

INTRODUCTION
A synopsis including names of important figures and information on the historical development of the disorder

MEDIA EXAMPLES
Many bushels of popcorn were consumed to find popular media characters portraying examples of each disorder

INTERVIEW CONSIDERATIONS
An outline of typical interview situations is given

PRESUMED ETIOLOGY
BIOLOGICAL - describes known or suspected biological links
PSYCHOSOCIAL - the presumed influences of parental, societal and individual factors are discussed

EPIDEMIOLOGY
Estimated prevalence are listed; if present, sex differences are also given

* Reprinted from the *Journal of Polymorphous Perversity*, Volume 10 (1), p. 9-13
© 1993, Wry-Bred Press. Used with permission.

EGO DEFENSES
Characteristic ego defense mechanisms are outlined

DIAGNOSTIC CRITERIA
Reprinted with permission from the DSM-IV

DIFFERENTIAL DIAGNOSIS
Other diagnostic possibilities are listed, as well as key features to help distinguish personality disorders from other conditions

OTHER DIAGNOSTIC CONSIDERATIONS
Additional information is included in certain chapters

MENTAL STATUS EXAMINATION
Typical mental status findings are given for: APPEARANCE, BEHAVIOR, COOPERATION, CONTENT OF THOUGHT, THOUGHT FORM, PERCEPTION, INSIGHT & JUDGMENT and SUICIDE/HOMICIDE

PSYCHODYNAMIC ASPECTS
An understanding of the psychodynamic principles underlying personality disorders is provided to give a conceptual framework applicable to all types of treatment

WHAT HAPPENS IN PSYCHODYNAMIC THERAPY?
A summary of psychodynamic-oriented psychotherapy principles is provided

TRANSFERENCE AND COUNTERTRANSFERENCE REACTIONS
Summarizes expectable patient and therapist reactions

SUMMARY OF THERAPEUTIC TECHNIQUES
Condenses the above information, along with other guidelines that do not require elaboration

PHARMACOTHERAPY
The rational use of medications is discussed

GROUP THERAPY
Various parameters of group of therapy are presented

COGNITIVE THERAPY
As an adjunct to psychodynamic considerations, cognitive and behavioral strategies are summarized

COURSE
Where known, prognostic features are discussed

INTRODUCTION:
DIAGNOSTIC PRINCIPLES

Why Study Personality Disorders ?

For many involved in the mental health profession, "personality disorder" is a term that lacks understanding, respectability or validity. As TYRER (1993) wrote, this term has historically, "been imbued with the negative qualities of *degeneracy, untreatability* and *conflict.*"

Personality disorders lack the consensus of the "major" psychiatric disorders. Difficult patients are often given the pejorative label of a "personality disorder," and once formulated as such, may well receive less support, empathy and tolerance from caregivers. Frequently, this decreases the initiative to try and help these patients. Their problems are seen only as their personal responsibility, given that no "formal" psychiatric condition exists.

Very often, reading the PERSONALITY DISORDER section brings about the immediate identification of several friends and relatives who fit the diagnostic criteria. A short time later, readers themselves fear that they suffer from one, or all of these disorders, usually simultaneously. This becomes the psychiatric equivalent of "medical student's disease," where one feels afflicted with the very condition being studied.

However, the clinical application of these concepts does not readily follow this initial sense of familiarity. Often, despite several assessments or lengthy hospital admissions, there is a lack of understanding of patients' personality styles. In case presentations or discharge summaries, the personality assessment is left out, fleetingly mentioned, or recorded as "no personality." The impact of a personality disorder contributing as a predisposing, precipitating or perpetuating factor is considered even less still.

This omission is unfortunate because it is a disservice to patients. Whereas many psychiatric conditions are episodic, a personality disorder is present throughout the majority, if not all, of patients' lives. Perception, thinking, feeling and behavior are affected just as in the major clinical disorders.

There are significant advantages to having a working knowledge of the diagnosis and management of personality disorders:

• planning treatment interventions (e.g. psychotherapies, medication)
• understanding the effect on the course of major clinical condition
• developing and maintaining effective therapeutic relationships

What is a Personality ?

The word "personality" is used in different contexts. We hear gossip about "TV personalities," learn that someone we haven't met yet "has a nice personality," and may refer to our favorite beer as "full of personality." An operational definition for use of the term personality is useful to have for work in clinical settings.

One definition of personality is, **a relatively stable and enduring set of characteristic behavioral and emotional traits.** Over time, a person will interact with others in a reasonably predictable way. However, as the adage warns "don't judge a book by its cover," circumstances can alter behavior, so that someone does something "out of character." For example, extreme circumstances like divorce or New Year's Eve can bring out behavior that is atypical for that person.

A Glass of Personality

Personality changes with experience, maturity, and external demands in a way that promotes **adaptation** to the environment. It is affected by genetic (internal), psychosocial and interpersonal (external) factors. While a discussion on the theory of personality is beyond the scope of this book, enumerating some of the etiologic factors is helpful in understanding personality disorders.

The majority of the behavior in non-humans is thought to be genetically programmed. The process of natural selection influences the survival of a species so that those having a better "fit" with their environment are more likely to endure. Our distant ancestors survived because of behaviors that sustained life and promoted reproduction. Predation, competition, attracting a mate or helper, banding together as a group, or avoiding overcrowding were all important adaptive strategies. One branch of our central nervous system is geared to a *flight, fright* or *fight* response, because these responses are essential for survival.

A degree of social judgment is inherent in deciding what determines a personality disorder. In different cultures, what is considered normal can vary widely, necessitating that behavior be understood in the context of a person's particular social milieu.

What is a Personality Disorder?

The preceding section on personality development sets the framework for understanding disorders of personalities. When genetic endowment is too loaded, early nurturing too deficient, or life experiences so severe (or interactions involving these variables) that emotional development suffers, a personality disorder results.

A **personality disorder** is a variant, or an extreme set of characteristics that goes beyond the range found in most people. The American Psychiatric Association defines a personality disorder as, **"An enduring pattern of inner experience and behavior that deviates markedly from the expectations of the individual's culture, is pervasive and inflexible, has an onset in adolescence or early adulthood, is stable over time, and leads to distress or impairment."**
SOURCE: DSM-IV, 1994, P. 629

While many other definitions exist, points consistently emphasized in defining a personality disorder are that it:

- is deeply ingrained and has an inflexible nature
- is maladaptive, especially in interpersonal contexts
- is relatively stable over time
- significantly impairs the ability of the person to function
- distresses those close to the person

Personality disorders are enduring patterns of perceiving, thinking, feeling and behaving that remain consistent through a majority of social situations. An essential point is that personality disorders are **egosyntonic**, meaning that behaviors do not distress the person directly. A fuller understanding can only be reached after taking into account how those close to the person are affected.

The criteria with which personality disorders are diagnosed are very much within the realm of common human experiences. Each one of us at times has been: hypervigilant, destructive, suspicious, shy, bossy, vain, striving for perfection, dramatic, afraid to be alone, fearful of rejection, purposely late for something, too independent, too needy, critical of others, resentful of authority, averse to criticism, bored, seductive, or experiencing rapidly shifting emotional states. None of these behaviors alone warrants the diagnosis of a personality disorder. Instead, clusters of behaviors existing over a lengthy time period and interfering with a person's level of functioning make up the criteria.

By basing diagnostic criteria on these common qualities and behaviors, the following important questions arise:

- How many criteria are needed to make a diagnosis?
- How long do they need to be present to make a diagnosis?
- What degree of severity is required to qualify for a diagnostic criterion?

Again, **adaptation** is a key point. Society has changed more rapidly than our innate adaptive strategies. A personality disorder can be considered as being an extreme degree of behavior that in a lesser way might benefit that person. Consider evolutionary-derived patterns that are either amplified or are a poor fit for our highly individualized and technological society:

BEHAVIOR	PERSONALITY DISORDER IF TAKEN TO AN EXTREME
Suspiciousness, vigilance about one's environment	Paranoid
Interest in one's self, "looking out for number one"	Narcissistic
Need to be attached to others	Dependent
Meticulous attention to detail, high level of productivity	Obsessive-Compulsive
Reluctance in social situations/ strong desire for solitude	Avoidant/Schizoid
Need to get others' attention or help	Histrionic
Taking advantage of available "opportunities," bending rules	Antisocial
Strong desire for individuality of style and non-conformity of thought	Schizotypal

At the time of writing, an evolutionary or social advantage to the Borderline Personality Disorder was less evident.

How Do I Diagnose a Personality Disorder ?

In 1952, the American Psychiatric Association (APA) published the first edition of the Diagnostic and Statistical Manual of Mental Disorders (DSM-I). There were five categories with a total of twenty-seven personality disorders. The diagnoses were made using a general clinical description, often influenced by psychoanalytic concepts.

The DSM-II was introduced in 1968. In this edition the number of personality disorders was reduced to twelve, though many from the DSM-I were shifted to other categories. Again, the diagnosis was based on a descriptive paragraph. Because of this, the DSM-II was deemed by many to lack validity, reliability and clinical effectiveness. Introduced at a time of sweeping cultural and social changes, its shortcomings necessitated significant changes in the next edition.

Introduced in 1980, the DSM-III listed specific diagnostic criteria for its fourteen personality disorders. These were first established from the psychiatric research done by Feighner, Robbins and Guze and later expanded by Spitzer. Five major changes were introduced:

• Descriptive features were based on presenting symptoms that were atheoretical, and not based on presumed etiologic factors
• Information beyond the criteria were given, such as demographic, etiologic and prognostic variables
• Particular criteria were used (symptoms, duration, exclusion criteria)
• In response to criticism about the potential misuse of labeling patients with a psychiatric diagnosis, the APA stressed using clinical judgment in addition to meeting criteria
• The concept of a multi-axial diagnosis was introduced, which fostered a multi-faceted approach towards understanding patients
Source: Adapted from Turkat, 1990

The DSM-III-R (R for revised) was introduced in 1987. Despite the many advances in DSM-III, there were problems with the validity, accuracy and clarity of some of the criteria. The personality disorders were put into phenomenologically similar clusters.

Cluster A - Odd or Eccentric, "Mad" - Paranoid, Schizoid, Schizotypal
Cluster B - Dramatic, Emotional or Erratic, "Bad" -
Antisocial, Borderline, Histrionic, Narcissistic
Cluster C - Anxious or Fearful, "Sad" -
Avoidant, Dependent, Obsessive-Compulsive, Passive-Aggressive

The DSM-III-R contained eleven personality disorders; three from DSM-III were amalgamated into a new category called *Personality Disorder Not Otherwise Specified.*

In 1994 the DSM-IV was released. It retains the multi-axial diagnostic approach and personality clusters listed above. The number of personality disorders was reduced to ten. The Passive-Aggressive Personality Disorder was removed and placed in Appendix B, where it has been renamed the **Negativistic Personality Disorder**.

GENERAL DIAGNOSTIC CRITERIA FOR A PERSONALITY DISORDER

A. An enduring pattern of inner experience and behavior that deviates markedly from the expectations of the individual's culture. This pattern is manifested in two (or more) of the following areas:

(1) cognition (i.e., ways of perceiving and interpreting self, other people, and events)
(2) affectivity (i.e., the range, intensity, lability, and appropriateness of emotional response)
(3) interpersonal functioning
(4) impulse control

B. The enduring pattern is inflexible and pervasive across a broad range of personal and social situations.

C. The enduring pattern leads to clinically significant distress or impairment in social, occupational, or other important areas of functioning.

D. The pattern is stable and of long duration and its onset can be traced back at least to adolescence or early adulthood.

E. The enduring pattern is not better accounted for as a manifestation or consequence of another mental disorder.

F. The enduring pattern is not due to the direct physiological effects of a substance (e.g. a drug of abuse, a medication) or a general medical condition (e.g. head trauma).
REPRINTED WITH PERMISSION FROM THE DSM-IV.
COPYRIGHT, AMERICAN PSYCHIATRIC ASSOCIATION, 1994

An Integrated Classification System

Clusters A, B and C listed in the previous section are based on descriptive, or phenomenological similarities. The integration of etiologic, therapeutic, prognostic and conceptual variables provides a method of classification based on **spectrum**, **self** and **trait** features.

Spectrum Disorders share a biological link to major disorders with a *spectrum* of expression; these disorders tend to have poor prognoses

Self Disorders cause severe dysfunction; often see turbulent personal backgrounds, a fragile sense of identity and an unstable course

Trait Disorders exist on a dimension with normality; may be subjectively distressed in social, occupational and cultural contexts

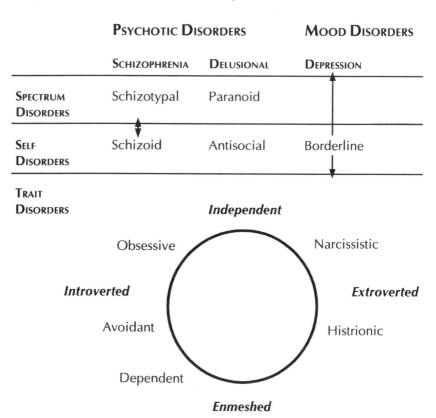

	PSYCHOTIC DISORDERS		MOOD DISORDERS
	SCHIZOPHRENIA	DELUSIONAL	DEPRESSION
SPECTRUM DISORDERS	Schizotypal	Paranoid	
SELF DISORDERS	Schizoid	Antisocial	Borderline
TRAIT DISORDERS		*Independent*	

Obsessive   Narcissistic

Introverted   *Extroverted*

Avoidant   Histrionic

Dependent

Enmeshed

Diagnostic Tidbits

The DSM uses five **axes** to make a complete diagnostic summary:

- **Axis I**: Major Psychiatric Syndromes or Clinical Disorders
- **Axis II**: Personality Disorders and Mental Retardation
- **Axis III**: General Medical Conditions
- **Axis IV**: Psychosocial and Environmental Problems
- **Axis V**: Global Assessment of Functioning (GAF Score from 0-100)

The DSM also uses Axis II to record prominent personality traits and defense mechanisms. For example, if a patient meets most, but not all of the criteria for a Paranoid Personality Disorder, this is recorded as "Paranoid Personality Features." If a personality disorder or strong features are not evident but the patient uses a defense mechanism to a maladaptive level, this is recorded as "Frequent use of projection." Another official coding for Axis II can be "No Diagnosis" or "Diagnosis Deferred."

The Paranoid, Schizoid, Schizotypal and Antisocial personality disorders are not diagnosed if they are coincident with certain Axis I conditions. Exclusion criteria are not listed for the other personality disorders. The Antisocial Personality Disorder is the only diagnosis with an age requirement and a prerequisite diagnosis. Patients must be at least age eighteen, and have met the criteria for a diagnosis of Conduct Disorder before age fifteen.

The personality disorders are not diagnosed exclusive of one another, allowing concurrent diagnoses to be made. In practice, there is usually one that is more prominent and this is recorded as the Axis II diagnosis with the others listed as "features." If two or more are equally apparent, they can all be recorded.

The residual personality diagnosis in the DSM-IV is called **Personality Disorder Not Otherwise Specified (NOS)**. This is used when the patient does not meet the complete criteria for a single personality disorder, but exhibits specific diagnostic features of other personality disorders. Additionally, if the criteria are met for the Depressive or Passive-Aggressive (Negativistic) personality disorders (considered research diagnoses in DSM-IV), the diagnosis of Personality Disorder NOS is used.

The diagnostic criteria for the personality disorders in DSM-IV are listed in decreasing order of their significance (where this is known).

PERSONALITY CHANGE DUE TO A MEDICAL CONDITION

This diagnosis is made when a personality disturbance is due to the direct physiological effects of a medical condition. This personality change must be persistent, and a clear change from previous patterns.

Some of the common manifestations are: aggression, lability, apathy, suspiciousness, poor judgment, or impulsivity.

When this is given as the diagnosis, it is coded on Axis I as: "Personality Change Due to . . . (Condition)." The medical condition is specified on Axis III.

DIAGNOSTIC CRITERIA

A. A persistent personality disturbance that represents a change from the individual's previous characteristic personality pattern.
(In children, the disturbance involves a marked deviation from normal development or a significant change in the child's usual behavior patterns lasting at least 1 year.)

B. There is evidence from the history, physical examination, or laboratory findings that the disturbance is the direct physiological consequence of a general medical condition.

C. The disturbance is not better accounted for by another mental disorder (including Mental Disorders Due to a General Medical Condition).

D. The disturbance does not occur exclusively during the course of a delirium and does not meet criteria for a dementia.

E. The disturbance causes clinically significant distress or impairment in social, occupational, or other important areas of functioning.

Specify Type:
Labile, Disinhibited, Aggressive, Apathetic, Paranoid,
Other, Combined, Unspecified
REPRINTED WITH PERMISSION FROM THE DSM-IV.
COPYRIGHT, AMERICAN PSYCHIATRIC ASSOCIATION, 1994

WHAT IS THE ICD-10?

The ICD-10 is the **International Classification of Diseases, Tenth Edition**, published by the World Health Organization in 1992. It is a diagnostic classification system used outside of North America (mainly in Europe). Preparation of the DSM-IV was coordinated with Chapter V of the ICD-10 called "Mental and Behavioral Disorders."

DSM-IV coding and terminology are compatible with the ICD-10, which is planned to be introduced in the United States in the late 1990's. The ICD-10 has in common with the DSM-IV the following personality disorders: **Paranoid, Schizoid, Histrionic, Dependent** and **Avoidant** (Anxious). The **Antisocial Personality** is called **Dissocial** (Dyssocial), and the **Obsessive-Compulsive** is **Anankastic** (Anancastic).

There is a diagnostic category called "Emotionally Unstable Personality Disorders" - with a *Borderline Type* and an *Impulsive Type*. The latter has no clear DSM-IV analogue. Narcissistic and Schizotypal personality disorders also have no equivalent category (this may account for some cultural differences).

How can Psychological Testing Help Make a Diagnosis?

Psychological testing (**psychometric testing**) provides a method for personality assessment beyond the criteria in the DSM-IV or ICD-10. Testing yields valuable diagnostic information and can be used to monitor progress or prognosis. Most commonly used instruments have a standard protocol for administration and scoring. This helps ensure the critical issues of **reliability** (the test gives consistent results) and **validity** (the test measures what it is supposed to measure).

Inherent in the scoring is a concept of normality. Since the tables used in these tests were assembled empirically, relatively "normal" people had to provide the raw data. Different concepts of normality exist. The model used in statistics is the bell-shaped curve, where some measure of behavior is plotted numerically with deviation seen at the extreme ends. While this lends itself nicely to numerical interpretations, it is somewhat artificial, in that aspects of a personality or behavior are not always amenable to a scoring system.

Many definitions of normality exist; common themes among them are:

- strength of character
- ability to learn from experience
- ability to work
- ability to achieve insight
- absence of symptoms/conflict
- ability to experience pleasure without conflict
- flexibility/ability to adjust
- ability to laugh
- ability to love another
- degree of acculturation

Psychological tests for personality disorders fall into two main categories. **Objective tests** contain specific questions, generally with right or wrong answers that yield numerical results. **Projective tests** have an ambiguous content requiring the examinees to *project* something of themselves in order to give an answer, which is neither wrong nor right. Projected answers reveal the needs, conflicts and defenses of those taking the test. Interpretation of these results requires a theory of personality development.

OBJECTIVE TESTS

Minnesota Multiphase Personality Inventory - MMPI-II
This test consists of five hundred and sixty-seven statements about thoughts and feelings, to which the subject answers true or false. Answers are graded on ten scales, designed to separate normal controls from psychiatric patients.

MMPI-II Scales:

1 Hypochondriasis	**2** Depression
3 Hysteria	**4** Psychopathic Deviance
5 Masculinity-Femininity	**6** Paranoia
7 Psychasthenia (anxiety/obsessive-compulsive traits)	
8 Schizophrenia	**9** Hypomania
0 Social Introversion	

There are also scales that report the validity of the test:

L Lie Scale	**F** Faking Bad (Infrequency)
K Faking Good (Suppressor)	**?** Cannot Say Scale

Frequently, a personality assessment is given based on the scores from the two highest scales (twin peaks). Typical elevations for the DSM-IV personality disorders are as follows:

Cluster A	**Elevated Scales**
Paranoid	1, 6, K
Schizoid	0
Schizotypal	2, 7, 8

Cluster B	
Antisocial	4, 9
Borderline	3, 4, 7
Histrionic	2, 3
Narcissistic	high 4, low 0

Cluster C	
Avoidant	8, 0
Dependent	2, 3
Obsessive-Compulsive	7, 8

Additionally, the MMPI may give information about patients' clinical state at the time of testing:
· An elevated 8 scale in Borderlines may signify deterioration.
· Histrionic patients in crisis may have an elevated score on 2.
· Violent patients may have elevated scores on scales 4, 6, and 8.

Millon Clinical Multiaxial Inventory-II

This MCMI-II consists of one hundred and seventy-five true or false questions. The results are scored on scales that correspond with DSM-III-R personality disorders. This inventory also contains scales measuring validity.

Other Objective Tests

- California Personality Inventory
- State-Trait Anxiety Inventory
- Jackson Personality Inventory
- Eysenck Personality Inventory
- Beck Depression Inventory

PROJECTIVE TESTS

Rorschach Test

Hermann Rorschach was a Swiss psychiatrist who standardized a set of inkblots that stimulated free association in his patients. There are ten cards (five colored, five black and white), shown in a specific sequence.

Thematic Apperception Test

The TAT consists of thirty cards demonstrating ambiguous social situations, to which subjects "project" their views onto the scene. Four questions are asked per slide:

- Relationships between people
- Thoughts and feelings of those in the pictures
- Events leading up to the scene
- Outcome

Themes are then discerned from the answers given.

Other Projective Tests

- Sentence Completion Test
- Word Association
- Draw-A-Person

REFERENCES

American Psychiatric Association
DIAGNOSTIC AND STATISTICAL MANUAL OF MENTAL DISORDERS, FOURTH EDITION
American Psychiatric Press; Washington D.C., 1994

N. Andreason, D. Black
INTRODUCTORY TEXTBOOK OF PSYCHIATRY
American Psychiatric Press; Washington, D.C., 1991

M. Fauman
STUDY GUIDE TO DSM-IV
American Psychiatric Press; Washington, D.C., 1994

H. Kaplan, B. Sadock, Editors
COMPREHENSIVE TEXTBOOK OF PSYCHIATRY, SIXTH EDITION
Williams & Wilkins; Baltimore, Maryland, 1995

H. Kaplan, B. Sadock & J. Grebb, Editors
SYNOPSIS OF PSYCHIATRY, SEVENTH EDITION
Williams & Wilkins; Baltimore, Maryland, 1994

J. Morrison
DSM-IV MADE EASY: THE CLINICIAN'S GUIDE TO DIAGNOSIS
The Guildford Press; New York, 1995

I. Turkat
THE PERSONALITY DISORDERS: A PSYCHOLOGICAL APPROACH TO
CLINICAL MANAGEMENT
Pergamon Press; Elmsford, New York, 1990

P. Tyrer and G. Stein, Editors
PERSONALITY DISORDERS REVIEWED
Gaskell/The Royal College of Psychiatrists; London, England, 1993

Parking Lot of the Personality Disordered

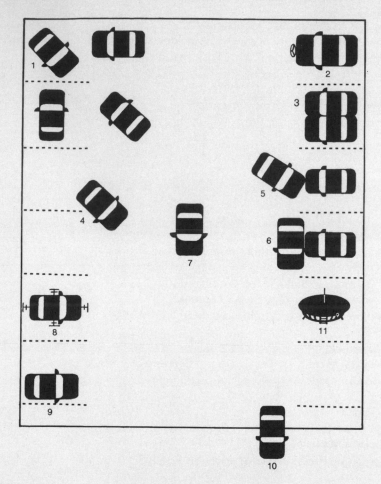

Key:

1. Paranoid — Cornered again!!
2. Narcissist — Largest car; prominent hood ornament
3. Dependent — Needs other cars to feel sheltered
4. Passive-Aggressive — Angles car to take two spaces
5. Borderline — Rams into car of ex-lover
6. Antisocial — Obstructs other cars
7. Histrionic — Parks in center of lot for dramatic effect
8. Obsessive — Perfect alignment in parking spot
9. Avoidant — Hides in corner
10. Schizoid — Can't tolerate closeness to other cars
11. Schizotypal — Intergalactic parking

INTRODUCTION:
THEORETICAL PRINCIPLES

The work of CHESS AND THOMAS has given strong evidence of a genetic contribution to personality, called **temperament**. They identified nine behaviors in the autonomic reactivity of infants:

- approach/withdrawal
- activity level
- adaptability
- threshold of responsiveness
- quality of mood
- rhythmicity
- intensity of reaction
- attention span or persistence
- distractibility

The ancient Greeks considered personality to be a mix of four temperaments: choleric (irritable), melancholic (depressive), phlegmatic (apathetic), and sanguine (hypomanic).

Recent advances in biological and neuropsychiatry have renewed interest in genetic and neonatal factors. Bio-genetic factors that can provide a more descriptive means of classification are being sought. This is fueled by the growing understanding of the genetics of many major psychiatric conditions, and some of the personality disorders.

Innate characteristics or tendencies can be reinforced or extinguished by the pattern of involvement with caretakers early in life. Whatever the temperamental contributions, social and psychological influences make an impact from the moment of birth. Early disruptive experiences with caretakers are strong influences for later personality disorders, though curiously not everyone exposed to such situations develops a disorder. Genes and experiences interact to shape personality, just as with other features like athletic or musical ability. Overall, genetic endowment sets a range of possibilities and, within that range, developmental experiences influence the outcome.

Personality development is theoretically based. The variables are too complex to establish an exact science. Many classification systems offer explanations for various stages of the personality development. Among the most famous are those of: **Margaret Mahler, Jean Piaget, Erik Erikson, John Bowlby** and **Sigmund Freud**.

The **Life Cycle** represents stages from birth to death. There are three assumptions about the progress through these stages.
1. Stages are completed in their given sequence.
2. Development proceeds only when an earlier stage is completed.
3. Each stage has a dominant feature, and various personality difficulties can be caused by arrested development at this stage, also know as **fixation**.

LIFE CYCLE STAGES IN SUMMARIZED FORM

MARGARET MAHLER
Birth to 4 weeks: Normal Autistic Phase
Feature: Main task is to achieve equilibrium with the environment

4 weeks to 4 months: Normal Symbiotic Phase
Feature: Social smile

4 to 10 months: Separation Individuation - Phase I, Differentiation
Feature: Stranger anxiety (development of recognition memory)

10 to 16 months: Separation Individuation - Phase II, Practicing
Feature: Separation anxiety

16 to 24 months: Separation Individuation - Phase III, Rapprochement
Feature: The child wants to be soothed by mother, but may be unable to accept her help

24 to 36 months: Separation Individuation - Phase IV, Consolidation and Object Constancy
Feature: Able to cope with mother's absence; finds substitutes for her

JEAN PIAGET
Birth to 2 years: Sensorimotor Phase
Schemata (pattern of behavior) dictates actions; environment is mastered through **assimilation** (taking in new experiences through one's own knowledge system) and **accommodation** (adjusting one's system of knowledge to the demands of the environment); **object permanence** is achieved by two years

2 to 7 years: Preoperational Phase
Feature: Uses symbolic functions; egocentrism; animism; illogical/magical thinking

7 to 11 years: Concrete Operations
Feature: Logical thinking emerges; able to see things from another's point of view; laws of conservation understood

11 years to Adolescence: Formal (Abstract) Phase
Feature: Hypothetico-deductive reasoning used; able to understand philosophical nature of ideas; more flexible thinking becomes possible

Erik Erikson
Birth to 1 year: Basic Trust versus Basic Mistrust
Feature: Consistency of experience provided by caretaker is crucial

1 to 3 years: Autonomy versus Shame and Doubt
Feature: Learns to walk, feed self and talk during this phase; firmness of caretaker, boundaries and guidelines necessary before autonomy

3 to 5 years: Initiative versus Guilt
Feature: Mimics adult world; Oedipal struggles occur at this age, with resolution via social identification

6 to 11 years: Industry versus Inferiority
Feature: Busy with building, creating, accomplishing; abilities in relation to peers increase in importance

11 years to Adolescence: Identity versus Role Diffusion
Feature: Preoccupied with hero worship, appearance; group identity develops

Adult Tasks: Intimacy versus Isolation
                 Generativity versus Stagnation
                 Integrity versus Despair

John Bowlby
Birth to 12 weeks: Phase I
• Olfactory and auditory stimuli used to discriminate people
• Initiates innate attachment behavior to any person - smiling, babbling, reaching and grasping; these behaviors increase the time spent closer to a caregiver
• Tracks movement with eyes; stops crying in the presence of a person

12 weeks to 6 months: Phase II
Feature: Phase I continues with increased intensity towards the primary attachment figure

6 months into Second Year: Phase III
Feature: Attachment to mother more solid, uses her as a base from which to explore; **stranger anxiety** towards others

2 years and beyond: Phase IV
Feature: Growing independence from mother; obtains sense of objects being persistent in time and space; observation of adult behavior

SIGMUND FREUD

Birth to 1 year: Oral Stage
· Main site of tension and gratification is the mouth, lips and tongue
· More aggressive with the presence of teeth after six months

1 to 3 years: Anal Stage
· Acquire voluntary sphincter control; anus and perineal become the major area of interest

3 years to 5 years: Phallic-Oedipal Stage
· Genital stimulation of interest; masturbation is common
· Intense preoccupation with castration anxiety
· In Freud's theory, penis envy was seen in girls at this stage
· **Oedipus Complex** (desire to have sex with and marry opposite sex parent and dispose of or destroy same sex parent)

5 to 11 years: Latency Stage
· **Superego** forms, the last part of the psychic apparatus (see p. 36)
· The **id** is present at birth and the **ego** develops as the child becomes aware of the external world
· Sexual drives channeled into socially acceptable avenues
· Quiescence of sexual drive as the oedipal complex is resolved

11 to 13 years: Genital Stage
· Final psychosexual stage
· Biologically capable of orgasm and able to experience true intimacy

FREUD EXPRESSES HIS OPINION ON ERIKSON'S STAGES BEING LISTED FIRST.

What is Ego Psychology?

In the early 1900's, Freud published the *Interpretation of Dreams* and developed his **topographical theory** which divided the mind into the Conscious, Unconscious and Preconscious. The unconscious mind contained wishes seeking fulfillment that were closely related to instinctual drives, specifically sexual and aggressive urges. A type of thinking called **primary process** was associated with the unconscious. Primary process is not bound by logic, permits contradictions to coexist, contains no negatives, has no regard for time, and is highly symbolized. This is seen dreams, psychosis and children's thinking.

The preconscious was an agency of the mind that developed over time and was involved in the censorship of wishes and desires. It facilitated bi-directional access between the conscious and unconscious. The preconscious and conscious mind use **secondary process** thinking. This is logical and deals with the demands of external reality. Secondary process is the goal-directed day-to-day type of thinking that adults use.

Over time, Freud encountered **resistance** to his therapeutic interventions. He observed that patients defended themselves against the recollection of painful memories. In the topographical model, the preconscious was accessible to consciousness. Clearly, there was an unconscious aspect of the mind responsible for repressing memories. Freud incorporated his findings into his structural theory, introduced with the publication of *The Ego and the Id* in 1923. This consisted of a *tripartite* structure containing the **Id**, **Ego** and **Superego**.

Present from birth, the **id** is completely unconscious and seeks gratification of instinctual (mainly sexual and aggressive) drives. The **superego** forms from an identification with the same sex parent at the resolution of the **Oedipal Conflict**. It suppresses instinctual aims, serves as the moral conscience in dictating what *should not* be done, and, as the ego ideal, dictates what *should* be done. The superego is largely unconscious, but has a conscious element.

The **ego** is the mediator between two groups: the id and superego; and the person and reality. The ego has both conscious and unconscious elements. The following are considered the conscious roles of the ego:

- Perception (sense of reality)
- Reality Testing (adaptation to reality)
- Motor control
- Intuition
- Memory
- Affect
- Thinking (the ego uses secondary process) and Learning
- Control of instinctual drives (delay of immediate gratification)
- Synthetic functions (assimilation, creation, coordination)
- Language and Comprehension

The fundamental concept in Ego Psychology is one of *conflict* amongst these three agencies. The **id, ego** and **superego** battle for expression and discharge of sexual and aggressive drives. This conflict produces anxiety, specifically called **signal anxiety**. This anxiety alerts the ego that a **defense mechanism** is required, which is an unconscious role of the ego. The events can be conceptualized as follows:

The id seeks expression of an impulse
↓
The superego prohibits the impulse from being expressed
↓
This conflict produces signal anxiety
↓
An ego defense is unconsciously recruited to decrease the anxiety
↓
A character trait or neurotic symptom is formed

The consequence of an ego defense can be thought of as a compromise which allows expression of the impulse in a disguised form. Such *compromise formations* can be part of adaptive mental functioning but, when pathological, are considered neurotic symptoms. Everyone, normal or neurotic, employs a repertoire of defense mechanisms in varying degrees. All defenses protect the ego from the instinctual drives of the id and are unconscious processes.

Freud directed most of his attention to **repression**, which he considered the primary ego defense. Repression is defined as expelling and withholding an idea or feeling from conscious awareness. He thought other defenses were used only when repression failed to diminish the anxiety. Freud's daughter, Anna, expanded the total to nine in her 1936 book, *The Ego and the Mechanisms of Defense*. Since then, many more defense mechanisms have been identified. Akin to the theories of life cycle development, there is a progression in the use of ego defenses with maturity.

George Vaillant catalogued defenses into four categories: **Narcissistic**, **Immature**, **Neurotic** and **Mature**. Explanations of these defenses can be found in standard reference texts. The principal defenses found in personality disorders are discussed in the individual chapters.

NARCISSISTIC DEFENSES
Denial
Distortion
Primitive Idealization
Projection
Projective Identification
Splitting

NEUROTIC DEFENSES
Controlling
Displacement
Dissociation
Externalization
Inhibition
Intellectualization
Isolation
Rationalization
Reaction Formation
Repression
Sexualization
Undoing

MATURE DEFENSES
Altruism
Anticipation
Asceticism
Humor
Sublimation
Suppression

IMMATURE DEFENSES
Acting Out
Blocking
Hypochondriasis
Identification
Introjection
Passive-Aggressive Behavior
Projection
Regression
Schizoid Fantasy
Somatization

Ego Defenses in Personality Disorders

An understanding of defensive mechanisms is essential for recognizing and treating Axis II disorders. "Understanding the defenses of another person allows us to empathize rather than condemn, to understand rather than dismiss." (Vaillant, 1992)

Personalities become *disordered* by the maladaptive use of ego defenses, both in terms of *which* defenses are used, and the *extent* to which they are used. A more detailed account of these defenses is contained in the following individual chapters, where they are explained in the context of the personality disorder. The major defenses seen in use by the different personality disorders are as follows:

Antisocial	Acting Out, Controlling, Dissociation, Projective Identification
Avoidant	Inhibition, Isolation, Displacement, Projection
Borderline	Splitting, Distortion, Acting Out, Dissociation, Projective Identification
Dependent	Idealization, Reaction Formation, Projective Identification, Inhibition, Somatization, Regression
Histrionic	Sexualization, Repression, Denial, Regression, Dissociation
Narcissistic	Idealization, Devaluation, Projection, Identification
Obsessive-Compulsive	Intellectualization, Undoing, Displacement, Isolation of Affect, Rationalization
Paranoid	Projection, Projective Identification, Denial, Splitting, Reaction Formation
Schizoid	Schizoid Fantasy, Intellectualization, Introjection, Projection, Idealization Devaluation
Schizotypal	Projection, Denial, Distortion, Primitive Idealization, Schizoid Fantasy

What's Happened Since Freud ?

As discussed, Ego Psychology proposes that drives such as sexuality and aggression are innate, or primary, and relationships with people are secondary. In this view, the most important task is to discharge the tension generated by these drives. **Attachment Theory** and **Object Relations Theory** postulate that human drives are geared towards seeking relationships, and not discharging primal urges. In these theories, tension emerges in the context of frustrated relationships.

What is Attachment Theory?

The central concept in **Attachment Theory** is that close, positive attachments are a fundamental human need. In this theory, the quality of early attachments to caretakers largely determines the success of future relationships. Deprivation of early attachments, with the loss (or threatened loss) of positive attachments to caretakers, creates a vulnerability resulting in adverse psychological reactions. The outcome of these reactions can be a diverse array of emotional conditions, including personality disorders.

A diagrammatic representation of the CAUSATION OF PSYCHOLOGICAL SYMPTOMS according to attachment theory appears on the next page. If the innate need for close attachment is satisfied by **pleasurable interpersonal relationships** (**PIRs**), normal growth and development occur. If these needs are frustrated by **disturbances in interpersonal relationships** (**DIRs**), an inevitable drop in self-esteem is followed by various consequences. Withdrawing, or the **flight response**, involves:

• building interpersonal walls to diminish emotional pain
• developing work habits that compensate for other deficiencies, or finding a structured "institutional" workplace as a substitute
• regressing to the need for earlier pleasures; others aren't needed to obtain pleasure (often "oral" habits like smoking or drinking alcohol)

The **fight response** brings about aggression. Anger that is not used constructively may be used destructively against the self, causing the emergence of suicidal feelings. Anger and hostility directed at others bring about a potent sense of guilt. Accompanying this sense of guilt is its unconscious analog - the fear of, or need for punishment.

A third response is a creative effort, involving learning more adaptive ways to deal with DIRs.

CAUSATION OF PSYCHOLOGICAL SYMPTOMS

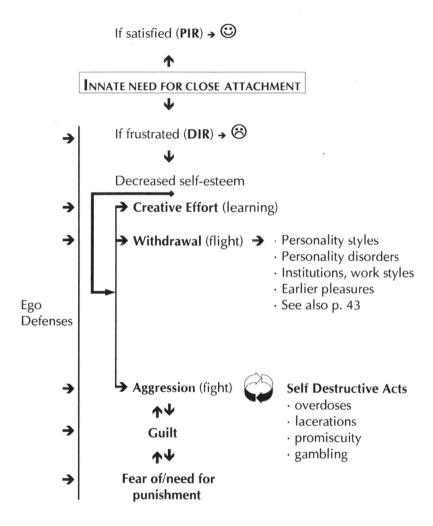

Disturbances in interpersonal relationships include:

• Threat of rejection or abandonment
• Loss of approval, acceptance, affection and attachment

SOURCE: J. MOUNT, 1995

What is Object Relations Theory?

The word *object* in this theory is an unfortunate substitute for *person*. Freud focused his attention on the subject who possessed the drives. Object, in this context, referred to the person at whom the drive was aimed. Object Relations developed from the contributions of a number of theorists, each with his or her own perspective. Some of the integral names associated with object relations are: **Melanie Klein**, **W.R.D. Fairbairn**, **Margaret Mahler**, **Otto Kernberg** and **Heinz Kohut**. Freud laid some of the groundwork for the development of this theory, and in many ways Object Relations is a refinement and reshaping of his ideas. There is no unified Object Relations theory. Each of the contributors listed above had a particular focus, though there is a common thread of agreement.

Central to an understanding of Object Relations is that *interpersonal contact* becomes *internalized* as a *representation* of that relationship. For example, in a developing child, it is not the mother who is internalized, but the whole relationship with her which is internalized. This process is called **introjection**. In Object Relations, an understanding of people and what motivates them stems from an awareness of how relationships are internalized and transformed into a sense of self or self-image in that person.

"Object Relations"

Object Relations theorizes that the most important relationship is with an early caregiver, most often the mother. The sense of alternating gratification and deprivation occupies so much of the life of an infant that this relationship becomes a template for subsequent relationships. Consider the following interactions in a hungry infant:

Positive experience of mother:
Attentive caregiver

Negative experience of mother:
Neglectful caregiver

Positive emotional experience:
Satiated with milk

Negative emotional experience:
Persistent hunger

Positive sense of self:
Loved and cared for

Negative sense of self:
Frustrated and angry

These two sets of interactions are **introjected** as the *good object* and *bad object*, partitioning or **splitting** the inner world of a child into good and bad experiences. It is important to note that what is introjected is the *experience* of the relationship, not necessarily the actual relationship. For example, a loving mother attending to other responsibilities might still be experienced as the bad object. Over time, this influences the sense of self, or one's sense of being. The notion of conflict in object relations is viewed as the clash between the internalized representations of feelings, self and objects.

From this point on, the various contributors focused on different applications of this theory - defense mechanisms (especially splitting and projective identification), individual disorders (Narcissistic and Borderline in particular) and the parameters affecting development.

An individual may find a substitute in order to compensate for deficient attachments. As a means of understanding substitution as symptom, STEINBERG (1995) has divided activities into three groups:

Direct Oral or Genital Somatic Satisfaction
· drug abuse; over indulgence in sex, food or alcohol

Narcissistic Satisfactions
· acquisition of fame/notoriety, money or power

Investment in an Institution
· excessive devotion to work, a social cause, a group, or recreational activity; close attachments to animals, plants or inanimate objects

Deficient attachment early in life influences one's style of relating as an adult. Early relationships are internalized as a negative self-image and negative view of others. This has a very strong influence over *how* we relate to others and to *whom* we relate. These early relationships tend to get repeated, called **repetition compulsion**.

The internalized image influences what is expected in future relationships and how others are perceived. These internal objects are **projected** onto others. With personality disorders comes an inability to realistically evaluate others. This is most obvious when individuals expect someone to behave a certain way when very little is known about that person. This process is called **transference** and is explained on page 45.

OBJECT RELATIONS TIDBITS

• Object relations considers the very substance of the human psyche to be made of concerns about relationships, not discharging drives.

• The focus in Freud's theory was on the father. By causing castration anxiety in boys and penis envy in girls he determines the success of the **Oedipal Complex** or **Stage**. In object relations, the focus is pre-oedipal and centers on the relationship with the mother. This places critical developmental issues in the first year of life instead of at the fifth or sixth year when Oedipal issues were thought to emerge.

BASIC PSYCHODYNAMIC PRINCIPLES

There are some time honored principles that form the basis of the psychodynamic approach and give it a unique perspective on diagnosis and treatment. As introduced earlier, the presence of the **unconscious** is an integral part of this theoretical perspective. Dreams and Freudian Slips (**parapraxes**) are the two most common ways the unconscious is accessed. Symptoms and behaviors are visible extensions of unconscious processes that defend against repressed wishes and feelings.

Experiences in childhood are considered crucial in the formation of the adult personality. It is in these early years that the repetitive interactions with family members are of etiologic significance in personality disorders. Early patterns of relating to others persist into adult life; in a sense, the past is repeating itself. This was aptly put by William Wordsworth as, "The child is the father of the man."

TRANSFERENCE

In therapy, the process of transference involves patients experiencing the therapist as though he or she is a significant person from the patients' past. Feelings, thoughts and wishes **projected** onto the therapist are borrowed from a previous significant relationship. In this way, the current therapeutic relationship is a repetition of the past. Properly handled, transference is fertile ground for learning in psychotherapy. Two key points need to be illustrated:
· the relationship is *re-enacted* in therapy, not just *remembered*; this becomes more obvious when one pays attention to the **process** of the session, instead of just the **content**
· the reaction to the therapist is inappropriate and anachronistic

Transference in not limited to therapy; it pervades all important relationships. Early attachments and internal representations are so firmly held that they color all future interactions. All relationships are a combination of the real relationship and transference reactions. In a sense, this guides the relationships we pursue. Our unconscious "controls" us to a larger extent than is often appreciated. We seek out the types of relationship(s) with which we are already familiar. This is part of the principle of **psychic determinism**, which asserts that almost all we do is for reasons dictated by our unconscious. Thankfully, we are not passive victims to our unconscious mental processes. There is room for choice and conscious intention in bringing about change.

COUNTERTRANSFERENCE

Harry Stack Sullivan said "we are all much more human than otherwise." Just as patients exhibit transference in their relationships with therapists, the converse also happens. Therapists are (usually) human beings who will, to some degree, unconsciously experience the patient as someone from their past. While many definitions of **countertransference** exist, KERNBERG (1965) has aptly summed it up as "the therapist's conscious and appropriate total emotional reaction to the patient." Whereas patients' transference is grounds for observation and interpretation, countertransference is not openly discussed in therapy. Constant internal scrutiny is required on the part of the therapists to be aware of countertransference. Though it can be tempting to act on it, doing so only causes a repetition of other relationships. Instead, countertransference can be used diagnostically and therapeutically. It gives a firsthand awareness of how patients interact with others.

USE YOUR COUNTERTRANSFERENCE - HOW DO YOU FEEL ABOUT THE PATIENT?

DISORDERED PERSONALITIES

Resistance

At virtually every turn in therapy, there is a strong drive on patients' part to oppose the treater's efforts. Change of any sort is difficult and accompanied by distress. There is an internal effort to preserve the psychic status quo. Resistance is as common as transference and should be expected in therapy. Whereas ego defenses are unconscious and are inferred, resistance can be conscious, preconscious or unconscious and is openly observed. It can take many forms: lateness or absence from sessions, prolonged silence, diversion to irrelevant material, questions of a personal nature about the therapist, "forgetting" the content of past sessions, avoidance or failure to arrange payment, non-compliance, etc.

Resistance is a self-protective mechanism against experiencing strong emotions - love, hate, jealousy, shame, anxiety, etc. As therapy progresses, these unacceptable feelings are less repressed, and are accompanied by some form of resistance. Just as countertransference is used therapeutically and not acted upon, resistance also provides information for the therapist. In other relationships, resistance is dealt with harshly. However, a psychodynamic understanding provides an opportunity to discover *what* the resistance conceals and *what* past situation is being reenacted in therapy. Resistance in a sense is a misnomer. Though the term implies that it is a process that impedes treatment, understanding resistance is a large part of the treatment.

The treatment of personality disorders is very much in the domain of psychotherapy. Medications are used to some extent, but by far the majority of interventions are made with "talk" therapies. Since these disorders are interpersonal in nature, it follows that interpersonal treatments are the prime modality. By understanding the processes of transference, countertransference and resistance, the therapeutic relationship can be used to increase awareness of how past relationships (object relations) affect current relationships, thus permitting conscious decisions about changing maladaptive patterns of interpersonal behavior.

What is Cognitive Therapy?

A **cognition** is a verbal or visual representation that comes into consciousness when one is confronted with a situation. Specifically, it is what one thinks *in* the situation and not *about* the situation. This type of therapy was developed by Aaron Beck and is based on his observation that "an individual's affect and behavior are largely determined by the way in which he or she structures the world." Beck originally developed this for use in depressive disorders. Here, he found the style of thinking depressed patients used reinforced a negative view of themselves, the world and their future (**the cognitive triad of depression**). Cognitive techniques are now available for treating anxiety disorders and personality disorders.

Cognitive therapy is short-term, structured and interactive. It has a "here and now" focus and is geared to solving current problems. The assumptions on which cognitive therapy is based are as follows:

Cognitions represent a synthesis of internal and external stimuli
↓
Individuals structure situations based on their cognitions
↓
Emotional and behavioral changes are caused by cognitions
↓
Cognitive therapy elicits an awareness of "cognitive distortions"
↓
Correction of these distortions leads to improved functioning

Adjusting the "cogs" in Cognitive Therapy

Cognitive Techniques

At the beginning of each session, the therapist sets the agenda, checks and assigns homework and introduces new skills. The components of cognitive therapy consist of eliciting automatic thoughts and identifying maladaptive assumptions, and then testing their validity

As patients' thoughts are elicited, their patterns of behavior, based on these assumptions, become obvious. The automatic thoughts are called **cognitive distortions**. Each disorder (Axis I and II) has its own profile of cognitive distortions. Common ones are: overgeneralizing, selective abstraction, excessive responsibility, catastrophizing, dichotomous thinking, self reference and assuming temporal causality.

Cognitive therapy has a different emphasis than analytically-based therapies. The cognitive therapist is required to be quite active (due to time constraints) and exude an *early* warmth and empathy. There is a large didactic component that explains the relationship between perception, thoughts, feelings and behavior, as well as a rationale for the treatment. Behavioral techniques are practical interventions designed to change maladaptive strategies. Techniques include: scheduling activities, graded task assignments, rehearsal, self-reliance training, role playing and diversion techniques.

WHAT IS GROUP THERAPY?

Group therapy is an effective treatment for a wide variety of disorders. Virtually any type of individual therapy is possible in a group setting: supportive, cognitive-behavioral, interpersonal, analytically-oriented or educational. Groups can be set up on an inpatient or outpatient basis, be open or closed to new members, be time-limited or open-ended, and have heterogeneous or homogeneous compositions.

Group therapy is an efficient treatment modality. In an age where the diminishing resources for therapy are under greater scrutiny, groups are gaining popularity and, in some cases, are an economic necessity.

While some personality disordered patients do well in a group setting, others typically do not. It is important to keep in mind that within a given diagnosis, there is a range of functioning that should be considered when determining suitability for a group.

Group therapy is different than the Bob Newhart show. A group has an identified leader or therapist, who uses therapeutic interventions *and* the group member interactions to facilitate change. Unlike individual therapy, a group provides opportunities for immediate feedback from peers. Also, the group functions as a micro-society and is perhaps a more "normal" setting in which to view patients' interactions. This is valuable, because it allows the therapist and the patient to observe transference reactions to a wider variety of people.

Groups conducted for personality disorders are generally ongoing and open to new members. Ideally, a group has is eight to ten members. Sessions are ninety to one hundred and twenty minutes once per week. Socialization outside the group is discouraged, as is participation in a concurrent therapy elsewhere.

The theoretical basis for treating personality disorders in groups is usually analytically oriented. Additionally, there are several powerful therapeutic factors unique to the group setting:

- Cohesion
- Interaction
- Universality
- Acceptance
- **Identification** (unconscious) or Imitation (conscious) of another member

- Validation by other group members
- Corrective emotional/familial experiences
- Learning from group members
- Interaction

References

N. Andreason, D. Black
INTRODUCTORY TEXTBOOK OF PSYCHIATRY
American Psychiatric Press; Washington, D.C., 1991

A. Beck, A. Freeman and Associates
COGNITIVE THERAPY OF PERSONALITY DISORDERS
The Guildford Press; New York, 1990

G. Gabbard
PSYCHODYNAMIC PSYCHIATRY IN CLINICAL PRACTICE, THE DSM-IV EDITION
American Psychiatric Press; Washington, D.C., 1994

H. Kaplan, B. Sadock, & J. Grebb, Editors
SYNOPSIS OF PSYCHIATRY, SEVENTH EDITION
Williams & Wilkins; Baltimore, Maryland, 1994

O. Kernberg -"Notes on Countertransference"
JOURNAL OF THE AMERICAN PSYCHOANALYTIC ASSOCIATION 13: p38-56, 1965

N. McWilliams
PSYCHOANALYTIC DIAGNOSIS
The Guildford Press; New York, 1994

J. Mount
CAUSATION OF PSYCHOLOGICAL SYMPTOMS
Personal Communication; 1995 Revision

P. Steinberg
THE PSYCHODYNAMIC FORMULATION
Personal Communication; 1995

G. Vaillant
EGO MECHANISMS OF DEFENSE
American Psychiatric Press; Washington, D.C., 1992

THE TRANSMUTATION OF EGO DEFENSES*

In his structural theory of the mind, Freud divided the psychic apparatus into the id, ego and superego. The ego, being the "middle child" in this arrangement, was set up to get nailed from both sides. It has to temper the wildly libidinous urges of the id, buffer the harsh prohibitions of the superego **and** do all this while acting as the press agent to the real world. Strategy dictates that a strong offense starts with a strong defense. Freud appreciated the need for defense mechanisms for the ego, and duly noted repression to be the mother of all defenses. A further cataloguing of ego defenses was provided by his daughter Anna, and Valiant[1] efforts have enumerated still more. Just as Freud's Drive Theory was overrun by **Objectionable Relations Theory**[2] and **Selfish Psychology**[3], ego defenses have had to make adjustments to the multifactorial changes in today's society.

NARCISSISY DEFENSES

Old: Primitive Idealization   **New:** American Expressization
EXPLANATION: The ultimate expression of "plasticity," allows the ego to function autonomously from the superego, until the end of the month.

Old: Projective Identification   **New:** Primate Identification
EXPLANATION: Used by over-socialized egos (primarily male) to seek psychic equilibrium through the imitation of primate behavior.

Old: Denial   **New:** Alibido
EXPLANATION: An amalgamation of two other defenses, *alibi* and *libido*, since the first is usually used to cover up the actions of the second.

PREMATURE DEFENSES

Old: Acting Out   **New:** Acting
EXPLANATION: This allows the ego to make the most of the "as if" personality by assuming identities of fictitious characters. Combined with **relocation**, this can be a lucrative defense.

Old: Regression   **New:** Digression
EXPLANATION: The spontaneous use of irrelevant and dated material in a rambling and verbose style assures complacency in others.

Old: Passive Aggression   **New:** Passé Aggression
EXPLANATION: Here, the ego becomes embroiled in the social milieu and struggles of a prior decade in order to avoid facing the demands of the current one. Some decades (e.g. the 1960's) seem heavily favored for use by this defense.

POST-MATURE DEFENSES

Old: Controlling   **New:** Remote Controlling
EXPLANATION: The ego is now able to achieve remarkable control over the external environment with this new defense. Not only is it effective with electrical devices, it can cause pronounced changes in humans as well.

Old: Displacement   **New:** Relocation
EXPLANATION: This defense allows the ego to displace itself across municipal, county and federal lines as a way of avoiding confrontation. It may be that egos using this defense cluster geographically (e.g. Hollywood).

Old: Isolation   **New:** Insulation
EXPLANATION: An evolved defense that now gives the ego materials with which to perform the isolating. The use of urea-formaldehyde insulation was one of the early misapplications of this defense.

VICTOR MATURE DEFENSES

Old: Humor   **New:** Humor
EXPLANATION: No comment.

Old: Altruism   **New:** Trumanism
EXPLANATION: Plainly stated, this enables the ego to have hard cash, as well as responsibility, to seek a final resting place on one's desk.

Old: Suppression   **New:** Supper-ession
EXPLANATION: The (usually unilateral) decision to postpone attention to a conscious impulse, at least until after dinner.

REFERENCES
[1] Valiant, Prince George: **The Hierarchical Structure of Ego Defenses**
Medieval Psychology; Round Table Press, Serf City, New England

[2] Maggie, Melanie and Bill
Driven to Detraction: **Objectionable Relations Theory**
British School Publishers; Grate Britain

[3] From Lilliputian to Kohutian:
The Advancement of Self Through Selfish Psychology
Chapter 1: Heinz 57 Manual of Therapeutic Interventions
Mirror, Mirror on the Wall Press; New York

* FROM THE *PsychoIllogical Bulletin*, VOL. 2, WINTER 1995, P. 18-20

PERSONALITIES 'Я' Us*

SENIOR MANAGEMENT

President: Narcissist

Vice-President: Paranoid

Personnel: Borderline

MIDDLE MANAGEMENT

Advertising: Histrionic	Legal Department: Antisocial
Research: Schizotypal	Customer Service: Passive-Aggressive

WORKFORCE - PREFERRED HOURS

Dependent: Whenever Told	Obsessive: Day and Night
Schizoid: Nights Only	Avoidant: Undesirable Shifts

* FROM THE *PsychoIllogical Bulletin*, VOL. 3, SUMMER 1995, P. 20

THE SCHIZOID PERSONALITY

Biographical Information

Name:	Wesley Wart
Occupation:	Toll booth collector from 1-7 a.m.
Appearance:	Stove-pipe pants and a circa '70's tie
Relationship with animals:	Brings "best friend" to session
Favorite Songs:	*Alone Again, Naturally*

At the Therapist's Office

Before Session:	Gets first appointment to avoid others
Waiting Room Reading:	Reads *Abstract Quarterly* in hallway
During Session:	Plays *Hide & Seek*; only won't seek
Fantasies Involve:	Liaison with philosophy course instructor
Relationship with Therapist:	Asks to play *Dungeons and Dragons*
Behavior During Session:	Teeters on edge of chair (and sanity)
Takes to Therapy:	Collection of mail-order catalogues

Diagnostic Shorthand

Mnemonic - "I PASSED"

Indifferent to praise or criticism

Pleasure from hobbies or activities is absent

Activities preferred are almost always solitary

Sexual experiences are not of interest

Solitary lifestyle

Emotionally detached

Desire lacking for close relationships

INTRODUCTION

Schizoid means "representing splitting or cleaving." This personality disorder is characterized by detachment from others, a restricted range of emotional expression and a lack of interest in activities.

Some of the key names associated with this disorder are:
• **Hoch** (1910) described a large percentage of schizophrenic patients as having a "shut-in" personality - reticent, seclusive and living in a world of fantasy; this was present before, and remained after, the florid signs and symptoms of a psychotic episode
• **Manfred Bleuler** (1924) used the term "schizoidie" to describe an apparent indifference to relationships or experiencing pleasure
• **Kraeplin** (1920's) made the comparison to an *autistic personality*; he considered this an attenuated form of schizophrenia
• **Kretschmer** (1925) identified two types of schizoid personalities:
· *overly sensitive* - resembling the avoidant personality disorder
· *insensitive* - a concept on which the current understanding is based
• **Fairbairn and Guntrip** (1969) made contributions to the description and understanding of this disorder; however, some of their work is more appropriately assigned to the schizotypal personality

The schizoid personality disorder (SzdPD) is characterized by social isolation extending even to family members. Emotional and physical intimacy are not desired. Men seem to marry rarely. Women may, if aggressively pursued by a man comfortable with the emotional distance. Patients with this disorder prefer solitary pursuits often with a degree of intellectual abstraction - computers, mathematics, astronomy, electronics, etc. They come across as bland, distant people lacking social graces. Their restricted affect does not inspire others to engage them in conversation or pursue relationships.

SzdPD was first clearly defined in DSM-III and expanded from three to seven criteria in DSM-III-R. *Schizoid* and *schizotypal* represent personality disorders consistent with the negative and positive symptoms (respectively) of schizophrenia (see DIFFERENTIAL DIAGNOSIS).

These patients virtually never seek attention for their personality disorder because they are not distressed by isolation. Commonly, an acute stressor or the encouragement of a family member brings them for help. They may have an increased risk of suffering from certain Axis I disorders - **Depression, Dysthymia** and **Anxiety Disorders** (especially **Phobias**).

MEDIA EXAMPLES

Schizoid characters are generally not interesting enough to play a prominent part in TV shows, movies or fictional bestsellers. They are typically recluses, loners, outcasts, or hermits. More interesting roles are as scientists or musicians, who are removed from society and care only for their work. However, a schizoid quality is one of the essential ingredients in heroism. Examples like the lone gunslinger who rides in from nowhere, takes out the badguys, and heads off into the sunset after refusing gracious invitations to stay in the town enhance the mystique of such characters. Here is a list of notable examples:

• **SHERLOCK HOLMES** - The famous Victorian detective embodies many schizoid elements. He craves contact with no one, and is distant, even with Dr. Watson. He immerses himself in scientific, musical and research pursuits when not absorbed in a case. Though mannerly, he only involves himself in what is germane to his investigation.

• **THE NET** - Sandra Bullock portrays a computer whiz who declines a dinner invitation in favor of ordering a pizza via a modem. Later, she plans her first vacation in six years. As the plot thickens, she has almost no one to turn to for help, because she doesn't know her neighbours or anyone at the company that employs her.

• **FLESH AND BONE** - Dennis Quaid gives a good performance as a schizoid vending machine owner. He travels from town to town absorbed only in replenishing his stock, until forced into interacting with Meg Ryan (he eventually has to; they're married in real life).

• **BATMAN** - While Bruce Wayne has many fine qualities that do not imply a personality disorder, he remains isolated, choosing to perfect his physical skills and secret weapons. In many instances he resists attempts to divulge his identity as Batman, or share his troubled past.

• **THE PROFESSIONAL** - This movie casts Jean Reno as Leon, an assassin. While his occupation surely makes him an antisocial personality, he leads an isolated, nomadic existence.

• **SCHIZOID** - This is an actual movie title starring Klaus Kinksi; however, the plot has nothing to do with this personality disorder.

Interview Considerations

Schizoid patients will seem at best modestly cooperative when interviewed. A lack of affective response will pervade the time spent with them. Often, responses are limited to a word or two and leave an impression of indifference to significant, or even catastrophic, events.

It is difficult to use a "strategy" to draw these people out. Often, general questions are used at the beginning of an interview to generate rapport. Their clipped responses may give the impression they are upset, but this is unlikely. Because they radiate little to no emotional warmth, it is difficult to use empathy to make a connection. Feelings are related in such a detached manner they may sound rehearsed.

Open-ended questions often do not evoke the desired response. Encouragement to provide more information, even on topics that patients choose, rarely succeeds. If a history cannot be obtained using open-ended questions, a closed-ended, structured "laundry list" of questions may be necessary. Schizoid patients are unlikely to be affected by even a barrage of questions. In particular, mention of an emotional state requires closer questioning. For example, these patients may exist in a state of "depression" that does not correspond with the symptoms of a major depressive disorder. Collateral social history is invaluable in making this diagnosis.

Schizoid Themes

- Prefers to do things alone
- Why bother?/Who cares?
- Withdrawn/reclusive
- Works below potential
- Observers, not participants
- Lacks interests and hobbies
- Deficient motivation
- Goes "through the motions"
- May show considerable creativity
- Aloof, distant, cold
- Humorless
- Constricted emotions
- No apparent desire to pursue relationships

Tidbit

- In some psychiatric literature, and in particular psychoanalytic writing, the term "schizoid" may refer to schizoid, schizotypal and/or avoidant personalities. These three diagnoses were introduced as separate disorders in the DSM-III.

Presumed Etiology

BIOLOGICAL: SzdPD has a debatable link to schizophrenia. Some studies consider it a personality variant consistent with the negative symptoms of schizophrenia. Other studies demonstrate that the schizotypal personality disorder has a stronger association with, and a similar outcome to, schizophrenia.

If there is a genetic component, neuroanatomic and neurochemical aberrations may serve as a marker. To date, a number have been postulated but not confirmed (e.g. autonomic hyperactivity, deficits in the reticular formation, congenital aplasia in the limbic system, etc.).

Temperamental factors include hyper-reactivity, a tendency to overstimulation, anhedonia and aversion to others. Introversion is a highly heritable trait; pupillary dilatation, elevated heart rate and elevated urinary catecholamines accompany the behavioral signs. Families of patients with schizoid personalities have a higher prevalence of schizophrenia, schizotypal and avoidant personality disorder than the general population.

PSYCHOSOCIAL: There is split (bad pun intended) in what is considered a "schizoidogenic" family milieu. The most obvious family history involves cold, distant, inadequate or even neglectful caregivers. Children raised in such a setting experience relationships as painful and unrewarding.

However, the other extreme may also contribute to the etiology of this disorder. Parents who are overinvolved, overinvested (and overdrawn), may foster an emotional withdrawal in their children. A common finding is that of a seductive mother who transgressed boundaries, and an impatient, critical father. Bateson coined the term **double bind** (the psychiatric equivalent of a Catch-22) to describe confusing and contradictory interactions with parents. This no-win situation may facilitate retreat into a fantasy state.

It is important to keep cultural factors in mind with this diagnosis. For example, a Scandinavian will very likely seem more reserved than someone from the Mediterranean. Even within a given culture, a rural versus urban environment may place different expectations and norms on an individual. Analytic observations generally hold that men suffer more from disorders characterized by excessive isolation, and women more from disorders having too much attachment (dependent personality disorder, depressive episodes, etc.).

Epidemiology

Estimates of prevalence range from 0.5 to 7%. By its very nature SzdPD is difficult to measure accurately. There appears to be a higher prevalence in males.

Ego Defenses

SzdPD is notable for the *absence* of common defenses, especially in higher functioning characters. The primary defense used in this disorder is appropriately named **schizoid fantasy**, a withdrawal into an inner world of imagination. The next most common defense used is **intellectualization**, excessive use of intellectual processes to avoid experiencing or expressing emotion. To a lesser extent other defenses used are:
· **projection** (see Paranoid Chapter)
· **introjection** (internalizing the qualities of an important person)
· **idealization** and **devaluation** (described in the Borderline Chapter)

Diagnostic Criteria

A. A pervasive pattern of detachment from social relationships and a restricted range of expression of emotions in interpersonal settings, beginning by early adulthood and present in a variety of contexts, as indicated by four (or more) of the following:

(1) neither desires nor enjoys close relationships, including being part of a family
(2) almost always chooses solitary activities
(3) has little, if any, interest in having sexual experiences with another person
(4) takes pleasure in few, if any, activities
(5) lacks close friends or confidants other than first-degree relatives
(6) appears indifferent to the praise or criticism of others
(7) shows emotional coldness, detachment, or flattened affectivity

B. Does not occur exclusively during the course of Schizophrenia, a Mood Disorder With Psychotic Features, another Psychotic Disorder, or a Pervasive Developmental Disorder and is not due to the direct physiological effects of a general medical condition.

Differential Diagnosis

Schizoid is one of five "schizo" terms occurring in psychiatry. In order to explain the differential diagnosis of this disorder, an understanding of these terms is necessary.

Schizophrenia: Literally a splitting of the mind, or "schism," between perception, thinking, feeling and behavior. Clinical features include delusions, hallucinations, disorganized speech and behavior, and **negative symptoms** (described on the next page).

Schizophreniform Disorder: This diagnosis is identical to schizophrenia except that the duration is not long enough to qualify for a diagnosis of schizophrenia. The deterioration in social and occupational function may be less affected than in schizophrenia.

Schizoaffective Disorder: This denotes the presences of a Mood Disorder (Major Depressive, Manic or Mixed Episode) concurrent with the symptoms of schizophrenia listed above, *as well as* a period with delusions or hallucinations without prominent mood symptoms.

Schizotypal Personality Disorder: This is a short form for "schizophrenic genotype" and is a Cluster A personality disorder.

The differentiation of SzdPD from schizophrenia is not difficult during the acute or psychotic phase of the latter. The presence of positive symptoms, and a clear decline in level of function, do not occur in this personality disorder. It may be more difficult to distinguish SzdPD from the residual or prodromal phases of schizophrenia.

Similarly, schizoid patients do not have the same severity of symptoms, or the decline in function seen in a Major Depressive Episode. There is little overlap between Mania or Mixed Mood Episode and this personality. However, brief psychotic episodes (**micropsychotic episodes**) lasting minutes to hours can occur in SzdPD.

Continued abuse of street drugs or alcohol can cause the emergence of schizoid-like characteristics. A schizoid personality disorder prior to the onset of schizophrenia is considered to be a poor prognostic feature.

SCHIZOPHRENIFORM
· lesser in time course and severity of symptoms than schizophrenia

SCHIZOAFFECTIVE
· combination of mood and schizophrenic symptoms

SCHIZOPHRENIA

positive symptoms are *added to* the clinical presentation

negative symptoms are *missing from* the clinical presentation

POSITIVE SYMPTOMS

Hallucinations
• of any sensory modality
• running commentary on actions

Delusions
• bizarre themes

Unusual Behaviour
• social/appearance
• stereotyped/aggressive

Formal Thought Disorder
• tangential/circumstantial
• illogical/incoherent
• thought insertion, withdrawal, broadcasting

Inappropriate Affect
• incongruous to situation

NEGATIVE SYMPTOMS

Affective Flattening
• unchanging facial expressions
• few spontaneous movements

Alogia
• poverty of speech
• poverty of content of speech

Avolition/Apathy
• poor grooming and hygiene
• physical anergia

Anhedonia/Asociality
• few recreational interests
• no relationships/intimacy

Attention
• social inattention
• testing on mental status exam

SCHIZOTYPAL PD

SCHIZOID PD

OTHER DIAGNOSTIC CONSIDERATIONS

Autism (markedly impaired development of social interaction, communication and a restricted repertoire of activities and interests), and **Asperger's Disorder** (similar to autism but without the delays in language, cognitive development or adaptive behavior), are examples of the pervasive developmental disorders mentioned in the diagnostic criteria. Generally, patients with these have stereotyped behaviors and demonstrate more impaired social interactions than is seen in SzdPD. Frequently, patients with SzdPD have an associated avoidant and/or schizotypal personality disorder.

MENTAL STATUS EXAMINATION

APPEARANCE:	None characteristic; inattentive to trends; clothes are functional, not fashionable; may be socially inept
BEHAVIOR:	Edgy, anxious; fidgety; clumsy; stilted; ill at ease; few facial expressions; little animation
COOPERATION:	Cooperative, but little revealed
AFFECT:	Restricted range, flat, withdrawn; may be dysphoric
SPEECH:	Goal directed but lacks detail; intonation rarely changes; monotonous; slow
CONTENT OF THOUGHT:	Little to no elaboration on any topic; one word answers, seemingly unaffected by material usually laden with emotion; may be aware of lack of interest in people or significant events; may have ideas of reference
THOUGHT FORM:	No characteristic abnormality; rarely have actual thought blocking (answer readily, just sparsely)
PERCEPTION:	No characteristic abnormality
INSIGHT & JUDGMENT:	Intact; not bothered by lack of interest; tend to be pessimistic and underestimate their abilities
SUICIDE - HOMICIDE:	Need to consider this in conjunction with any Axis I disorder; not likely to be dangerous to others or themselves; isolation from relationships tends to minimize DIRs as a precipitant for seeking help

PSYCHODYNAMIC ASPECTS

Melanie Klein hypothesized that an infant in about the third or fourth month of life passes through a **paranoid-schizoid position**. Here, the infant splits off (the schizoid part) libido from aggression that is then projected (the paranoid part) onto the mother, leaving the infant in fear of maternal persecution. At about six months, this progresses to the **depressive position** which involves a fear the infant may destroy the loved object, and via **reparation**, acts towards the mother as if to repair the damage inflicted either in fantasy or reality. Remember, this is just a theory. However, to Klein's credit, later in life schizoid patients struggle with basic safety (paranoid aspect) and have split off their desires (schizoid aspect) to the point where they are aptly viewed as spectators, instead of participants.

To schizoid patients, the world looms with the potential for being consumed, engulfed, or absorbed. The usual appetitive drives (sex, food, etc.) are not experienced as coming from within, but instead as coming from the external world. In fact, the body habitus of many schizoid patients tends to be thin (a link to **Anorexia Nervosa** has been proposed), accentuating their withdrawal from sustenance. Emotional expression causes trepidation spanning a spectrum from outright fear to deep ambivalence. When overwhelmed, these patients hide either literally, or defensively.

The retreat into fantasy as a coping mechanism happens reflexively in a wide variety of situations. Fantasies may contain violent themes and be manifested by an interest in sordid movies and literature: horror films, true-crime books, heavy metal, mild bondage magazines, games with omnipotent or destructive roles for players, etc. The hunger fueling these interests is usually well-defended. Schizoid personalities usually seem pleasant, low-key and even transparent.

It would be a mistake, however, to assume that no emotional experiences occur *within* these patients. Schizoid patients can be in touch with emotions on a level of genuineness not often seen. Difficulties may stem from a lack of *validation* of emotional and intuitive experiences, not the complete absence of them. Schizoid patients perceive what others ignore, and may feel out of place with those oblivious to what is so apparent to them. Social practices may appear so contrived that it seems fraudulent to participate. A detached, sarcastic and faintly contemptuous attitude helps fend off a world perceived as overcontrolling and overintrusive.

What Happens in Psychodynamic Therapy?

Schizoid characters may be unfairly thought of as lower functioning across a spectrum of behaviors (social, career, interpersonal, etc.) due to the presumed connection to schizophrenia, especially to the negative symptoms. It is important to keep in mind that this diagnosis can be applicable at any level of functioning - from a withdrawn, chronically hospitalized patient to a highly creative artist. It is common for these people to be drawn to intellectual pursuits often removed from direct contact - philosophy, theoretical sciences, mathematics, theological studies, computers and creative arts. The level of personality functioning is not necessarily related to the level of occupational functioning.

Although the interpersonal dynamics mentioned above keep patients from entering relationships and seeking professional help, the constraints of psychotherapy may well be appealing. The customary boundaries of time limits, a professional office setting, ethical restrictions against social and sexual relationships, and a clearly outlined therapeutic contract all decrease fears of engulfment.

Frequently, a crisis may precipitate the initial visit - an Axis I disorder (depression, anxiety), dysphoria over a loss, or the wish for a limited social life (they often long for unattainable sexual partners while ignoring available ones). Interpersonal difficulties are revealed early in therapy. Though experiencing emotional pain, patients may not be able to clearly express themselves, leaving awkward pauses. It is critical early on to create an atmosphere of patience, respect and safety. Avoid probing too deeply or pressing for an immediate disclosure. By letting patients share *what* they want to, *in the way* they want to, and *at the speed* they want to, a trusting relationship has a chance to develop.

In a non-critical atmosphere, their highly-tuned perceptual abilities become more apparent and provide fertile ground for the therapeutic process to continue. Regardless of how bizarre or incomprehensible internal experiences seem, being able to express them in an intimate and supportive atmosphere is a prime therapeutic factor.

As therapy proceeds, the withdrawal into fantasy as a defense can eventually be addressed. Imagination can be reframed as a talent, rather than being seen as an immutable barrier. A key factor that promotes self-esteem is the encouragement of self-expression through creative activity.

Schizoid patients frequently need reassurance that they are not deviant or grotesque to others. Here, confirmation of their sensitivity and uniqueness can be valuable. This can be accomplished by communicating that their inner world is not only comprehensible, but gifted. This can be aided by the use of artistic or literary sources, depending on the erudition of the therapist.

In his book SOLITUDE, Storr emphasizes that many of the world's great thinkers lived alone for the majority of their lives. Descartes, Newton, Locke, Pascal, Spinoza, Kant, Leibniz, Schopenhauer, Nietzsche, Kierkegaard and Wittgenstein are just a few examples. Even among notably creative individuals who did marry, there is an almost universal observation that their work was carried out in solitude.

We must reserve a little back-shop, all our own, entirely free, wherein to establish our true liberty and principal retreat and solitude.
     MONTAIGNE

As therapy proceeds, patients hopefully internalize the experience of being accepted without being engulfed or dominated. Eventually, increased self-esteem allows the experience of being misunderstood as potentially due to the limitations of others, not because of some deficiency on their part. Once achieved, practical gains outside therapy may start taking place: friendships, creative endeavors, etc.

The main feature contrasting this SzdPD with the Avoidant Personality Disorder is that schizoid patients *appear* not to desire close relationships. However, attachment theory postulates that relationships are a fundamental human need. In schizoid patients, early experiences have walled off the desire to form relationships.

McWilliams outlines helpful techniques to draw patients out:

• support taking risks in the direction of relationships
• be playful or humorous in ways lacking in the patient's past
• respond with attitudes that counteract the tendency to "go through the motions" of emotionally connecting with others
• a more responsive therapeutic style may make the patient's transference more accessible to interpretation; the patient needs the therapist's active participation as a warm and empathic person
SOURCE: MCWILLIAMS, 1994, P. 202

Transference and Countertransference Reactions

Schizoid patients generally are appreciative and cooperative within the boundaries of a therapeutic relationship.

Countertransference can involve boredom, impatience, derision and giving a prematurely negative prognosis. Patients can be seen as resisting a process that requires disclosure on their part. It may be tempting to "get to the heart of the matter," finish patients' sentences, or become amused by their maladroit mannerisms.

Later, there may be an unwitting tendency to form an emotional world, or cocoon, within therapy. This is enhanced when a feeling of being special or unique exists because patients have no other close relationships. Under such circumstances, therapy can become a solution for a schizoid person, instead of a catalyst for growth outside the office. This is more likely to happen in two instances:

• when collusion occurs with patients' sense of helplessness and fragility by seeking to protect them from the harsh external world
• with patients who are creatively gifted, therapists may find themselves in the role of an agent or advocate - taking on a parental role (the parent they never had) to promote special talents

Summary of Therapeutic Techniques

• Don't rush the patient into early disclosure, be patient, however don't use too many open-ended techniques at the outset
• Provide structure; initial sessions may need to be tactfully spaced
• Be aware of the setup in your office; locate your chair comfortably away from patients; respect physical and emotional distances
• By nature, these patients disregard convention - keep an open mind
• Try to understand the latent or symbolic content of their speech
• Involve education or social skills training to increase assertiveness

Pharmacotherapy

The use of medication for schizoid personalities has not been established. Axis I disorders may require **antidepressants**, **anxiolytics** or **hypnotics**. Antipsychotics are rarely indicated. In some cases, it may be easier to develop a therapeutic relationship by initially using a medication and then easing into a form of psychotherapy.

GROUP THERAPY

Some schizoid patients are suited to the group process. Meeting with a consistent group of people is an important step in beginning to value relationships and developing a social network. Social learning and deciphering of facial expressions are early therapeutic gains.

Schizoid patients can be accused of passively drawing attention to themselves. Their manner can also be reminiscent of a "co-therapist" and both of these situations can draw ire from the more attention-seeking members of a group. If a therapist experiences countertransference difficulties with silence, he or she may covertly encourage ganging-up on withdrawn patients. Forcing patients to contribute to the group may repeat earlier interpersonal trauma.

COGNITIVE THERAPY

Basic Cognitive Assumptions:
- "Relationships are just trouble."
- "I'm a social outcast."
- "Nothing excites me."
- "Life is easier without others."
- "It is better to walk softly, and walk away."

ADAPTED FROM BECK, FREEMAN & ASSOCIATES, 1990

Cognitive therapy with schizoid patients is a test of perseverance for the therapist. Because thoughts are linked to feelings, and since these patients express few feelings, it takes considerable time to generate something to examine. Additionally, the indifference expressed towards others removes a useful catalyst for change. Frequently these patients enter therapy because of anxiety or depression. While undergoing cognitive therapy for these conditions, interventions can be made toward correcting their isolated lifestyle:

- Pay more attention to positive emotional details
- Use limited self-disclosure to develop a rudimentary relationship
- Teach social skills, assertiveness training
- Add "booster" sessions to prevent relapse

COURSE

SzdPD appears to be stable over time; little is known about prognosis.

REFERENCES

American Psychiatric Association
DIAGNOSTIC AND STATISTICAL MANUAL OF MENTAL DISORDERS, FOURTH EDITION
American Psychiatric Press; Washington, D.C., 1994

N. Andreason, D. Black
INTRODUCTORY TEXTBOOK OF PSYCHIATRY
American Psychiatric Press; Washington, D.C., 1991

A. Beck, A. Freeman & Associates
COGNITIVE THERAPY OF PERSONALITY DISORDERS
The Guildford Press; New York, 1990

G. Gabbard
PSYCHODYNAMIC PSYCHIATRY IN CLINICAL PRACTICE, THE DSM-IV EDITION
American Psychiatric Press; Washington, D.C., 1994

H. Kaplan, B. Sadock (editors)
COMPREHENSIVE GROUP PSYCHOTHERAPY, THIRD EDITION
Williams & Wilkins; Baltimore, 1993

H. Kaplan, B. Sadock (editors)
COMPREHENSIVE TEXTBOOK OF PSYCHIATRY, SIXTH EDITION
Williams & Wilkins; Baltimore, 1995

N. McWilliams
PSYCHOANALYTIC DIAGNOSIS
The Guildford Press; New York, 1994

E. Othmer and S. Othmer
THE CLINICAL INTERVIEW USING DSM-IV
American Psychiatric Press; Washington, D.C., 1994

R. Pies
CLINICAL MANUAL OF PSYCHIATRIC DIAGNOSIS AND TREATMENT
American Psychiatric Press; Washington, D.C., 1994

A. Storr
SOLITUDE
Collins Publishing Group; Great Britain, 1988

You're just about to do computer battle with Zorgon for control of the thirteenth level of Hell when the doorbell rings. After avoiding your neighbours for seven years, why would they pick today to meet you?

And after all you've done to ensure your privacy - working nights, eating take-out food, and choosing a basement apartment at the end of the hallway. You can run, but you'll just have to meet them tired.

Have no fear!! Eau D'Hermit is here!!

An antiperspirant foul enough to
keep even this gregarious horde away.

Eau D'Hermit

The Antiperson Antiperspirant

THE PARANOID PERSONALITY

Biographical Information

Name:	Perry Noyd
Occupation:	Full-time movie projectionist
Appearance:	Wears glasses with rear-view mirrors
Relationship with animals:	Questions his dog's fidelity
Favorite Song:	*I Spy* theme song

At the Therapist's Office

Before Session:	Checks to see if he was followed
Waiting Room Reading:	Authenticates therapist's diploma
During Session:	Questions partner's fidelity
Fantasies Involve:	Demanding a full explanation of therapist's jokes
Relationship with Therapist:	Questions therapist's fidelity
Behavior During Session:	Complains about lack of warmth in office
Takes to Therapy:	Scrapbook of injustice collection

Diagnostic Shorthand

Mnemonic - "HUGS FAR"

Hidden meanings seen in others' remarks
Unjustified doubts about others
Grudges held
Suspects others of exploitation and deceit

Fidelity of partner doubted
Attacks on character are perceived
Reluctant to confide in others

Introduction

The paranoid personality disorder is characterized by unwarranted suspiciousness and a tendency to misinterpret the actions of others as threatening, or deliberately harmful.

Paranoia is an ancient term, preceding even Hippocrates. Literally translated from Greek it means "a mind beside itself" and was originally used to describe insanity. Over time, it has been inconsistently applied to a diverse number of conditions.

Some of the key names associated with the concept of paranoia are:
• **Heinroth** (1818) reintroduced use of the term in its current form
• **Kahlbaum** (1863) used the term to designate a group of disorders that remained essentially unchanged over time
• **Adolf Meyer** (1910's) used the term *paranoid personality disorder*
• **Kraeplin** (1915) described a "pseudoquerulous" type of personality that predisposed patients to delusional disorders
• **Freud** (1911) in his analysis of the jurist Daniel Paul Schreber (who suffered from paranoid schizophrenia), thought the core conflict in paranoia was a homosexual wish; to Schreber, this consciously unacceptable (denial) wish was transformed (reaction formation) into a male companion hating him (projection); thus, he was only aware of feeling persecuted; Freud introduced the defense mechanism of projection in 1894, how did you celebrate its centennial?
• **Melanie Klein** (1952) in developing object relations theory, proposed a **paranoid-schizoid position**, in which destructive thoughts and feelings are split off (schizoid) from the ego and projected outwards (paranoid) as an early means of separating intrapsychic representations of good (nurturing mother) and bad (depriving mother)

Due to the early descriptions of paranoid behavior, it has become a traditional diagnostic category in most classification systems. The paranoid personality disorder (PPD) was included in the DSM-I and in each revision since. The ICD-10 also contains a diagnostic category for paranoid personalities, though the definition is broader than the DSM-IV. Other features that have historically been part of the description of PPD are: hypersensitivity to criticism, disproportionate reaction to setbacks and an aggressive pursuit of individual rights (when not being threatened).

PPD has been hypothesized to be part of the **schizophrenic spectrum** of disorders and has also been linked to **Delusional Disorder**.

Media Examples

Paranoid personalities are frequently cast in "us versus them" situations. As main characters, they garner audience support for their battles against authority figures. An element of heroism is involved when the underdog triumphs against oppression. Frequent portrayals are characters such as private investigators or police officers, who prepare to do battle with the "forces of evil."

• The Caine Mutiny - Humphrey Bogart plays a classic paranoid personality as Captain Queeg. Soon after taking command of the ship, he begins to demonstrate his suspiciousness of others. He becomes ruthless when he believes he is being humiliated by some of his men. The scene where he is called as to testify at the court martial is an excellent illustration of this disorder.

• Doctor Strangelove - this movie is virtually a study in paranoia. Even the character names Jack D. Ripper, T. J. "King" Kong, Ambassador de Sadesky, Lothar Zogg, and Premier Kissoff have a sinister ring to them. We see the clearly paranoid General Jack D. Ripper ordering his bomber squadron to launch a nuclear attack on Russia. Later, we learn his motivation for doing so - fluoridation of water. He perceives this to be a communist plot to destroy his precious bodily fluids. As Strangelove, Peter Sellers demonstrates the suspiciousness, lack of humor and grandiosity seen in this disorder.

• Guilty by Suspicion - paranoia is exemplified by the menacing committee driven to eradicate communism at the time of the McCarthy witch hunts.

• Invasion of the Body Snatchers - deals with a paranoid theme, (Capgras Syndrome - replacement of a close person by a double) though this is on the scale of a delusion.

• The Treasure of the Sierra Madre - Bogie again portrays a paranoid character who becomes increasingly suspicious of his prospecting partners as their dig proceeds.

• Falling Down - Michael Douglas plays a paranoid character who acts with outrage against those who cross him.

• Unstrung Heroes (novel and movie) - Michael Richards portrays one of the eccentric and very paranoid uncles of the main character.

Interview Considerations

Paranoia of moderate (or greater) severity is usually not difficult to recognize. Hypervigilance, anger, hostility and vindictiveness become obvious early in the interview. Considerable energy is expended trying to foil the efforts of those whom patients perceive as trying to shame and humiliate them. In most instances, these convictions are revealed readily, with a long list of experiences to support and justify them. With time, patients become aware others see them as paranoid, and they can suppress their tirades, especially when there is an obvious gain in doing so (e.g. avoiding hospitalization).

With higher functioning patients, paranoia can be much less obvious and detected only over time. For example, a request for assertiveness training or relaxation therapy may be veiled paranoia. The important question to keep in mind is "*why is this patient making this request?*" Further investigation might reveal a sense of being picked on, or not being able to relax because of constant vigilance. Dealing with the surface manifestation may miss the underlying suspiciousness.

Interviewing paranoid patients can be difficult because they expect to be exploited, taken advantage of, or even humiliated. Questions and intentions will be scrutinized for "hidden" meanings. Frequently, inquiries are made about how information will be used. Issues of confidentiality may be magnified. Regardless of how the interview is conducted, a lack of trust predominates.

Paranoid patients frequently act on their misperceptions. When sufficient "information" is collected, a detailed account of betrayal is delivered in a heated manner. They are able to confront others without being able to accept confrontation themselves.

This tirade can be quite difficult to endure. It may be tempting to respond with indignation, defensiveness, or by "setting them straight." Paranoid thinking lacks flexibility, but highlighting obvious logical incongruities usually has no impact. Arguing with patients simply increases their suspiciousness. Being genuine, open and frank is more likely to be a successful strategy. An example of such an intervention might point out how everything is twisted to fit their expectations.

Small gains in trust are all that can be expected, and may be short-lived. At any moment, patients can launch a counterattack if they feel betrayed. They are more prone to lash out rather than endure the anxiety of what they consider to be inevitable mistreatment.

PARANOID THEMES

• Externalize blame for difficulties - see themselves as the continual target of abuse; constantly complain about poor treatment
• Repeated difficulty in dealing with authority figures
• Over-estimate minor events - "Make mountains out of molehills"
• Search intensively to confirm suspicions to the exclusion of more reasonable conclusions - "Miss the forest for the trees"
• Cannot relax; display little to no sense of humor
• Project envy or even pathological jealousy - "They're out to get me because they want what I have"
• Critical of those who they see as weaker, needy, or defective
• Difficulty exuding warmth or talking about their insecurities
ADAPTED FROM BECK, FREEMAN & ASSOCIATES, 1990

PREVENTION OF VIOLENCE

An old adage advises, "Just because you're paranoid doesn't mean you're not being followed." If there is some realistic aspect to issues of safety, it is vital to establish the actual risk. Frequently, a kernel of truth exists in even the most flagrant paranoid thoughts. Paranoid patients are among the most likely to be violent. Below is a list of recommendations to help prevent such an occurrence.

• Don't challenge beliefs, especially shortly after initiating an interview
• Give explanations for your actions; demonstrate openness
• Respect patients' autonomy
• Maintain your composure
• Stress *verbalization*, not *action*
• Allow an adequate, even ample space for patients; sitting close to the door or exit can facilitate your escape if necessary
• Do not block the door should the patient bolt
• Seating arrangements can be discussed with the patients
• Introduce others and explain their purpose in the room
• Be attuned to your feelings; don't react with anger or sarcasm

Presumed Etiology

BIOLOGICAL: Chess and Thomas found the following temperamental qualities associated with later paranoia: irregularity, nonadaptability, high intensity of reaction, negative mood and a tendency to hyperactivity. Innate aggression or irritability may result in the angry and threatening qualities seen in this disorder.

First-degree relatives of those affected with schizophrenia have a higher incidence of PPD. This disorder is considered part of the **schizophrenic spectrum** (see page 103). It is not uncommon for those who develop late onset schizophrenia to have had PPD premorbidly.

Paranoid traits have also been associated with developmental handicaps (e.g. impaired vision or hearing; physical deformities).

PSYCHOSOCIAL: Paranoid patients have often had repeated experiences of feeling overwhelmed and humiliated during childhood. Environmental factors often include: criticism, teasing, ridicule, arbitrary punishment, parents who cannot be pleased and being used as a scapegoat. Children become vigilant for cues to impending sadistic treatment from caregivers, leading to their defensive attitude.

Children who grow up in environments filled with condemnation incorporate parental warnings about the outside world, even though they may find more kindness outside their homes. Negative reactions reinforce in children a sense that outsiders are persecutory. Reality and feelings become incongruous. Fear and shame become instilled, instead of a sense of being understood.

Children learn to believe that their feelings and complaints have a strong destructive power. Interactions with parents in such situations (e.g. being insulted) increase anger and frustration. While relieving none of the distress, the confusion about feelings and perception is magnified.

Paranoid behavior can also be modeled. **Folie à deux** is a disorder in which the delusion(s) of one person induce another to believe the idea. Though this disorder is usually seen in the context of a delusional or psychotic disorder, it illustrates the power of environmental influences.

Epidemiology

The very nature of PPD makes it difficult to study and assess accurately. Estimates of prevalence range from 0.5% to 2.5%. No sex differences have been reported.

Ego Defenses

Defense mechanisms in PPD induce the very feelings or actions in others that they are being accused of in the first place. The principal ego defense used in this personality disorder is **projection**. This substitutes an external threat for an internal one, while keeping out of awareness struggles with power, aggression, desire for same-sex closeness, racial or religious biases, etc. Other defenses used are: **projective identification, denial, splitting** and **reaction formation**.

Depending on ego strength, projection can take place on a psychotic, borderline, or neurotic level. In PPD, this does not progress to a psychotic level, but an understanding of this defense is important in all paranoid conditions.

Projective Identification is a three step process:
• First, as in projection, a threat is externalized toward the therapist
• Second, the therapist is then shaped or controlled by the projection (interpersonal pressure from the patient), and starts to feel or act in a way that is congruent with the projection
• Third, the projected material is processed by the therapist and incorporated (re-introjected) by the patient, further modifying his or her internal experience

This is a conceptually difficult defense. In essence, projective identification binds others to patients. It facilitates a degree of control over the behavior of other people. An alternate explanation is as follows: a patient tries to get rid of (project) certain feelings, but maintains a connection with them and needs reassurance that they are realistic. The projections "fit" the person on whom they are targeted.

This can provoke strong reactions in others. This happens because within everyone exists the repertoire of reactions, defenses and attitudes that are being projected. Weathering this emotional barrage is an integral part of dealing with paranoid patients. There is a "self-fulfilling" aspect to this defense. An example is as follows:

POSITIVE EXCHANGE:
Patient: I know this is just our second session. I don't have a reason to feel this way, but I already think that you're waiting to expose and humiliate me. You just hide it better than others."
Therapist: In what way do you think that I will expose you?

NEGATIVE EXCHANGE:
Patient: You headshrinkers are all the same. You keep notes about me and I can't even see them. I don't care what you say. You don't know me and you've been wrong about everything so far.
Therapist: Now look here. I'm trying to help you. If you can't relax and trust me this is going to be a waste of time.

In the first example, the patient projects a persecutory fantasy onto the therapist and is aware that it seems irrational. It was done in a way that shows an "observing ego" and allows the therapist to explore the fantasy and work with the patient. The second is an example showing, not only that the patient has similarly projected onto the therapist, but already feels humiliated. The accusation hasn't lessened the patient's suspicion, which is the purpose of the defense. The angry counterattack to the perceived threat has already mobilized defensiveness on the therapist's part, provoking what the patient feared in the first place. Kernberg described this as "maintaining empathy" with what has been projected.

Splitting and **Reaction Formation** are discussed in the BORDERLINE and OBSESSIVE-COMPULSIVE PERSONALITY chapters respectively.

DIAGNOSTIC CRITERIA

A. A pervasive distrust and suspiciousness of others such that their motives are interpreted as malevolent, beginning by early adulthood and present in a variety of contexts, as indicated by four (or more) of the following:

(1) suspects, without sufficient basis, that others are exploiting, harming or deceiving him or her
(2) is preoccupied with unjustified doubts about the loyalty or trustworthiness of friends or associates
(3) is reluctant to confide in others because of unwarranted fear that the information will be used maliciously against him or her
(4) reads hidden demeaning or threatening meanings into benign remarks or events

(5) persistently bears grudges, i.e., is unforgiving of insults, injuries, or slights
(6) perceives attacks on his or her character or reputation that are not apparent to others and is quick to react angrily or to counterattack
(7) has recurrent suspicions, without justification, regarding fidelity of spouse or sexual partner

B. Does not occur exclusively during the course of Schizophrenia, a Mood Disorder With Psychotic Features, or another Psychotic Disorder and is not due to the direct physiologic effects of a general medical condition.
REPRINTED WITH PERMISSION FROM THE DSM-IV.
COPYRIGHT, AMERICAN PSYCHIATRIC ASSOCIATION, 1994

DIFFERENTIAL DIAGNOSIS

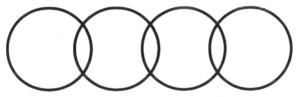

| NORMAL | PARANOID | DELUSIONAL | PARANOID |
| VIGILANCE | PERSONALITY | DISORDER | SCHIZOPHRENIA |

Feelings of being watched, talked about, lied to, or taken advantage of are universal human experiences. It is not difficult to connect with non-bizarre delusions expressed in the above disorders. The ability to perceive and react to danger in our environment is clearly an adaptive mechanism, and is the first line in assuring our safety. In Erikson's life cycle theory, this is the first need to be met, and is essential for further development to proceed.

PPD and **Delusional Disorder, Persecutory Type** may have a genetic link, and distinguishing between the two disorders can be difficult. A delusional disorder involves a systematized, encapsulated non-bizarre delusion (for example, it is possible that a person is being sought by organized crime). **Systematization** involves a logical scheme of precautions and concerns *if the initial premise is taken as correct.* **Encapsulation** indicates that the activities of the person outside the delusion are not obviously unusual. Paranoid personalities are hypervigilant, suspicious, and self-referential, *but fall short of having delusions.* Additionally, this behavior is not encapsulated - it is pervasive throughout their interactions with others.

Differentiation from **Paranoid Schizophrenia** is easier; bizarre delusions, hallucinations, and a formal thought disorder are not present in PPD. Patients with well-controlled paranoid schizophrenia (residual phase) may still be prone to experience delusions. This, as well as the history, helps distinguish these disorders. The diagnosis of PPD cannot be made in the presence of **Schizophrenia, Delusional Disorder** or **Other Psychotic Disorders**.

OTHER DIAGNOSTIC CONSIDERATIONS

Mood disorders (Mania or Depression) can manifest paranoid elements. However, the mood disturbance is present first, and is usually significant enough that differentiation is not difficult.

Use of amphetamines or marijuana can also induce paranoid reactions, though this has been described as being closer to paranoid schizophrenia. Paranoia has been reported to be the most common psychological reaction in cocaine use.

MENTAL STATUS EXAMINATION

APPEARANCE:	None characteristic; may be wary and have shifting eyes; in some cases physical abnormalities or sensory deficits may be present
BEHAVIOR:	Hypervigilant, anxious, or tense
COOPERATION:	Usually suspicious, guarded, or challenging
AFFECT:	Often anxious, hostile, humorless
SPEECH:	Fluent; goal directed
CONTENT OF THOUGHT:	Will try to decipher "true" intentions and confront them when revealed; otherwise, will generally speak about the plots and conspiracies of others; may have ideas of reference
THOUGHT FORM:	No characteristic abnormality
PERCEPTION:	Generally intact; heightened awareness to all stimuli
INSIGHT & JUDGMENT:	Impaired; continually justify suspiciousness and hypervigilance
SUICIDE - HOMICIDE:	More likely to be dangerous to others than to themselves, but may be self-injurious to preempt danger they perceive as inevitable

Psychodynamic Aspects

At the core of this diagnosis is extremely low self-esteem. Paranoid personalities are outwardly demanding, superior, mistrustful, vigilant, lacking in sentimentality and moralistic. Internally, they are timid, plagued with doubt, gullible, unable to grasp the big picture, and can be quite inconsiderate. They exude a stilted, grandiose manner in an attempt to compensate for their inner selves. Special attention is given to those with a higher rank, or more power, as they desire strong allies, but are also fearful of being attack. Self-referential grandiosity is evident in that everything patients notice must somehow be directly related to them. Self-esteem is enhanced by exerting power against authority and important people. Feelings of vindication and moral triumph provide a fleeting sense of safety and righteousness. They are litigious and live out a need to challenge and defeat a persecutory parent.

The initial understanding of PPD involved an underlying conflict over homosexuality. This evolved into the current understanding, which is wish for a same-sex relationship. First attachments outside the home are generally to same-sex friends. In their isolation, patients tend to repeat this tendency. However, it can be misinterpreted as homosexuality, triggering a series of ego defenses. Another view is that they are more worried about passive surrender to others than about homosexuality (Shapiro, 1965).

Homosexuals, minorities and deviants may serve as an easy target for the projected feelings of intimacy and dependency. Interestingly, the persecutory group often bears a close resemblance to the patient.

Paranoid patients are constantly warding off humiliation, transforming any sense of their own culpability into a threat from the outside. They are fearful of shocking others with their depravity. For this reason, intimacy is avoided. They expect to be "found out" and are continuously trying to find the evil intent in others' behavior towards them. In paranoid thinking, showing weakness invites an attack.

Because of past experiences, and the unacceptability of unconscious yearnings for closeness, intimacy is avoided. Love is feared as much as hate. Wishes for closeness are abhorred, denied and projected.

An example of this his process is as follows:

Yearning for closer relationship to someone of the same gender
↓
Unconscious misinterpretation of the impulse as sexually motivated
↓
Denial of unacceptable impulse
↓
Projection of impulse onto external group   UNCONSCIOUS
↓ ——
Suspicions of a conspiracy   CONSCIOUS

Here, this person would only be consciously aware of being
persecuted, while the other steps are carried out on an unconscious
level. Treating PPD can be difficult because of the many steps
between the initial feeling and its subsequent defensive handling.

WHAT HAPPENS IN PSYCHODYNAMIC THERAPY?

The goal with paranoid patients is to try and create trust via a solid
working alliance. When trust is truly achieved, the therapeutic process
has been successful. The process of acknowledging weaknesses,
making disclosures and attempting an enduring relationship are
important steps in treatment.

There is a strong tendency to try and talk patients out of their
persecutory thoughts. Because people are not universally benevolent,
it is difficult to persuade patients against being bothered by the "clues"
they uncover. In fact, they may perceive the attempt as a ploy to get
their guard down, with the possible effect of increasing their level of
suspicion. It is more helpful to NOT confront paranoid ideas. To do
this, adopt a "let's agree to disagree" understanding. Paranoid patients
are incredibly attuned to the emotions and attitudes of those around
them. Their disorder involves a *misperception* of what happens, not
missing details. Challenging their beliefs is seen as an overt comment
on their sanity, not that they have misinterpreted their environment.

If asked directly about your beliefs, try an empathic statement that
validates their feelings, but also offers an alternative explanation. For
example, "I can see why you are upset about people at work talking
about you. Anyone would find that uncomfortable. However, could it
be possible, just *possible* that there is another explanation for what is
happening?" This at least opens the door to a future re-examination by
patients but gives them the option, in the short term, of feeling
supported, and taking or leaving what you've said.

The usual practices in psychotherapy are less likely to be successful with paranoid patients. Interpretations that attempt to probe the depth of their conflicts are not going to be graciously received. Consistency is another critical element in the therapeutic process. Regardless of the details of how therapy is carried out (missed sessions, telephone calls, vacations etc.), it is important that this be consistent.

Attention to behavior or verbal slips (**parapraxes**) only increases anxiety. Early scrutiny of ego defenses evokes unmanageable anxiety, regression and use of even more primitive defense mechanisms.

Another maxim in therapy is to, "Analyze resistance before content." In the interest of building an alliance, it may be better to provide straightforward answers to their questions. Giving answers, instead of trying to get at a deeper meaning, conveys an openness and genuineness lacking in their experiences with others.

However, observance of boundaries is especially important. Every action or statement can be misinterpreted and prove to be a complication. Patients are preoccupied with being used for personal gain. They need to be shown that their tirades can be withstood, and not alter a therapist's customary stance.

A sense of humor can be a critical therapeutic factor in treating paranoid patients (also in writing books). While there are risks, they are outweighed by the potential benefits. Obviously, a sense of appropriateness is warranted. Patients can model the behavior of the therapist laughing at himself or herself, life's coincidences and objects of humor without being degraded. Humor can be used in therapy by making light of **your** mistakes, idiosyncrasies and pretensions. Paranoid patients' hypervigilance makes it very likely that your deficiencies will have been noticed. For example, should a patient mention that you yawned in his or her presence, try a light-hearted response about "not being able to get away with anything," instead of justifying a hectic schedule.

Another technique is to search for precipitants when patients are upset (look for the DIR). Avoiding confrontation, and focusing on the cause, can help reduce paranoid thinking. When patients do this outside of therapy, fear of malevolence from others gradually gives way to a focus on their own motives.

PROJECTIVE IDENTIFICATION IN TWO CLINICAL SCENARIOS

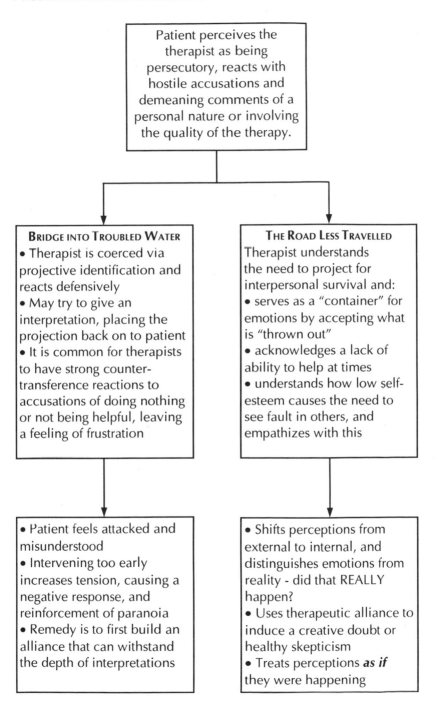

Patient perceives the therapist as being persecutory, reacts with hostile accusations and demeaning comments of a personal nature or involving the quality of the therapy.

BRIDGE INTO TROUBLED WATER
• Therapist is coerced via projective identification and reacts defensively
• May try to give an interpretation, placing the projection back on to patient
• It is common for therapists to have strong counter-transference reactions to accusations of doing nothing or not being helpful, leaving a feeling of frustration

THE ROAD LESS TRAVELLED
Therapist understands the need to project for interpersonal survival and:
• serves as a "container" for emotions by accepting what is "thrown out"
• acknowledges a lack of ability to help at times
• understands how low self-esteem causes the need to see fault in others, and empathizes with this

• Patient feels attacked and misunderstood
• Intervening too early increases tension, causing a negative response, and reinforcement of paranoia
• Remedy is to first build an alliance that can withstand the depth of interpretations

• Shifts perceptions from external to internal, and distinguishes emotions from reality - did that REALLY happen?
• Uses therapeutic alliance to induce a creative doubt or healthy skepticism
• Treats perceptions *as if* they were happening

Patients also learn by modeling. By making a distinction between thoughts and actions, they can learn that it is acceptable to have morbid fantasies. Patients can model their therapist's capacity to experience baser feelings and emotions without acting on them. One does not become bad or evil for simply having thoughts. Patients can learn to enjoy feelings and fantasies and use therapy as a place to discuss them.

The inner world of aggression, hostility, destruction and confusion between thought and action leaves patients concerned their ideas can injure or annihilate. Convey to patients a personal strength and frankness that can withstand their fantasies. Over time, this can be a rewarding therapeutic effort. After their haranguing, a warmth and appreciation for your devotion and honesty can emerge. Patients are capable of deep attachment and protracted loyalty to those for whom they care.

TRANSFERENCE AND COUNTERTRANSFERENCE REACTIONS

Paranoid patients are quite active. Their transference is swift, intense and negative. Their universal tendency to project is the basis for transference, as there is a great need to disavow upsetting attitudes. Therapists are often seen as humiliating, hostile and derogatory. They experience authority figures as superior and out to expose them. Consequently, they seem grim, humorless and poised to criticize.

In response to early transference reactions, raise the possibility that there may be a way to help them, and that their best interests are being kept in mind. This may be difficult. It takes requires considerable comfort to deal with the hatred and suspiciousness of their negative transference. Serving as a "container" for emotions helps patients learn that they can't destroy others with their bad thoughts. Acceptance of their strong feelings conveys a sense of safety from retaliation. Patients eventually come to acknowledge that the human qualities they consider unacceptable exist within everyone.

Same-sex therapists need to be aware that erotized transference can occur as a result of the patient's deprivation and confusion between thoughts and actions. Should this occur, examine the precipitants to their reaction, and explore the feelings behind the precipitants. Differentiate their fantasies from the boundaries in the therapy.

Much of the initial time is spent with the therapist being the target of **projection** and **projective identification.** It is very easy to respond with a sense of vulnerability and defensiveness. Countertransference is often anxious or hostile, and quite strong. These powerful feelings can eventually cause a hatred for patients because they have the freedom to vent their feelings. However, using countertransference is the best guide to understanding the affect, or impulse, that patients are defending against.

Even when therapy has progressed in a stable and dependable fashion, one minor disappointment can erase "credibility" and leave patients feeling convinced the therapist has finally been revealed. If countertransference reactions become an impediment, arrange for transfer or supervision. Personal therapy can be an invaluable asset in understanding countertransference reactions to patients.

SUMMARY OF THERAPEUTIC TECHNIQUES

• The cardinal modalities in treating paranoid patients are: respect, integrity, tact and patience
• Don't challenge negative views or their recollection of events, instead, get details; empathize with feelings
• Don't deflate grandiosity - behind it is their low self-esteem
• Share notes if requested
• Seek suggestions of how to improve therapy
• Encourage and demonstrate openness
• Accept tirades; avoid the issue of fault; make connections with feelings - "You must be exhausted. . ." "It must be difficult . . ."
• Don't return projections in the early stages of therapy
• Observe your actions for possible legitimacy of patients' observations
• Encourage elaboration; facilitate this by using silence

PHARMACOTHERAPY

Antipsychotics have been tried but without consistent results. Brief psychotic episodes (minutes to hours) can occur, but since PPD is not a psychotic disorder, neuroleptics may be needed for short periods only. Anxiolytics or antidepressants may be used from time to time. PPD can be a premorbid condition to an Axis I disorder.

Cognitive Therapy

Cognitive strategies stress the use of action over words to help gain trust. The initial task is to increase self-efficacy through improving coping skills, or if these skills are adequate, patients' *sense* of self-efficacy. If they feel confident they can handle the "attacks" of others, they will be less bothered by them. The step next involves a modification of their basic assumptions and interpersonal reactions. For example:

Basic Assumption: "The world is a rotten place. It's a dog-eat-dog world and if you aren't careful, you'll get chewed up and spit out."

Interpersonal Reaction: Sees others as threats and alienates them with poor treatment (e.g. unjustified accusations or unwarranted suspicion).

Result: Other people (understandably) react harshly and increase the strength of the negative basic assumption.

The next focus is on testing their negative views by trusting others with small things and evaluating the outcome. By doing so, patients become aware the world has a spectrum of people in it ranging from malevolent to benevolent. Once this is achieved, assertiveness training is used to increase social skills so they can learn to deal with others in a way that does not provoke hostility.

Hypersensitivity to criticism is a reaction that can be targeted with a behavioral approach. Initially, patients are taught a type of anxiety-reducing response (progressive muscular relaxation or a cognitive intervention). Next, biofeedback via physiologic indicators such as Electromyography **(EMG)** or Galvanic Skin Response **(GSR)** is used. When anxiety is generated via a hierarchy of criticisms, it can be diminished using the methods previously learned.

Other interventions that can be used are:

• Teaching patients to attend to a wider range of social stimuli, not just what they selectively abstract. (e.g. watch a video tape together)
• Correcting interpretation of ambiguous stimuli
• Adjust appearance, hygiene, grooming, tone of voice, etc.

GROUP THERAPY

Paranoid patients generally do poorly in group therapy due to their active misinterpretation of others' motives, and the difficulty in understanding, and dealing, with **projective identification.**

Factors that make group therapy more likely to succeed are:

• well-timed introduction - no active confrontational crisis occurring in the group when paranoid patients begin therapy
• well-balanced composition of the group
• ability of the therapist to act as an ally for the paranoid patient
• coincident introduction of a PPD patient with another newcomer

The ability of the group to provide a consensus about suspicions or projections is a powerful intervention, and may be more successful than in individual therapy.

COURSE

Comparatively little research has been conducted on PPD because of its tradition of being poorly treatable.

PPD tends to run a chronic course, remaining generally resistant to therapeutic efforts. Patients readily find evidence from their surroundings and interactions with others to reaffirm their suspiciousness. On a daily basis, newspapers, TV, and radio programs pass along the details of personal tragedies, buttressing the vigilance of paranoid patients.

In general, patients have enduring problems in occupations and relationships. Little is known about the longitudinal course of this disorder. However, later in life paranoid ideation becomes an increasingly common finding. As cognitive faculties wane, exaggerated issues of safety emerge. Many geriatric patients come to therapeutic attention by families tired of the endless accusations of theft. Elderly patients not infrequently limit their travels outside their dwellings, and in extreme cases, barricade themselves in.

As mentioned, PPD can be an antecedent to an Axis I disorder.

REFERENCES

American Psychiatric Association
DIAGNOSTIC AND STATISTICAL MANUAL OF MENTAL DISORDERS, FOURTH EDITION
American Psychiatric Press; Washington, D.C., 1994

N. Andreason, D. Black
INTRODUCTORY TEXTBOOK OF PSYCHIATRY
American Psychiatric Press; Washington, D.C., 1991

A. Beck, A. Freeman & Associates
COGNITIVE THERAPY OF PERSONALITY DISORDERS
The Guildford Press; New York, 1990

G. Gabbard
PSYCHODYNAMIC PSYCHIATRY IN CLINICAL PRACTICE, THE DSM-IV EDITION
American Psychiatric Press; Washington, D.C., 1994

H. Kaplan, B. Sadock (editors)
COMPREHENSIVE GROUP PSYCHOTHERAPY, SECOND EDITION
Williams & Wilkins; Baltimore, 1983

H. Kaplan, B. Sadock (editors)
COMPREHENSIVE TEXTBOOK OF PSYCHIATRY, SIXTH EDITION
Williams & Wilkins; Baltimore, 1995

N. McWilliams
PSYCHOANALYTIC DIAGNOSIS
The Guildford Press; New York, 1994

E. Othmer & S. Othmer
THE CLINICAL INTERVIEW USING DSM-IV
American Psychiatric Press; Washington, D.C., 1994

D. Shapiro
NEUROTIC STYLES
Basic Books; New York, 1965

I. Turkat
THE PERSONALITY DISORDERS: A PSYCHOLOGICAL APPROACH TO CLINICAL
MANAGEMENT
Pergamon Press; Elmsford, New York, 1990

PARANOPOLY

THE BOARD GAME

The Schizotypal Personality

BIOGRAPHICAL INFORMATION

Name:	Aldrina Q. Cosmos
Occupation:	Developer for a UFO landing pad
Appearance:	Tin foil hat, unpaired socks, mood ring, dress hemmed with staples
Relationship with animals:	Laments pet budgie remains dead, despite séances
Favourite Song:	*Dark Side of the Moon*

AT THE THERAPIST'S OFFICE

Before Session:	Reads palms, tea leaves and tarot cards of others in the waiting room
Waiting Room Reading:	*Astrology Weekly*
During Session:	Initiates session by talking to herself
Fantasies Involve:	A management position with the *Thought Broadcasting Corporation*
Relationship with Therapist:	Casts a spell on therapist
Behavior During Session:	Plays with voodoo Barbie doll
Takes to Therapy:	An autographed copy of new book on neologisms, *"How to Call 'Em as I see 'Em"*

DIAGNOSTIC SHORTHAND

MNEMONIC - "UFO AIDER"

Unusual perceptions
Friendless except for family
Odd beliefs, thinking and speech

Affect is inappropriate or constricted
Ideas of reference
Doubts others - suspicious and paranoid
Eccentric appearance and behavior
Reluctant in social situations, anxious

INTRODUCTION

The word *schizotypal* is an abbreviation for *schizophrenic genotype*. This diagnosis is characterized by deficits in interpersonal relationships and distortions in both cognition and perception.

Some of the key names associated with this disorder are:
• **Kraeplin** (1920's) noted that relatives of schizophrenic patients often had **schizophrenic spectrum** traits
• **Bleuler** (1924) described **latent** and **simple schizophrenia**; these were precedents for this diagnosis (see DIFFERENTIAL DIAGNOSIS)
• **Fairbairn and Guntrip** (1969) made contributions to the description and understanding of this disorder
• **Kety** (1971) in his Danish adoption studies reported on a condition that resembled schizophrenia, but was not as severe; this was initially called *borderline schizophrenia*, but the name was changed to avoid confusion with the borderline personality disorder
• **McGlashan** (1983) conducted a long-term study demonstrating similar outcomes in schizophrenia and schizotypal personalities

The schizotypal personality disorder (SztPD) was first included in the DSM-III. This is the only personality disorder defined empirically on the basis of a genetic relationship to an Axis I disorder (schizophrenia). The symptoms are schizophrenia-like, but expressed to a lesser degree, and cause a less severe impact on social and occupational functioning. Patients exhibit peculiar behavior, exaggerated social anxiety and idiosyncratic speech.

SztPD has an overlap with the positive symptoms of schizophrenia, while the schizoid personality has more of an overlap with the negative symptoms (see P. 63 in the SCHIZOID PERSONALITY CHAPTER).

These patients rarely seek medical attention because of their personality eccentricities alone. Usually an acute stressor or the encouragement of a family member brings them for help. In response to stress, these individuals may experience psychotic episodes that last from minutes to hours. These episodes are often referred to as **micropsychotic episodes**, usually do not last as long as twenty-four hours, and therefore do not meet the criteria for a Brief Psychotic Disorder. There is also an increased risk of suffering from Mood (**Depression, Dysthymia**) and Anxiety disorders (**Social Phobia, Generalized Anxiety Disorder**).

Media Examples

Schizotypal characters are frequently cast as: fortune tellers, clairvoyants, mystics, psychics, mediums and mind readers. The presumptive ability of these characters to predict the future, or make revelations about other characters enhances development of the plot. The visions, predictions and warnings offered by these characters often turn into self-fulfilling prophecies for the main characters. Additionally, with the "suspension of disbelief" required for the enjoyment of many movies, these inspired predictions can come true. Here is a compilation of some schizotypal characters:

• **Ghost** - Whoopi Goldberg won an Oscar for her performance as a storefront medium who conveys messages from a wrongfully murdered banker to his girlfriend. The humorous scenes involving her fraudulent attempts to contact the deceased relatives at a séance make her actual abilities that much more memorable.

• **Hello Again** - Judith Ivey turns in an endearing performance as Zelda, the witch-like sister, who resurrects the main character one year after her death. Her apparel, name, supernatural bookstore and various incantations all add to a colorful portrayal.

• **Benny & Joon** - Mary Stuart Masterson portrays Joon, a troubled young woman, who alternates between being a creative spirit when things are good, to a raging arsonist when she is upset. Though her diagnosis is not directly addressed in the film, she likely suffers from schizophrenia. Her difficulties with relationships, along with her eccentricities, provide a flavor of schizotypal qualities.

• **Macbeth** (Shakespearean play, movie versions released in 1948 & 1971) - The three witches who issue puzzling prophecies to Macbeth and Banquo have schizotypal features. They use unusual speech ("Fair is foul, and foul is fair"), perform a ritualistic dance and concoct a magical brew in a cauldron.

• **Seinfeld** (1990's TV) - The character of Kramer has many schizotypal personality features: quirkiness, unusual beliefs, odd speech, etc.

Other schizotypal characters can be seen in: **Live and Let Die**, **Pet Sematary**, **The Addams Family** (1960's TV show, movie versions in 1991 & 1993) and **Beetlejuice**.

Interview Considerations

Schizotypal patients often seem unusual in interviews. Empathy and nonjudgmental acceptance of (but not agreement with) their irrational perceptions is necessary in order to establish rapport. Once achieved, persistent inquisitiveness reveals a sanctuary of unusual ideas. Often these patients will reveal insights, references, eccentricities and connections that make them sound like they are from another planet.

It is not usually difficult to maintain the interview once these patients feel accepted. Use facilitating techniques such as open-ended questions and ask for specific information and examples to illustrate answers. As long as patients feel you can appreciate their experiences, they will be cooperative.

In a well conducted interview, schizotypal patients may sense a connection, and ask if you share the same experiences. In this situation it is important to preserve the tone you have set. Do not dismiss their views or prematurely confront them with reality. "Agree to disagree" on the idea/point/issue in order to preserve rapport.

Schizotypal Themes

- Clairvoyance
- Ideas of reference
- Suspiciousness
- Emotional Reasoning

- Premonitions
- Alternative/Fringe interests
- Existential concerns
- Magical Thinking

Presumed Etiology

BIOLOGICAL: The schizotypal personality disorder has a strong genetic link to schizophrenia. Adoption and family studies have consistently found an increased prevalence of **schizophrenic spectrum** disorders in the relatives of patients with SztPD.

Similarly, there is an increased prevalence of SztPD in the relatives of patients with schizophrenia. Epidemiologic studies have shown the prevalence of SztPD to be three times that of schizophrenia in the general population. It may be that the SztPD is a milder and more common expression of the schizophrenic genetic diathesis.

Biological and physiological findings in schizophrenia may also be abnormal in patients with SztPD:

• Smooth pursuit eye movement (**SPEM**) abnormalities. When following a moving object, rapid eye movements (**saccades**) occur.
• Auditory evoked potentials (**EP**) measure neural activity in response to a sound. Potentials are identified by polarity (positive or negative - P or N) and latency after the stimulus (in milliseconds). In these patients, there is a decrease in the size of the positive peak at 300ms (P300) which may represent a defect in cognitive processing. Impairment is also seen on other tests of visual or auditory attention.
• Elevated levels of homovanillic acid (**HVA**) in the cerebrospinal fluid and plasma may be associated with positive symptoms.
• An abnormally high ventricle-brain ratio (**VBR**) is seen on CT scans.

PSYCHOSOCIAL: The concordance rate for schizophrenia in monozygotic twins approaches fifty percent. Put another way, if one twin develops schizophrenia, the other has a fifty percent chance of doing so. This emphasizes the role of psychosocial factors in the development of psychiatric disorders. Due to the relatively recent description of SztPD as a separate disorder, there are few theories about what may constitute a definite psychosocial contributor.

A number of psychosocial theories have been advanced regarding schizophrenia and may be operative in the pathogenesis of SztPD:

• **Social Causation:** This theory postulates that being a member of lower socioeconomic classes is significant in causing mental illness.

• **Learning Theory:** Emotionally disturbed parental figures act as models for the irrational behavior seen in patients.

• **Double Bind:** Conflicting messages within a family cause patients to withdraw into a regressed state to avoid unsolvable problems.

• **Schisms and Skews:** This theory postulates these abnormal patterns of interaction within families lead to an unhealthy alignment of a parent with a child, or an abnormally dominant caretaker.

• **Pseudomutual and Pseudohostile Families:** These forms of communication suppress emotional expression. Such a family develops an idiosyncratic pattern causing difficulties when children are required to relate to others.

• **Expressed Emotion (EE):** This is defined specifically as showing hostility, criticism, or becoming overinvolved with patients. This is an important educational point for the families of affected individuals, and also has therapeutic and prognostic implications.

Given the genetic correlation with schizophrenia, and difficulties with cognitive processing, it can be hypothesized that such a stimulus barrier could create difficulties at all stages of development. In the **vulnerability-stress model**, a person is genetically "loaded" (vulnerability or diathesis), and then a stressor causes the emergence of the disorder. The actual stress can take many forms:

• Parents who are too indulgent, neglectful, authoritarian or just overly *something.*
• Substance abuse or dependence.
• Break-up of a relationship, or other losses.
• The stresses of leaving home and/or academic hardship.

In summary, an inherited schizophrenic genotype causes deficits in neural integration, which combined with environmental influences, lead to an abnormally organized personality.

EPIDEMIOLOGY

The prevalence is estimated to be 3% of the population. While there is no sex difference, women may display more "positive" symptoms.

EGO DEFENSES

Ego defences in SztPD are generally primitive or narcissistic, and used to extreme degrees (psychosis in some cases):

•**Projection:** see PARANOID CHAPTER
•**Denial:** abolishment of external reality; may see replacement with a wish-fulfilling fantasy
•**Distortion:** reshaping reality to meet inner needs, leading to unrealistic beliefs, overvalued ideas, hallucinations, etc.
•**Primitive Idealization:** external objects are seen as being "all good" and perceived as being omnipotent
•**Splitting:** dividing external objects into all good or bad with abrupt shifts between the categories
•**Schizoid Fantasy:** an autistic retreat to resolve conflicts and avoidance of intimacy

DIAGNOSTIC CRITERIA

A. A pervasive pattern of social and interpersonal deficits marked by acute discomfort with, and reduced capacity for, close relationships as well as by cognitive or perceptual distortions and eccentricities of behavior, beginning by early childhood and present in a variety of contexts, as indicated by five (or more) of the following:

(1) ideas of reference (excluding delusions of reference)
(2) odd beliefs or magical thinking that influences behavior and is inconsistent with subcultural norms (e.g., superstitiousness, belief in clairvoyance, telepathy, or "sixth sense"; in children and adolescents bizarre fantasies or preoccupations)
(3) unusual perceptual experiences, including bodily illusions
(4) odd thinking and speech (e.g., vague, circumstantial, metaphorical, overelaborate, or stereotyped)
(5) suspiciousness or paranoid ideation
(6) inappropriate or constricted affect
(7) behavior or appearance that is odd, eccentric, or peculiar
(8) lack of close friends or confidants other than first-degree relatives
(9) excessive social anxiety that does not diminish with familiarity and tends to be associated with paranoid fears rather than negative judgments about self

B. Does not occur exclusively during the course of Schizophrenia, a Mood Disorder With Psychotic Features, another Psychotic Disorder, or a Pervasive Developmental Disorder.
REPRINTED WITH PERMISSION FROM THE DSM-IV.
COPYRIGHT, AMERICAN PSYCHIATRIC ASSOCIATION, 1994

DIFFERENTIAL DIAGNOSIS

Schizotypal is one of the five "schizo" terms defined in the SCHIZOID CHAPTER. The term **schizophrenic spectrum** has been used to describe disorders that seem to share a genetic basis, with a variable degree of expression. This spectrum is illustrated on the next page. These disorders have an overlap of mental status findings and symptoms. In many cases, differentiation is made by the *degree* to which they are expressed, as well as the *presence* or *absence* of certain features.

Schizophrenic Spectrum

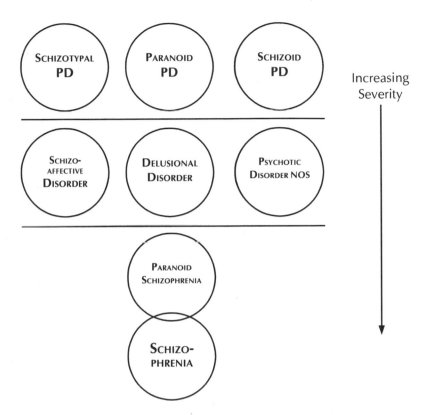

SztPD is differentiated from **Schizophrenia, Delusional Disorder** and a **Mood Disorder With Psychotic Features** by the absence of enduring psychosis. The presence of one of these disorders excludes the diagnosis of SztPD. Patients with SztPD also lack the clear change in level of function that occurs with more severe disorders. In order to distinguish this personality disorder from the residual or prodromal stages of schizophrenia, collateral history may required. Additionally, thought form and content in SztPD are disturbed to a lesser degree than in schizophrenia.

Brief psychotic episodes lasting minutes to hours can occur in SztPD. The diagnosis of **Brief Psychotic Disorder** requires that a psychotic disturbance lasts at least one full day, but less than one month, with a florid thought disorder. Disorders due to **Substance Use** or due to a **General Medical Condition** must be considered in the differential diagnosis of all psychiatric patients.

Other Diagnostic Considerations

As with SzdPD, any disorder that is marked by eccentric behavior, isolation and peculiarities of language needs to be differentiated from: **Autism, Asperger's Disorder, Expressive** and **Mixed Receptive-Expressive Disorders.** Language Disorders are established by the primacy and severity of these difficulties in relation to other features.

Prior to the DSM-III, schizotypal features were incorporated under certain subtypes of schizophrenia. Although the terms below are not included in the DSM-IV, they are still used occasionally and encompass descriptions that overlap with the concept of SztPD:

Latent Schizophrenia: Occasional behavioral peculiarities or thought disorders; progression to clear psychotic pathology does not occur. Also knows as *borderline* or *pseudoneurotic* schizophrenia.

Simple Schizophrenia: Gradual, insidious loss of drive, interest and initiative. Vocational performance deteriorates and there is marked social withdrawal. Hallucinations or delusions may be present, but only for brief periods of time.

In the ICD-10, the schizotypal personality is called the *Schizotypal Disorder* and is considered a major psychiatric disorder, along with Schizophrenia and Delusional Disorder.

Mental Status Findings

The most notable abnormalities in the mental status examination of a schizotypal patient occur in the areas of perception, thought content and thought form. Examples of these findings are as follows:

Perceptual Abnormalities

A **hallucination** is a perception of a non-existent external stimulus, occurring in any of the five senses; most frequent are auditory then visual, other types are more indicative of general medical conditions (e.g. epilepsy). An **Illusion** is a misperception of an existing external stimulus, which can also occur in any of the five sensory modalities.

Depersonalization: The subjective sense of feeling unreal, unfamiliar, or that one's identity is lost. **Derealization** is the subjective sense that the environment is unreal or strange.

THOUGHT CONTENT
Thought content refers to **what** a person is thinking or talking about.

Delusion: A fixed, false belief out of keeping with cultural norms, and inappropriate for the level of education or intelligence.

Overvalued Idea: Similar to a delusion, but of lesser intensity.

Idea of Reference: Belief that the actions of others refer to that person; radio or television broadcasts may contain special messages for that person; if unshakable, it is called a **Delusion of Reference.**

Idea of Influence: Belief that another person or force controls that person. If not amenable to change, called a **Delusion of Influence.**

Magical Thinking: Belief that thoughts, words, or actions have special powers. For example, something can happen simply by wishing it.

THOUGHT FORM OR PROCESS
Thought form refers to **how** a person is thinking or talking.

Neologism: A new word with an idiosyncratic meaning. Sniglets are made-up words that have an understandable meaning:

Neologism: Flogblock - the name for the tongue on a shoe.
Sniglet: Charp - the green, mutant potato chip found in every bag.

Circumstantiality: An indirect type of speech that eventually addresses the point or answers the question, but is overinclusive of detail.
If A is the starting point and B is the goal, circumstantial speech is:

$$A \rightarrow C \rightarrow D \rightarrow E \rightarrow F \rightarrow G \rightarrow B$$

Tangentiality: An inability to express goal directed thought.
If A is the starting point and B is the goal, tangential speech is:

$$A \rightarrow C \rightarrow D \rightarrow E \rightarrow F \rightarrow G \rightarrow H$$

Loosening of Associations: Flow of thought where ideas do not follow an understandable or logical sequence.
If A is the starting point and B is a logical connection, loose associations are:

$$A \rightarrow G \rightarrow X \rightarrow J \rightarrow K \rightarrow V \rightarrow O$$

Mental Status Examination

APPEARANCE: Often peculiar; may have amulets, charms, odd jewelry; don't reflect social convention or current styles; accessories/colors may have special meaning

BEHAVIOR: May be anxious towards a skeptical interviewer; behavioral oddities may include unusual facial expressions; odd affectation

COOPERATION: Cooperative, especially in a receptive atmosphere

AFFECT: Ranges from restricted/flat to animated; varies from topic to topic

SPEECH: Unusual or idiosyncratic meaning to some words; context can be odd; may use neologisms

CONTENT OF THOUGHT: Paranoid ideas; suspiciousness; magical thinking; telepathy; premonitions; "sixth sense"; out of body experiences; bizarre coincidences; extra sensory perception (ESP); "other worldly" matters

THOUGHT FORM: No characteristic abnormality; may be tangential, circumstantial, vague, overelaborate or metaphorical

PERCEPTION: May have unusual perceptual experiences

INSIGHT & JUDGMENT: Partial; may be aware others consider them odd; judgment is based heavily on their perception of reality which is not verifiable

SUICIDE - HOMICIDE: Need to consider this in conjunction with any Axis I disorder; not generally dangerous to others or themselves; risk increases with the presence of a formal thought disorder or marked paranoia

Psychodynamic Aspects

The psychodynamic theories regarding schizophrenia and SztPD are similar and can be considered as varying only in degree of severity. Freud hypothesized that schizophrenic patients are fixated at an early stage of development. The resulting defects in ego structure facilitate psychotic regression in response to conflict or frustration. Additionally, Freud thought that schizophrenic patients reinvest psychic energy (known as **cathexis**) back into the self, instead of towards people (objects) around them. This contributes to the development of an autistic world with subjective thinking, introversion and personal use of language, which are features also seen in SztPD.

There are other psychoanalytic views of schizophrenia that enhance the understanding of schizotypal personality development:

• **Object constancy** is not achieved. This is defined as the ability to develop *evocative* memory and create a stable intrapsychic image of a caregiver. Without this, the person faces difficulty in progressing beyond the *oral stage* of development, typified by complete dependence on a caregiver. Such a defect in developing a separate identity predisposes a patient to a personality structure which is vulnerable to disintegration under stress. Primitive ego defenses are used, due to the fixation of development at this early stage.

• Conflict between the ego and id is theorized to cause neurotic conflict, characterized by anxiety, hypochondriasis, obsessions, compulsions, etc. The conflict in psychosis is between the ego and the external world, where reality is disavowed and reconstructed via hallucinations, delusions, etc.

• Psychotic thought processes or mental status findings have a symbolic meaning for the patient. Schizotypal patients may be overwhelmed by demands and stresses, creating an alternate reality that is more manageable and comprehensible. Perceptual abnormalities and delusions may represent inner wishes or fears. Magical thinking and ideas of influence represent a wishes for child-like omnipotence over uncontrollable or unpleasant events.

An infant having a temperamental difficulty with attachment may perceive mother as rejecting, and then withdraw from her. However, the infant's needs grow until they seem insatiable. At this point, the infant may fear that its own greed will devour mother, with subsequent abandonment. As adults, schizoid and schizotypal patients are affected by highly conflicting feelings, on the one hand fearing that their neediness will drive others away, but also fearing that others will devour them (projected greed) if they get too close. These oral issues of devouring others, or being devoured stem from stasis at the oral stage of development.

As with the schizoid patients, a *schism* exists within schizotypal patients, and results in a diffusion of their identity. They seek distance to maintain their safety and separateness, and though desiring closeness, may complain of alienation and loneliness.

What Happens in Psychodynamic Therapy?

In the therapy of all psychiatric conditions, a higher level of functioning prior to entering therapy generally predicts a better outcome. Diagnosis is only one parameter that needs to be considered in a treatment plan. A comprehensive assessment of a patient's strengths, coping skills, intelligence and ability to form attachments is essential in guiding psychotherapy of any type.

In general, Cluster A patients are vulnerable to decompensation under stressful conditions. Along the continuum of techniques, a supportive focus is recommended over an exploratory or confrontative one. Typically, a "here and now" directive approach is more useful.

In previous sections, schizotypal patients have been described as using primitive ego defenses because of fixation at the oral stage of development. The importance of establishing and preserving rapport is critical for initiating therapy. An interested and accepting stance needs to be maintained, regardless of what patients reveal.

The most frequent complication arises when patients seek to test their perceptions, or ask for reassurance about them. It may be more profitable to address the feelings expressed (fear, sadness, etc.) with these unusual ideas and experiences than it is to confront reality directly. Internalization of a non-judgmental, respectful relationship is much more therapeutic for schizotypal patients than is an interpretation regarding their use of the psychic hotline.

As in any therapy, alteration of the style of relating to others will be met with resistance. In schizotypal patients, this is likely to take the form of silence because their fundamental difficulty is that of relating to other people (criteria eight and nine). Just as with the expression of unusual perceptions and ideas, silence should be non-judgmentally accepted. Silence in this situation is a defensive retreat on the patient's part. Use of **projective identification** evokes similar distancing responses from therapists as it does from others in the patient's life.

As therapy proceeds, the therapist may need to serve as an auxiliary ego. Schizotypal patients have a tendency to misinterpret reality and focus on a possible or symbolic meaning, rather than the intended one.

SztPD shares two features with **Schizophrenia:**

• **concrete thinking:** a style of thinking characterized by literalness and lack of generalization or abstraction; patients often miss the humor or irony in a situation

• difficulties with **ego-boundaries:** patients do not have a well-developed sense of themselves and may be confused about where they end and another person begins

Other situations may arise where patients need help with practical matters or guidance with decision-making. Once trust has developed, entertaining a creative or benevolent skepticism about patients' ideas and perceptions can improve and support reality testing. Over time, the goal of therapy is to help patients develop a more cohesive, integrated sense of self. Internalization of the therapeutic relationship facilitates an awareness of unconscious conflicts and an opportunity to reduce conscious fears about intimacy.

TRANSFERENCE AND COUNTERTRANSFERENCE REACTIONS

The initial transference reaction schizotypal patients manifest is to test whether the therapist is concerned enough about them to tolerate their peculiarities and distant interpersonal style. Long silences may need to be endured, as these patients are prone to detach and withdraw while overcoming the fear of being dismissed as amusing crackpots.

Countertransference manifestations are generally due to the painstakingly slow progress made by these patients. Therapists must be able to tolerate the limited gains that may be made initially in areas outside of interpersonal relationships. Therapists must also be wary of the process of projective identification and monitor their reactions without ridiculing, or falling into a state of counterdetachment.

SUMMARY OF THERAPEUTIC TECHNIQUES

• Be patient; the process of therapy outweighs the content
• Consistency and punctuality help foster a stable image of the therapist, the therapy and, ultimately, the patient
• Try to understand the latent or symbolic content of perceptions and unusual thoughts
• Be flexible in giving advice, or assisting in making decisions
• Maintain firm ego boundaries; clarify distortions when they occur

Pharmacotherapy

Intuitively, it would seem that antipsychotic medication would be beneficial for schizotypal personalities. Neuroleptics are the mainstay of treatment for schizophrenia and work best for positive symptoms, which are manifested in SztPD. However, there is virtually no systematic research to support this. Use of these medications may be justified during times of crises, or with patients who are more severely affected with marked perceptual abnormalities, anxiety, or an obvious thought disorder. As a general rule, medications should be used to treat symptoms and not the personality. The presence of an Axis I disorder requires treatment with an appropriate medication.

Group Therapy

Group therapy can be of considerable benefit to schizotypal patients, particularly in the area of increasing their socialization. The group functions as an extended family providing corrective emotional experiences that increase schizotypal patients' comfort with others. Difficulties can arise with patients who are too bizarre, or too different from other members. Prolonged silences and lack of contribution may cause the group to ignore or ridicule schizotypal patients.

Cognitive Therapy

Basic Cognitive Distortions:
• Mistrust, suspiciousness or frank paranoid ideation
• Ideas of Reference - "There are special messages for me"
• Magical thinking - "I can make something happen just by wishing it"
• Illusory precepts - "I see important historical figures everyday"
Adapted from Beck, Freeman & Associates, 1990

The automatic thoughts in SztPD often reveal the distortions of **emotional reasoning** and **personalization.** In emotional reasoning, the person has a negative emotion and automatically forecasts that there will be a negative occurrence. Personalization is similar to an idea of influence in that a person falsely believes he or she is responsible for, or has control over, an external situation. **Concrete thinking** is also a feature, the best example being:
Q. What brought you to hospital today?
A. An ambulance.

After establishing a solid working alliance, cognitive strategies focus on increasing social appropriateness. This helps improve day to day functioning in the areas of hygiene, social skills and personal management. These skills are reinforced through modeling, role-playing, structured sessions and setting short-term goals that are subject to frequent review.

The next step involves the critical aspect of teaching patients to look for objective evidence in the environment with which to evaluate their automatic assumptions. Along with this, patients are asked to consider the consequences of relying only on their emotional responses. Practice and patience are required because schizotypal patients have many distorted cognitions, and not all are amenable to change over a short time period. This can be achieved by having patients first record their predictions and later assess their accuracy.

It is unlikely that these patients will ever completely eradicate their bizarre notions, but can gain some emotional relief by recognizing inaccuracies. A realistic goal is to teach coping skills that decrease behavioral and emotional responses, and increase patients' awareness of their inappropriateness. An example is repeating a coping statement such as, "Just because I have this thought/feeling doesn't mean that it is really happening."

Finally, schizotypal patients may need help with their communication style. Some patients overlook essential information in a situation and need to focus their attention to detail. Other patients may get lost in a sea of irrelevant detail and can be encouraged to make summary statements to streamline their circumstantiality.

COURSE OF SztPD

The overlap of genetic, biological and phenomenological findings with schizophrenia give SztPD one of the more pessimistic outcomes of all the personality disorders. At long term follow-up, ten to twenty percent of patients go on to develop schizophrenia. The remainder appear to have a stable course. Three characteristics of this personality disorder have been positively correlated with later onset of schizophrenia: magical thinking, paranoid ideation and social isolation.

REFERENCES

American Psychiatric Association
DIAGNOSTIC AND STATISTICAL MANUAL OF MENTAL DISORDERS, FOURTH EDITION
American Psychiatric Press; Washington, D.C., 1994

N. Andreason, D. Black
INTRODUCTORY TEXTBOOK OF PSYCHIATRY
American Psychiatric Press; Washington, D.C., 1991

A. Beck, A. Freeman & Associates
COGNITIVE THERAPY OF PERSONALITY DISORDERS
The Guildford Press; New York, 1990

G. Gabbard
PSYCHODYNAMIC PSYCHIATRY IN CLINICAL PRACTICE, THE DSM-IV EDITION
American Psychiatric Press; Washington, D.C., 1994

R. Hall and Friends
SNIGLETS
Macmillan Publishing Company; New York, 1984

H. Kaplan, B. Sadock (editors)
COMPREHENSIVE GROUP PSYCHOTHERAPY, 3RD EDITION
Williams & Wilkins; Baltimore, 1993

H. Kaplan, B. Sadock (editors)
COMPREHENSIVE TEXTBOOK OF PSYCHIATRY, 6TH EDITION
Williams & Wilkins; Baltimore, 1995

N. McWilliams
PSYCHOANALYTIC DIAGNOSIS
The Guildford Press; New York, 1994

E. Othmer & S. Othmer
THE CLINICAL INTERVIEW USING DSM-IV
American Psychiatric Press; Washington, D.C., 1994

R. Pies
CLINICAL MANUAL OF PSYCHIATRIC DIAGNOSIS AND TREATMENT
American Psychiatric Press; Washington, D.C., 1994

DID THE ANCIENTS HAVE VALUABLE INSIGHTS INTO MODERN DAY LIFE?

COULD PREHISTORIC WISDOM SOLVE TODAY'S PROBLEMS?

STILL BOGGED DOWN IN THAT FLORIDA SWAMPLAND DEAL?

Now,
in a desert
excavation site
surprisingly close to Las
Vegas, archeo-entrepreneurs
discovered amulets that contain the
wisdom of the ages. Contained within these
hieroglyphics are fundamental existential truths that are
as valid today as they were upon inscription, perhaps millennia ago.

AMULET 1
Timeless advice
for travelers[Ω]

AMULET 2
Sound financial
wisdom[Ω]

ORDER TODAY! QUANTITIES ARE LIMITED[II]

[Ω] be careful when walking between parked cars
[Ω] a fool and his money soon part ways
[II] to the first five thousand, and then we'll make more

THE HISTRIONIC PERSONALITY

BIOGRAPHICAL INFORMATION

Name:	Cindi L. Valentine
Occupation:	Cosmetician & Aesthetician
Appearance:	Coordinated shoes, earrings, purse, nails and accessories
Relationship with animals:	Has cats named Puffy, Buffy & Muffy
Favourite Song:	*Love Me Tender*

AT THE THERAPIST'S OFFICE

Before Session:	Flirts with others in the waiting room
Waiting Room Reading:	Does quiz from fashion magazine
During Session:	Gives quiz results to therapist
Fantasies Involve:	Becoming a radio sex therapist
Relationship with Therapist:	Writes best-selling novel based on sex fantasies with therapist
Behavior During Session:	Faints when quiz results interpreted
Takes to Therapy:	Hides a perfumed business card in the seat cushion

DIAGNOSTIC SHORTHAND

MNEMONIC - "I CRAVE SIN"

Inappropriate behavior; seductive or provocative

Center of attention
Relationships are seen as closer than they really are
Appearance is most important
Vulnerable to the suggestions of others
Emotional expression is exaggerated

Shifting emotions
Impressionistic manner of speaking, lacks detail
Nice, to a fault

INTRODUCTION

The word *histrionic* is derived from **hysteria**, a disorder originally used to describe phobias, dissociative and amnestic phenomena, as well as conversion and somatoform disorders. This diagnosis is characterized by excessive emotional expression and attention-seeking behavior.

Some key names associated with development of this disorder are:
• **Sydenham** (17th century) gave a description of hysterical patients: "Tears and laughter succeed each other . . . all is caprice . . . the worst passions of the mind arise without cause"
• **Charcot** (19th century) delineated and classified differing manifestations of hysteria, and demonstrated that some symptoms had a psychological etiology
• **Janet** (1889) demonstrated a relationship between trauma and an hysterical dissociation of feelings or memories of the experience
• **Kraeplin** (1904) characterized hysterical personalities as having multiple symptoms, capricious and inconsistent behavior, histrionic exaggeration and a life of illness
• **Freud** (1905) focused on the childhood sexual investment and conflicted eroticization of the opposite-sex parent
• **Schneider** (1923) was influential in making the distinction between an "attention-seeking" personality and hysteria

The histrionic personality disorder (HPD) was first called the Hysterical Personality in DSM-II. The name was changed in DSM-III, and the conditions previously called "hysteria" were distinguished from each other as **Somatoform Disorders.**

The term histrionic is derived from the Greek word *hysteria*, meaning uterus. Descriptions of hysterical conditions date back to antiquity when it was thought that the uterus could dislodge itself and wander throughout the body causing symptoms at different sites. Due to the ambiguity and possible pejorative connotation of the term **hysteria,** it no longer appears in diagnostic nomenclature.

Separation of associated Axis I conditions and the development of psychoanalytic theory have helped define HPD as a discrete disorder. These patients have an increased rate of **Somatoform Disorders** (Somatization Disorder, Conversion Disorder, Hypochondriasis) and **Mood Disorders.** There is also a considerable overlap with other Cluster B personality disorders.

MEDIA EXAMPLES

Histrionic characters are frequently cast in romantic roles and comedies. Their capricious style and vanity are qualities around which the plot or sub-plots can be built. They are very good at attracting other characters and are a natural for "center of attention" situations. A classic pairing is that of a histrionic female with an obsessive-compulsive male. Here, her unpredictability and unmodulated affect contrast his emotional constriction and pedantic nature. A variation on this theme sets the flair and *joie de vivre* of a histrionic character against the rigid, oppressive rules of society.

• **GONE WITH THE WIND** - Vivien Leigh won an Oscar for her performance as Scarlett O'Hara, the southern belle caught in the drama of the Civil War. At the beginning of the film she teases two brothers into a competition for her company at a barbecue. When there, we see her in her element, surrounded by men vying for her affection. Leigh also portrayed another histrionic southern belle, Blanche DuBois in **A STREETCAR NAMED DESIRE**.

• **THE PRIME OF MISS JEAN BRODIE** - Maggie Smith won an Academy Award for her witty caricature of a romantic crackpot teacher in an upscale private girls' school. With her romantic notions of art, music and politics, she assembles a coterie of adoring students. She readily displays histrionic elements: snobbery, raving, ranting, cooing and other dramatic affectations. Her "jumble-shop" mind and ill-advised admiration of fascism set the plot.

• **PRIVATE BENJAMIN** - Goldie Hawn plays a "Jewish-American Princess" who impulsively signs up for a stint with the Army. Fully believing the recruiter's outrageous offers, she is shocked when the promised amenities do not materialize and responds with indignation.

• **MADAME BOVARY** (Gustave Flaubert character from 19th Century France; movies made in 1934, 1949, 1991) - Madame Bovary is a famous character from French literature. She is carried away from the void of rural life by romantic longings which are stirred by her shallow and selfish personality.

Other histrionic characters can be seen in:
• **SABRINA** - 1954 movie starring Audrey Hepburn; re-released in 1995 with Julia Ormond.
• **BREAKFAST AT TIFFANY'S** - 1961 drama also starring Audrey Hepburn.

INTERVIEW CONSIDERATIONS

Histrionic patients give dramatic and exaggerated interviews. Histories are often erratic with inconsistencies becoming obvious as more information is obtained. Open-ended questions usually lead to long, animated answers peppered with gestures, affectations and segues. Despite the abundance of "talk" there is a paucity of detail. Answers are frequently vague and evasive, dealing with only superficial elements. Additionally, the outpouring of emotion lacks substance, with discrepancies readily observed between reported symptoms and genuine emotional investment. **La belle indifférence** refers to an obvious emotional detachment from symptoms. This is also seen in other conditions such as **Conversion Disorder** and strokes.

It is not usually difficult to initiate an interview with histrionic patients. In any setting, time is given at the outset for patients to "tell their story." They revel in this opportunity and respond to the attention of an interested listener. As the interview proceeds, there is a "lot of weather" but a "lack of news." Redirection does not usually affect the interview, as new topics are pursued with the same relish.

Maintaining the interview requires structure, by redirecting answers back to the presenting complaint or other central focus. The major challenge is obtaining complete and accurate information. Polite persistence, curbing answers, closed-ended questions and asking for concrete examples help complete the history.

Histrionic patients can present difficulties at the outset of the interview. Commonly, patients of the opposite sex to the interviewer become flirtatious and seductive; patients of the same same sex see the interviewer as a rival. A continual search is made for signs of interest and approval, even in professional settings. Should the interview become difficult due to inappropriate answers or behavior, keep in mind that these patients are largely unaware of their actions. Histrionic patients often experience rejection that does not make sense to them. Confronting their behavior, or contradictory history, will just cause the emergence of more dramatization.

It can be difficult to preserve rapport with these patients. They carry out their internal agenda with flattery and overt seductiveness. A polite but firm return to the presenting problem can help assuage this. It may be necessary to have another person present or even to terminate the interview if there is a medical-legal concern.

Histrionic Themes

- Emotional instability
- Egocentricity/Vanity
- Suggestibility/Dependence
- Self-dramatization

- Exhibitionism
- Sexual provocativeness
- Fear of sexuality
- Overreaction/Immaturity

Presumed Etiology

BIOLOGICAL: There is an increased prevalence of HPD in the first-degree relatives of patients. As discussed, HPD and Somatization Disorder have been associated historically. Some studies have found a genetic link between the two disorders, as well as associations between HPD, ASPD and Substance Abuse (particularly alcohol).

Certain temperamental factors may predispose individuals to an histrionic personality style: intensity, hypersensitivity, extroversion and reward dependence. There is a strong "orality" or appetitive desire within histrionic individuals. They crave love, attention and gratification, but may be overwhelmed by too much stimulation.

Cognitive processing is one of the remarkable features of this personality, and may also be an innate quality. Histrionic people tend to give overly *impressionistic* answers to questions. This has been described by SHAPIRO (1965) as, "global, relatively diffuse, and lacking in sharpness, particularly in sharp detail . . . the hysterical person tends to cognitively respond to what is immediately impressive, striking, or merely obvious." For example, when asked to describe another person, global impressions such as, "He's wonderful" or, "She's so funny. We're really good friends" are typical replies.

In the left brain-right brain scheme, Histrionic people are considered to be right-brain dominant. Obsessive-compulsive personalities are the prototype for left-brain dominance. Instead of answering questions, histrionic patients give vivid impressions, whereas obsessive personalities relate a plethora of factual information.

PSYCHOSOCIAL: The family dynamics of HPD patients often reveal a power distribution perceived as, or actually favoring, males. In such families, females or temperamentally affectionate males, may have received attention only for their physical appearance or cute antics. Neglectful parents may unconsciously or unwittingly encourage their children to dramatize and exaggerate in order to get attention.

Mothers who are weak or ineffectual may also have an etiologic contribution. Without a strong and mature role model, children may learn to depend on seduction or "feminine" wiles to deal with others.

Another consistent feature is a father who was both intimidating and seductive. Narcissistic qualities such as criticism, angry outbursts and selfishness, transmit the message that males must be approached with caution. Some patients have fathers who turned to them for gratification not available in the marriage. The father who turned to open collusion, overt sexuality or even incest, creates the **approach-avoidance conflict** that is a prominent feature of this disorder.

Histrionic patients are fixated in a range between **oral** and **oedipal stages**. A diagrammatic representation for a female is as follows:

Child constitutionally predisposed to intense reactions or neediness
↓
Unsatiated by mother; oral needs remain unmet
↓
Devalues mother as reaction to unmet attachment needs
↓
Turns to father for gratification of dependency needs; idealization magnified by unmet oral needs
↓
Learns that flirtatiousness and exhibitionism get attention
↓
Family dynamics as outlined above
↓
Fixation at oedipal level: conflictual erotic attachment to father; devaluation of mother, self and other female figures
↓
Coexistence of sexual exhibitionism and inhibition

The **Oedipal Complex** (**Electra Complex** in females) is usually resolved by repression of impulses towards the opposite sex parent, and identification with the same sex parent. This resolution is not satisfactorily achieved in HPD because the patient:

· rejects identification with her (devalued) mother
· represses her sexuality to remain "Daddy's little girl"
· learns she cannot possess her father and feels rejected by him; this is also facilitated by a father feeling uncomfortable with his daughter's physical and sexual maturity, and withdrawing from the closeness they shared at an earlier time

Epidemiology

The prevalence is estimated to be 3% of the population. There is a sex bias, with women being diagnosed more frequently than men. Some structured analyses have found an equal prevalence among men and women and rates as high as 15% in some psychiatric populations. Sociocultural factors also need to be considered (e.g. GONE WITH THE WIND). There may be a higher prevalence among homosexual men.

Ego Defenses

Ego defences used in HPD are: **Repression, Regression, Dissociation, Sexualization** (giving an object or act a sexual significance) and **Denial** (avoiding an awareness of some painful aspect of reality)

Repression is defined as expelling from consciousness unacceptable wishes, feelings and fantasies. It is an unconscious process. ***Primary Repression*** refers to the process whereby ideas or feelings are prevented from reaching consciousness. ***Secondary Repression*** is the exclusion of what was once a conscious experience. Freud observed that although repressed memories are consciously inaccessible, they are still "known" and cause hysterical symptoms. Histrionic patients' cognitive style facilitates the use of repression and denial. Sketchy retention of an experience is later recalled in an impressionistic manner, facilitating **repression**. With attention easily distracted, elements of reality are disavowed (**denial**). The distinction is that **repression** defends against inner experiences, such as thoughts and impulses, whereas **denial** blocks out an awareness of external reality.

Regression is seen when patients are faced with challenges that stimulate unconscious fear or guilt. The return to a helpless, child-like state may be an attempt to disarm potential rejecters or abusers.

There is a three-fold contribution to the use of **dissociation**:
· high level of unconscious guilt and anxiety
· fears of intrusion and rejection
· temperamental predisposition to intense reactions

Histrionic individuals are easily overwhelmed and detach from an event that overstimulates them. This dissociation manifests itself in many ways: poor recollection of childhood memories, obliviousness to their flirtatious manner, **la belle indifférence**, fugue states, hysterical rages, predisposition to conversion disorders, etc.

Diagnostic Criteria

A pervasive pattern of excessive emotionality and attention seeking, beginning by early adulthood and present in a variety of contexts, as indicated by five (or more) of the following:
(1) is uncomfortable in situations in which he or she is not the center of attention
(2) interaction with others is often characterized by inappropriate sexually seductive or provocative behavior
(3) displays rapidly shifting and shallow expressions of emotions
(4) constantly uses physical appearance to draw attention to self
(5) has a style of speech that is excessively impressionistic and lacking in detail
(6) shows self-dramatization, theatricality, and exaggerated expression of emotion
(7) is suggestible, i.e., easily influenced by others or circumstances
(8) considers relationships to be more intimate than they actually are
Reprinted with permission from the DSM-IV.
Copyright, American Psychiatric Association, 1994

Differential Diagnosis

Many disorders have stemmed from the initial concept of hysteria. These are classified in the DSM-IV under **Somatoform Disorders**, **Dissociative Disorders** and **Anxiety Disorders**. The pervasive and virtually life-long traits of HPD and the absence of the cardinal symptoms help distinguish these disorders. Histrionic personalities may, however, have a greater propensity to develop these disorders.

Patients who are distractible, gregarious, attention-seeking, and who exaggerate emotions with inappropriate sexuality may be suffering from a **Manic** or **Hypomanic Episode** or **Cyclothymia**. The distinction can be made on the basis of other mental status findings, collateral information and medical history.

Dramatic or histrionic responses can also be seen in individuals with **Dysthymic Disorder**. There is a syndrome called **Hysteroid Dysphoria** that bridges dysthymia and HPD. The concept of hysteroid dysphoria is not included in the DSM-IV. This condition closely resembles an atypical depression and is defined as an abrupt change in mood in response to feeling rejected (**rejection sensitivity**). It almost exclusively affects those women who are particularly prone to seek approval, praise and romantic attention and who experience a surge in energy and mood state when these yearnings are satisfied. When euthymic, such patients have a considerable overlap with HPD and some of the features of the Borderline Personality Disorder. When depressed, the clinical picture is that of multiple somatic complaints, anxiety, emotional overreactivity, interpersonal rejection sensitivity and reversal of the vegetative symptoms. This disorder may respond preferentially to the Monoamine Oxidase Inhibitors (MAOIs).

Because of their suggestibility, patients can develop **Substance Use Disorders**. The overlap of histrionic qualities is particularly reminiscent of stimulant use (cocaine, amphetamines, etc.), but can occur with other substances. A careful history focusing on the reported changes after use of the substance will help sort this out.

With the attention to physical appearance that Histrionic personalities display, an **Eating Disorder** must also be considered. Additionally, they may suffer from **Sexual Disorders** such as **Vaginismus, Dyspareunia**, and **Arousal/Orgasmic Disorders**. Finally, there are **General Medical Conditions** that can cause an overlap with histrionic symptoms, e.g. Multiple Sclerosis, Strokes, Dementia, etc.

MENTAL STATUS EXAMINATION

APPEARANCE:	Often very fashionable; pay particular attention to grooming, accessories, designer clothing, dyeing hair
BEHAVIOR:	Vivid expressions; frequent, dramatic gesticulations
COOPERATION:	Notably cooperative
AFFECT:	Wide range of affect expressed; can change quickly
SPEECH:	Animated, highly-modulated voice
CONTENT OF THOUGHT:	Superficial descriptions; use colorful adjectives; global impressions lack detail; use of hyperbole
THOUGHT FORM:	No characteristic abnormality; may be tangential, circumstantial, vague, overelaborate
PERCEPTION:	No characteristic abnormality
INSIGHT & JUDGMENT:	Partial; often unaware of flirtatious manner; can place themselves in danger with provocativeness
SUICIDE - HOMICIDE:	Need to consider this in conjunction with any Axis I disorder; can overreact to losses or abandonment

Psychodynamic Aspects

As discussed in the Psychosocial Etiology section, histrionic individuals are left with unresolved oral and oedipal elements. This fixation is characterized by immaturity. These patients seem like caricatures of femininity by appearing shallow, vain, dependent, dramatic and selfish. Their internal existence is that of a powerless and fearful child trying to navigate a world dominated by powerful figures. They fear intrusion (retaliation from mother), and rejection (internal experience of losing father).

The central psychodynamic feature in histrionic patients is anxiety. The classical explanation is that defenses are recruited in response to **signal anxiety**, an unconscious process in which the ego is mobilized against internal or external threats. In other personalities, sexual energy is expressed or sublimated, but histrionic patients have **repressed** sexuality as part of their development. However, repression is soon overwhelmed because this defense covers normal impulses that are continually aroused and seek discharge. Because of this, other defenses are needed, and histrionic patients act in ways to cope with the "left over" anxiety.

The DSM-IV diagnostic criteria emphasize the behavioral aspects of HPD, which achieve three goals for these patients:
· security and sanctuary from an environment perceived as hostile
· increasing self-esteem
· attempting mastery of frightening situations by initiating them

As outlined in the Psychosocial Etiology section, histrionic patients see male figures as strong and exciting, but also dangerous. Because of their idealization of father figures, they are attracted to men they see as powerful, though this remains steeped in conflict. They seek the protection that such men offer, while fearing abuse of this power, and may unconsciously hate men for it. They learned that flirtatiousness gets attention, but this left a conflict over erotic impulses. Sexuality is used in a defensive manner instead of as a true expression of libido. Thus, patients may appear highly seductive (a return of repressed impulses), but are largely unaware of the sexual nature of their invitations, and are often surprised when their actions are interpreted as an invitation. Should they proceed with the encounter, it may well be to placate a threatening internal object, and to reduce the guilt which emerges after being confronted with their seductive behavior. These two factors drastically reduce enjoyment of the experience.

Histrionic patients regard power as a male attribute. As mentioned above, they idealize powerful men and attach to them, thereby increasing their self-esteem, as if it can be transferred by association. Histrionic patients, seeing their only strength as sexual attractiveness, become highly invested in appearance, and have particular difficulties with aging.

These patients also increase security and self-esteem by initiating frightening situations which they attempt to master. The term **counterphobic attitude** is used to describe behavior in which feared situations are sought out. **Acting out** is the process of living out an unconscious wish or impulse in order to avoid becoming aware of the idea, or the emotion (affect), that accompanies it. Much like patients who take up activities like parachuting after a heart attack, histrionic patients **act out** in **counterphobic** ways, often related to their preoccupation with the fantasied power and the dangerousness of the opposite sex. Examples include:

- seductive behavior, when sex is frequently not enjoyed
- flirtatiousness, which covers a sense of bodily shame
- craving and attracting attention while feeling inferior to others
- launching into dangerous situations when aggression is feared
- provoking authority, when it is actually feared

The anxiety underlying HPD also manifests itself in dramatization. Because of early experiences, patients do not expect to be taken seriously, or to receive respectful attention. Their behavior invites this reaction, an example of **repetition compulsion**. As adults, they yearn for acceptance, but relate to others in a mixed fashion. Emotional expression teems with conflict. Feelings are conveyed in a way that allows retraction in case patients are ignored by the more "powerful" people present. Coquettish mannerisms and flowery adjectives facilitate a retreat in such instances. Another view holds that the combination of intensity, shallowness and impressionistic style defends against an awareness of stronger emotions (hate, envy, etc.).

The situation for histrionic males is similar to females. They also experience maternal deprivation and look to their fathers for nurturance. When not provided, some men develop an effeminate identity influenced by their mothers. Others model themselves after cultural stereotypes of hypermasculinity. Both are fraught with difficulties in relationships. The former may remain celibate to preserve loyalty to an idealized mother; the latter may be promiscuous in order to reaffirm a sense of masculinity.

What Happens in Psychodynamic Therapy?

Psychoanalysis was developed by Freud for the treatment of patients with hysteria/histrionic personality qualities. Psychodynamic-oriented psychotherapies remain the preferred treatment for HPD. Histrionic patients who function in a moderate or better range can thrive in psychotherapy. To a significant degree, they "make themselves well" with modest guidance.

It is important to establish a therapeutic contract, or working alliance as soon as possible. The parameters and goals of psychotherapy should be clearly explained and conveyed in an open, professional manner. Some patients have the expectation that therapists "know all about them" or "know them better than themselves." This perception needs to be corrected at the outset. Patients should be encouraged to be as open as possible about their feelings, regardless of the degree of embarrassment involved. Exploring reactions and resistance, instead of "demanding" they tell all, avoids making therapy an experience of submitting to yet another authority figure.

One of the first therapeutic interventions with histrionic patients is to obtain a detailed account of their present functioning and history. Redirection and persistence will be required to get past the "I don't know" and "I told you everything already" replies. The vague and impressionistic cognitive style seen in HPD is a form of resistance against deeper thoughts and feelings. Additionally, some patients benefit from developing a cohesive account of their lives.

By encouraging patients to be more reflective and attend to internal and external experiences in greater detail, repression is lessened. The increased amount of emotional information allows an examination of both ideas and feelings, and most importantly, the connection between the two. Awareness of this association, with the ability to discuss thoughts and feelings in detail increases the interest in, and tolerance for, deeper experiences. Patients benefit by internalizing the therapist's interested attitude and using this awareness to alter relationship patterns.

Caution is also advised in using interpretations too quickly. To histrionic patients, who **sexualize** experiences, this can have a "penetrating" quality and cause feelings of powerlessness or being violated. A more profitable approach is to raise questions that do not occur to patients, and have them search for answers instead of being "told what to think."

Histrionic patients express considerable interest in finding out about therapists' lives. This form of resistance becomes apparent at times of stress, either in or out of the therapeutic relationship. This defensive maneuver camouflages difficulties in accessing their own feelings. Regardless of the tenacity of the attempts, it is critical to avoid self-disclosure. While questions of a general nature can be answered, much can be gained by not gratifying the attempts at **sexualizing** the therapy. In a sense, "failing" in the seduction has therapeutic value. Having strong desires that are not exploited in a relationship with a powerful figure who considers their best interests is unique. This encourages patients to become more autonomous and to value themselves.

As with all personality disorders, HPD occurs in a range of severity from the healthier "oedipal" to less functional "oral" histrionics. Patients who function at lower psychological levels will require a more active and educational approach. Such patients may particularly benefit from construction of a detailed history focusing on their maladaptive responses to anxiety. For example, pointing out that a wish to flee from therapy is part of the same process interfering with their relationships and jobs, helps patients gain some perspective and maintain the therapeutic relationship.

Lower functioning patients are more prone to experience physical symptoms with emotional difficulties. Somatic manifestations may herald regression, or even psychotic decompensation. Still, these symptoms have a psychodynamic relevance and an awareness is helpful in dealing with them. Conversion symptoms achieve the **primary gain** of anxiety reduction by resolving the conflict between wishes and their prohibition. **Secondary gain** is a real-world advantage from others (attention from others, relief from duties, etc.). **Tertiary gain** refers to the benefit that others receive from the patient's secondary gain (e.g. financial).

Another important issue is that of incest and childhood seduction. Freud initially believed the accounts he heard from his patients. Later, he ascribed them to fantasies related to oedipal wishes. Currently, therapists must consider many facets of this issue. Many patients are victims of sexual abuse from male relatives, which is an etiologically significant contributor to the severity of HPD. Some patients had fathers that were not frankly abusive, but were sexually inappropriate. Histrionic patients can express vivid fantasies and wishes involving fathers or father-figures, whether there was abuse perpetrated or not.

Transference and Countertransference Reactions

Just as Freud's work in hysteria led him to develop psychoanalysis, the concept of transference became obvious to him in dealing with these patients as well. He found it anachronistic that patients misperceived current relationships because of past trauma and, in particular, the relationship with him. Again, he recognized the phenomenon that what is not consciously accessible remains active in the unconscious, being expressed in symptoms and reenactments.

Histrionic patients are quite emotionally expressive and develop strong transference manifestations early in therapy. The gender of the patient-therapist dyad influences the transference. For example, female patients frequently reenact oedipal conflicts, and respond to male therapists in an excited, provocative and seductive manner. Female therapists may be viewed by female patients as competition, and treated in a hostile manner. Irrespective of the gender differences, histrionic patients frequently have intense reactions to their therapists.

Working through the transference is the main intervention by which patients benefit from therapy. Transference has been variously referred to as a "gold mine" or a "minefield." The outcome of therapy depends on how successfully transference is handled. It gives therapists a first-hand understanding of how patients interact in other current relationships, and the effects of previous ones. A rule of thumb is to make interpretations about transference only when it becomes resistance. A complete interpretation involves making a three-way connection between past relationships, current relationships (outside therapy) and the therapeutic relationship.

A most difficult aspect to manage is **eroticized transference**, which is the development of overt sexual feelings for the therapist. In healthier patients this develops gradually and is egodystonic. They recognize that it is inappropriate to act on these feelings, as this will sabotage the therapy. Lower functioning patients have a more immediate, overwhelming eroticized transference. In these situations, it is advisable to ask for consultation and supervision. Transfer of care to a same-sex therapist may become necessary.

Higher-functioning patients may still need encouragement to discuss their feelings. Shame and embarrassment often accompany the eroticized component. The strength of the therapeutic alliance often determines whether patients continue or are frightened by their feelings and terminate therapy.

It is important to keep in mind that eroticized transference is another manifestation of histrionic patients' defensive handling of their anxiety. **Sexualization** is a smoke-screen that obscures deeper, more germane issues. It is more "grist for the mill" and is best managed in an nonexploitative, accepting manner. Patients may need to be reminded that a variety of feelings will emerge in therapy and that their discussion is the work of therapy. Patients may **act out** the transference long before they verbalize it. Examples include: starting a relationship with someone who has the same name as, or is similar in appearance to, the therapist; over-dressing for appointments (especially with liberal amounts of cologne or perfume!); and giving gifts. While eroticized transference may be seen as a positive feature, it is quite the opposite. Histrionic patients may unconsciously need to defuse "powerful" people (like therapists), while seething with hostility and aggression under the veneer of sexuality.

Countertransference reactions can be intense. It can be gratifying to have patients take an eager and apparently genuine interest in our lives. Additionally, the flirtatiousness of attractive, well-groomed patients of the opposite sex can be difficult to resist; this behavior reflects their adaptation, not therapists' qualities. Therapists need to monitor their reactions to patients. Particular concerns are:

• contributions therapists make to patients' eroticized transference
• personal narcissistic needs being met by adoring patients
• voyeuristic enjoyment of patients' fantasies
• a sense of disgust being conveyed at patients' disclosures
• a sadistic enjoyment from being "unavailable" to patients

It takes skill to manage the eroticized transference material in an accepting and non-exploitative manner. While the difficulties with overinvolvement have been mentioned, countertransference distancing from patients can also occur. Through the use of **projective identification** or **regression**, histrionic patients may also provoke infantilizing or condescending reactions from their therapists.

SUMMARY OF THERAPEUTIC TECHNIQUES

• Encourage *reflection*; aim for a *proactive*, not reactive style
• Guide patients to build self-esteem in areas other than attractiveness
• Be attuned to transference and countertransference issues
• Encourage patients to use their own resources to solve problems
• Resist self-disclosure, giving advice, or other departures from therapy

Group Therapy

Histrionic patients can present in assessments as charming, outgoing and verbal. They are often chosen readily and can serve as valuable figures in group therapy. Their energy activates the more passive members, and their seductiveness can stir transference reactions that fuel group interaction.

However, there are drawbacks to having histrionic members in a group. Craving attention, they shift allegiances frequently and may escalate their dramatic ways if overshadowed by others. Flirtatious behavior may well attract more than one group member, creating a rivalry in addition to one already existing between patients and the therapist. Histrionic patients may also view group sessions as a forum to express themselves, not learn about their interactions.

Histrionic patients can also be seen as **help rejecting complainers.** These individuals play the role of victim and induce caregiving behavior from others (advice giving, offering favors, etc.). When this is done, the patient devalues the effort and resumes complaining. This can be a very difficult situation to deal with for a group.

Histrionic patients can benefit from group therapy when they understand that their loquaciousness and endless dissatisfaction serve to isolate them from others and perpetuate their unhappiness.

Cognitive Therapy

Basic Cognitive Distortions:
- "I am incapable of looking after myself. I can't do it on my own."
- "I need to have a powerful man's interest at all times."
- "If I'm not fun and exciting, no one will want me around."
- Overgeneralized, diffuse, impressionistic, or catastrophic thinking
ADAPTED FROM BECK, FREEMAN & ASSOCIATES, 1990

The central cognition in HPD is, "I am inadequate and unable to manage by myself." This is not unique to HPD - it is also seen in depression and dependent personalities. Unlike patients with these disorders, histrionic patients find others who will accept them and attend to their needs. This perpetuates a cycle in HPD. Patients feel they are inadequate, use emotional reasoning ("if I feel this way, I must be this way"), and then set out to find someone to take care of them, reinforcing their initial sense of inadequacy.

Histrionic patients are so focused on external approval and acceptance that they have little consideration left for their own internal existence. While capable of introspection, they do not initially attend to details. Frequently, patients are not able to identify what they need and avoid self-knowledge because it feels foreign. The cognitive-behavioral treatment of HPD is less well-established than in other personality disorders. These treatments require the time and patience to examine thoughts and test alternatives, which is contrary to the histrionic temperament. However, histrionic patients can benefit from the following interventions:

• developing a more systematic, problem-focused style of thinking by setting a reasonable agenda and attending to one item at a time
• considering the long-term costs of impulsivity; look for alternatives such as drawing up pro and con tables for decisions
• assertiveness training may take time to work; when patients directly ask for what they want, they fear the possibility of rejection
• role-playing involving exposure to small rejections

It is important to reassure patients that their "basic character" will not be altered in cognitive therapy. On a practical level, patients can be encouraged to seek employment that satisfies their need for high-visibility: acting, dancing, politics, teaching, the arts, etc. Histrionic patients can be quite creative when integrating their emotions with their work.

PHARMACOTHERAPY

With the widely fluctuating mood and affect seen in this disorder, clinicians may be tempted to prescribe mood stabilizers. These medications are not generally beneficial except in co-existing, clearly diagnosed mood disorders. Changes in mood and affect are not usually sustained long enough to warrant a trial of medication. From time to time, judicious use of antidepressants, sedative-hypnotics and anxiolytics may be needed to help patients through crises.

COURSE OF HPD

Little is known definitively about long-term outcome. As with other Cluster B disorders, it takes a lot of energy to maintain this personality configuration. Patients may "burnout" and show fewer symptoms with time. Because HPD is among the Axis II disorders most amenable to therapeutic intervention, the outcome can be viewed optimistically.

REFERENCES

American Psychiatric Association
DIAGNOSTIC AND STATISTICAL MANUAL OF MENTAL DISORDERS, FOURTH EDITION
American Psychiatric Press; Washington, D.C., 1994

A. Beck, A. Freeman & Associates
COGNITIVE THERAPY OF PERSONALITY DISORDERS
The Guildford Press; New York, 1990

G. Gabbard
PSYCHODYNAMIC PSYCHIATRY IN CLINICAL PRACTICE, THE DSM-IV EDITION
American Psychiatric Press; Washington, D.C., 1994

H. Kaplan, B. Sadock (editors)
COMPREHENSIVE GROUP PSYCHOTHERAPY, THIRD EDITION
Williams & Wilkins; Baltimore, 1993

H. Kaplan, B. Sadock (editors)
COMPREHENSIVE TEXTBOOK OF PSYCHIATRY, SIXTH EDITION
Williams & Wilkins; Baltimore, 1995

N. McWilliams
PSYCHOANALYTIC DIAGNOSIS
The Guildford Press; New York, 1994

H. Merskey, in
THE DSM-IV PERSONALITY DISORDERS; J. LIVESLEY, EDITOR
The Guildford Press; New York, 1995

E. Othmer & S. Othmer
THE CLINICAL INTERVIEW USING DSM-IV
American Psychiatric Press; Washington, D.C., 1994

R. Pies
CLINICAL MANUAL OF PSYCHIATRIC DIAGNOSIS AND TREATMENT
American Psychiatric Press; Washington, D.C., 1994

D. Shapiro
NEUROTIC STYLES
Basic Books; New York, 1965

You've got a *hectic* day . . .
A hair appointment at 10 downtown, nails at 11 uptown
and a power luncheon at 12 cross-town . . .
You've got greetings, eatings & meetings all afternoon . . .

You have to make an impression, you simply
must!! Whatever you do, do it ***El flagrante!!***
That's your trademark, and you have to look
good doing it!! You need makeup that won't let
you down when you're in the spotlight . . .

Dramatique

Cosmetics for the woman who wants to leave an impression,
not just a business card.
live it . . . wear it . . . live it . . . wear it . . . live it . . . wear it . . . live it

FILL-IN-THE-BLANK PERSONALITIES:
ANATOMY OF A ROMANCE NOVEL

ACT I
A beautiful, unspoiled <u>histrionic</u> lives a marginal and repressed existence under the cruel tyranny of her husband. However, she gave her word on the altar and remains deeply committed to this <u>schizoid</u> lout even though he is just a shell of the man she married. His distant manner and frequent business trips don't arouse her suspicions until she is tipped off by his <u>paranoid</u> secretary that he is having an affair (with the same woman who broke up her own marriage). She seeks the comfort of her hapless <u>obsessive</u> boss who, seeing an opportunity, cannot contain himself and confesses his undying love for her.

ACT II
Reeling from the betrayal of this trusted friendship, she enters a trance-like state and wastes away in her still elegantly fashioned apartment. In the nick of time, her trusty but highly <u>dependent</u> confidant offers her some banal advice which depresses her even more. Summoning her last ounce of strength, she sets out on a journey of recovery. Her life takes an intriguing twist when she takes the advice of a <u>schizotypal</u> fortune-teller and leaves for a distant, enchanting land.

ACT III
The heat and plush, undulating landscape cause her to let down her guard and fall prey to the affections of a dashing, wealthy <u>narcissist</u>. Unbeknownst to her, libidinal strivings are simultaneously aroused in this man's nefarious, but strikingly handsome, <u>antisocial</u> brother. While being royally courted by these two, she catches a glimpse of a kindred spirit, the mysterious <u>avoidant</u> who works as a stable-hand.

ACT IV
The long-seated rivalry between the two brothers reaches a fever pitch and they agree their dignity can only be settled by a duel. As high noon approaches on the appointed day, the <u>borderline</u> ex-lover of one of the brothers returns and quells his ire with her own passion. Besides, the <u>passive-aggressive</u> matriarch of the family was fed up with her ill-tempered sons and loaded blanks in their duelling pistols. As our heroine takes up with her man of mystique, clouds the shape of wedding bells form on the horizon.

From the *PsychoIllogical Bulletin*.

THE BORDERLINE PERSONALITY

Biographical Information

Name: Wanda Cutter

Occupation: Emotional hotline counselor

Appearance: Dresses completely in black or white; today it's black

Relationship with animals: Sleeps with pet cat and an assortment of stuffed animals

Favourite Song: *Love Rollercoaster*

At the Therapist's Office

Before Session: Fights with ex-lover outside office

Waiting Room Reading: Castrates pictures of men

During Session: Smells *Histrionic's* perfume and goes into a rage

Fantasies Involve: Ménage with therapist and partner

Relationship with Therapist: Threatens blackmail over fantasy

Behavior During Session: Widens hole made by *Antisocial*

Takes to Therapy: Suicide note with weekly changes

Diagnostic Shorthand

Mnemonic - "AMID A RISE"

Abandonment frantically avoided
Mood instability
Identity disturbance
Dissociative symptoms

Anger is poorly controlled

Relationships are unstable
Impulsive
Suicidal behavior is recurrent
Emptiness

INTRODUCTION

The word *borderline* refers to the "border" between neurosis and psychosis. Prior to the narrowing of criteria in the DSM-III, the diagnosis of schizophrenia encompassed a wider range of symptoms and behaviors. Borderline personalities were initially thought to have a variant or atypical form of schizophrenia. In the DSM-IV, Borderline Personality Disorder is characterized by impulsivity, and instability in the areas of mood, self-image and relationships.

Some key names associated with development of this disorder are:
• **Hoch and Polatin** (1949) called this condition **pseudoneurotic schizophrenia**, characterized by "panneurosis, pananxiety and pansexuality" (these were all considered neurotic symptoms)
• **Knight** (1950's) identified a group of patients in his hospital practice who had severely impaired ego functions, manifested by **primary process thinking** and an inability to suppress primitive impulses
• **Grinker** (1968) pioneered research into the phenomenology of this disorder, finding four consistent features: anger as the main affect; poorly established self-identity; pervasive moodiness (usually depression or dysthymia); and deficiencies in the capacity to form intimate relationships
• **Gunderson** and **Singer** (1975) and **Gunderson** (1984, 1990) identified criteria that clearly discriminated the borderline personality from other psychiatric conditions
• **Kernberg** (1967, 1975) described borderline patients from a psychoanalytic perspective, finding four key features that allowed a definitive diagnosis: nonspecific manifestations of ego weakness; shift toward primary process thinking; specific defensive operations; and pathological internalized objects; he also developed the concept of the **borderline personality organization** (see PSYCHODYNAMIC ASPECTS)

The borderline personality disorder (BPD) was first described in the DSM-III, which helped narrow use of the term. Previously, borderline had been used to refer to: a spectrum of disorders, a difficult patient, diagnostic uncertainty and a type of personality organization. From its initial description as a subtype of schizophrenia, BPD has also been thought of as an atypical mood disorder. Further research has supported BPD as an independent diagnostic entity.

Many complete textbooks have been written on BPD, which remains a controversial, complex and convoluted diagnosis. The material in this chapter is confined to the DSM-IV description of BPD.

Media Examples

Borderline characters are unpredictable, emotional, vindictive and intense. For these reasons, they are cast as main characters or "movers and shakers" in plot development. Borderlines frequently fill the roles of: "boyfriend/girlfriend/roommate from hell," or a spurned lover. Their mission of revenge adds considerable drama, and is usually the climax of the movie. They differ from sociopathic characters in that they seek revenge for perceived rejection, whereas Antisocial Personalities (ASPDs) do not require this prerequisite for their actions.

• FATAL ATTRACTION - Glenn Close portrays a classic borderline personality in this thriller. She readily agrees to an uninhibited weekend affair with a married man, and then becomes pathologically attached to him. When he subsequently distances himself from her, she becomes frantic in her attempts to woo him back. Finally, she terrorizes him, vandalizes his car, stalks his family and kidnaps his daughter. This character evoked such strong reactions (see TRANSFERENCE section) that audiences were not satisfied with the original ending in which she did not die. It is of interest to note that movie reviewers describe her behavior as "psychotic" and "loco," illustrating some of the confusion over the diagnosis of the condition.

• THE CRUSH - Alicia Silverstone portrays a teenage Lolita who becomes obsessed with a male boarder in her parents' home. She gains his attention with her talents, but can't comprehend the inappropriateness of a relationship with him. He suffers her increasingly destructive wrath when he pursues another relationship.

• MALICIOUS - Molly Ringwald portrays a borderline medical student in this film. Expanding on the glimpse of etiology seen in FATAL ATTRACTION, this movie illustrates some of the family dynamics that lead to her troubled state.

• PRESUMED INNOCENT - Greta Scacchi portrays a more subtle variation of the borderline personality, emphasizing the rapid idealization and devaluation, and shifts in mood that also characterize the diagnosis.

Other borderline characters can be seen in:

• THE TEMP - the role played by Lara Flynn Boyle
• THE HAND THAT ROCKS THE CRADLE - the Rebecca De Mornay character
• SINGLE WHITE FEMALE - the role played by Jennifer Jason Leigh

Interview Considerations

Borderline patients are often quite verbal and difficulties are not usually encountered in initiating an interview. They may even interrupt introductions to relate the details about something that is upsetting them.

A formidable obstacle in interviews is the intensity of affect expressed by borderline patients. They are often in a state of turmoil and express anger readily. These patients will also abruptly shift allegiances. At one moment, they idealize any interpersonal contact, only to devalue it in the next. While the content of the interview may bring about a heated tirade, a response to internal cues may also leave an interviewer quite bewildered about the source of the affect.

Borderline patients present unique difficulties because their arsenal of primitive defenses and potent anger can be readily aimed at the interviewer. Caregivers are perceived either as all powerful and placed on a pedestal, or as depriving and discarded to a dumpster. Abrupt changes occur between these two perceptions. This can occur when patients receive something they want (medication, admission, sick leave, etc.), or when they are denied these requests.

To maintain rapport, interviewers need to recognize that these patients interact with everyone in this way, and not to take such difficulties personally. Acknowledging instability as an issue for further exploration may help sustain the interview. Use of open-ended questions, redirection back to clinically relevant material, and simply hearing patients out can be helpful.

Borderline patients can develop **micropsychotic episodes** under stressful situations and display features such as hallucinations, delusions (particularly paranoid), and loosening of associations.

Borderline Themes

- Chaotic childhood
- Parental neglect and abuse
- Impulsivity
- Disrupted education
- Legal difficulties
- Substance abuse or dependence
- Sexual abuse; early onset of sexual activity; promiscuity
- Fears abandonment, maintains self-destructive relationships
- Failure to achieve potential or long-term goals
- Frequent suicidal ideation or gestures (burns, lacerations, etc.)

PRESUMED ETIOLOGY

BIOLOGICAL: BPD may have a genetic contribution. Studies have found familial tendencies towards poor regulation of mood and impulses.

BPD patients may be temperamentally aggressive and have intense attachment needs. Low serotonin levels have been found in individuals who have been aggressive or suicidal. Dysfunction of serotonin regulation has been well established as an etiologic factor in mood disorders. Additionally, dopamine seems to facilitate aggression, and is the major neurotransmitter system implicated in psychosis. It has been proposed that dysregulation of either, or both, systems may provide a neurobiological mechanism for some of the features of BPD. Another possibility implicates a lowered threshold for excitability in the limbic system.

The extended families of borderline patients have increased rates of **Substance Use Disorders**, Cluster B personality disorders (particularly Antisocial), **Conduct Disorders**, **Learning Disabilities** and **Mood Disorders**.

PSYCHOSOCIAL: The adage that "Borderlines are made, not born" rings particularly true when virtual carbon copies can be made of their personal histories. While not universal, there is still an uncanny similarity in the family and social situations of many patients.

Development is thought to be interrupted at Mahler's **rapprochement subphase of separation-individuation.** At sixteen to thirty months of age, children begin to explore the world around them as entities separate from mother. They venture away from caregivers cautiously, returning readily for reassurance and security. Caregivers who interpret this return as an indication that children do not want to be autonomous will squash future attempts. Similarly, caregivers who have pathologically strong desires to be loved and needed may engender strong separation fears in their children. Children may subsequently be punished for attempts at autonomy.

Borderline patients can be viewed as constantly reliving this struggle with autonomy. They do not develop **object constancy**, and fear that attempts to separate will result in disappearance of caregivers, with subsequent abandonment. This can result in such children being unduly intolerant of being alone, and more difficult to parent.

Initial stimulation, followed by later frustration of attachment, causes children to find maternal substitutes. The first **transitional object** often takes the form of a cuddly toy, usually a teddy bear. It is a frequent sight on inpatient units to see adults bring in stuffed animals to comfort them during their admission. One study investigating this phenomenon reported a sixty-one percent correlation with BPD.

In general, failure to provide adequate attention invalidates feelings and experiences. Without this, children do not develop a stable image of themselves or others, and rely instead on substitutes.

Other contributions may be due to erratic caregiving such as:

• Parental absence; substance abuse; episodes of mood disturbance
• Inadequate maturity or characterological disturbances of parents
• Divorce; frequent moves; relationship break-ups or other losses

Disturbed parent-child relationships cause particular difficulty in the handling of anger. Pre-borderline children may sense that the expression of anger has a destructive potential, and instead deal with it by **splitting** it off or **dissociating**.

Severe childhood trauma is also correlated with adult BPD. This most often is present in the form of emotional, physical and, especially, sexual abuse. These devastating occurrences overwhelm children to such a degree that use of the above defenses is necessary to cope with the trauma.

While a genetic component may be present, a more accurate etiologic understanding is that BPD is more likely "made" than "born." This is supported by the emergence of this disorder after accumulated developmental insults, usually in late adolescence or early adulthood.

EPIDEMIOLOGY

The prevalence is estimated to be approximately 3% of the general population. BPD is by far the most common personality disorder diagnosis made in clinical settings. Here, the prevalence can be as high as 10% on inpatient units, and 20% in outpatient clinics. There is a strong sex difference, with women being diagnosed at least three times as often as men. This may also reflect cultural stereotypes in that men exhibiting the same symptomatology are likely to be diagnosed with an Antisocial or Narcissistic Personality Disorder.

EGO DEFENSES

The use of ego defences in BPD is readily apparent. The defensive structure used by these patients evokes strong reactions in others and is not as subtle as with other personality disorders. As with other "self" disorders, the defenses are primitive in nature and used to extreme degrees, including psychosis in some cases.

Foremost among the defenses in BPD is **splitting**. This is defined as a process whereby external objects are seen as "all good" or "all bad," with sudden shifts between these perceptions. Patients express a firm attitude, while regarding the opposite view as being completely unconnected. What makes this such an obstacle in dealing with borderline patients is the intense affect occurring with these "splits." Borderlines have not been able to integrate co-existing good and bad images of themselves or others. They have not developed to the point of tolerating ambivalence. People are either unrealistically idealized as nurturing rescuers, or devalued as the personification of evil and neglect. Splitting can be seen in:

• self-representation; patients experience rapidly fluctuating views of themselves (also referred to as **identity disturbance** or **diffusion**)
• attitudes and behaviors towards other people (singly)
• groups of people also become divided; this is frequently seen on inpatient units where staff members are split into those who feel either sympathy or antipathy for these patients

Other defenses are used in BPD:

• **Denial** is the abolition of external reality. This is used particularly in BPD to disavow the other side of the "split."
• **Distortion** is the reshaping of reality to meet inner needs or to fulfil fantasies. Use of this defense leads to unrealistic beliefs and overvalued ideas, and may facilitate **micropsychotic episodes**. This defense reinforces the narrowing of perception that maintains splitting.
• **Dissociation** is a temporary disconnection from a situation that is too painful to deal with. While dissociated, there is usually a drastic change in character. While this can be a benefit under certain circumstances, the drawback to this defense is its use automatically in situations where a less dramatic defense or adaptation would suffice.
• **Projective Identification** works in concert with splitting to induce others into behaving according to the projections (side of the split they are on) of the patient. It operates like a self-fulfilling prophecy.

DIAGNOSTIC CRITERIA

A pervasive pattern of instability of interpersonal relationships, self-image, and affects, and marked impulsivity beginning by early adulthood and present in a variety of contexts, as indicated by five (or more) of the following:

(1) frantic efforts to avoid real or imagined abandonment. **Note:** Do not include suicidal or self-mutilating behavior covered in Criterion 5.

(2) a pattern of unstable and intense interpersonal relationships characterized by alternating between extremes of idealization and devaluation

(3) identity disturbance: markedly and persistently unstable self-image or sense of self

(4) impulsivity in at least two areas that are potentially self-damaging (e.g., spending, sex, substance abuse, reckless driving, binge eating). **Note:** Do not include suicidal or self-mutilating behavior covered in Criterion 5.

(5) recurrent suicidal behavior, gestures, or threats, or self-mutilating behavior

(6) affective instability due to a marked reactivity of mood (e.g., intense episodic dysphoria, irritability, or anxiety usually lasting a few hours and only rarely more than a few days)

(7) chronic feelings of emptiness

(8) inappropriate, intense anger or difficulty controlling anger (e.g., frequent displays of temper, constant anger, recurrent physical fights)

(9) transient, stress-related paranoid ideation or severe dissociative symptoms

REPRINTED WITH PERMISSION FROM THE DSM-IV.
COPYRIGHT, AMERICAN PSYCHIATRIC ASSOCIATION, 1994

DIFFERENTIAL DIAGNOSIS

Borderline personality disorder in its more florid forms is not difficult to diagnose. These patients frequently present to emergency rooms, day programs and outpatient clinics in a state of turmoil. Usually, a psychosocial crisis that threatens a relationship (DIR) causes an upheaval. In response to this, borderline patients become overwhelmed and regress, making suicidal gestures or attempts. They often require admission because they cannot trust their impulses, therby forcing caregivers into a protective, "parental" role. As outpatients, they remain "stably unstable" and often make demands for ongoing therapy.

In its less obvious forms, BPD can present a diagnostic challenge. Historically, syphilis was referred to as the "great imitator" because of its protean physical manifestations. Currently, the manifold expressions of AIDS and HIV seropositivity would claim this title. BPD may be the "great imitator" of psychiatry because of the enormous overlap with other conditions, as indicated below.

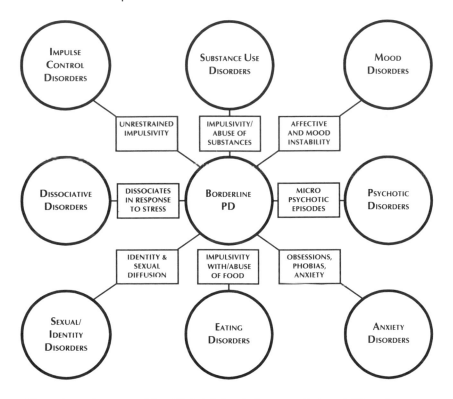

There is an increased familial risk for **Substance-Related Disorders**, **Mood Disorders** and **ASPD**. **Somatization Disorder** shares many etiologic factors with BPD. Because borderline patients make numerous demands for medication and hospitalization, **Factitious Disorder** and **Malingering** also need to be considered when constructing a differential diagnosis. There is a good deal of overlap with other Cluster B disorders. Borderline patients can run afoul of the law when acting impulsively, often for motor vehicle offenses or shoplifting. More overt antisocial acts are usually directed at gaining the attention of lovers, partners, caregivers, friends or employers.

Studies have shown that over ninety percent of patients with BPD warranted a second diagnosis, and over forty percent had two or more diagnoses.

OTHER DIAGNOSTIC CONSIDERATIONS

The development of BPD as a diagnostic entity separate from schizophrenia has been mentioned previously. **Latent, simple** and **pseudoneurotic schizophrenia** referred to atypical and mild forms of this condition. DSM-IV criteria for BPD have little overlap with these earlier concepts, or the current definition of schizophrenia. The major change from DSM-III-R was the inclusion of *criterion nine* - transient stress-related paranoid ideation or severe dissociative symptoms. The **micropsychotic episodes** occurring in BPD do not appear to indicate a future psychotic disorder, even if they fulfill the criteria for a **Brief Psychotic Disorder**. Studies comparing BPD and Schizophrenia have repeatedly shown a distinctly different course and outcome.

BPD has more recently been associated with **Mood Disorders**. There is considerable overlap with the symptoms and clinical course of these conditions. The mood disorder having the greatest overlap with BPD is **Dysthymic Disorder**. Borderline patients appear chronically empty, bored, lonely and have a pervasively negative affect. In BPD, vegetative signs are usually absent and there is a reactivity of mood symptoms to social situations.

Several characteristics are common to BPD and **Depression**: low self-esteem, feelings of worthlessness, depressed mood and suicidality. However, the "depression" in BPD is qualitatively different than in mood disorders. One of the main distinguishing factors, as with Dysthymia, is the absence of vegetative signs. Although there is a high lifetime prevalence for major depressive episodes in BPD, this is not a finding unique to this personality disorder.

BPD has also been posited to be an atypical bipolar disorder, most closely resembling **Cyclothymia**, with which it shares a long term vacillation of mood. Additionally, the amplitude of mood change is dramatic enough to be in the cyclothymic spectrum. Despite the similarities, the "up" phase in BPD rarely encompasses the required number of criteria of severity for a hypomanic episode. Also, elevated mood states in BPD usually have interpersonal precipitants.

Despite the many similarities between BPD and Mood Disorders, there are important phenomenological differences that support the existence of BPD as a separate disorder. In the ICD-10, BPD is called the **emotionally unstable personality disorder, borderline type**.

MENTAL STATUS EXAMINATION

APPEARANCE: May be dramatic; many prefer black - clothing, hair dye, nail polish; overabundance of eyeliner and excessive eyebrow plucking; pierced body parts (other than ears); tattoos, may have unusual hair styles - multiple lengths and colors; forearms, neck or other areas may have scars from slashing

BEHAVIOR: Often sit cross-legged, curled up, or sideways in chair or sit on floor; may get up and pace due to agitation; in extreme cases can be violent towards property, self or others

COOPERATION: Highly variable, may be ingratiating or hostile; will cooperate as long as interviewer remains sympathetic; can change abruptly to a rage if denied requests, or confronted about behaviors

AFFECT: Intense and labile; ranges from seductive to outbursts of emotion (anger, tears, etc.)

SPEECH: May be punctuated with epithets; otherwise normal

CONTENT OF THOUGHT: Generally related to questions; spontaneous elaboration about interpersonal difficulties, themes of idealization and devaluation; obvious contradictions

THOUGHT FORM: No characteristic abnormality; may be tangential, circumstantial, overinclusive

PERCEPTION: Generally unremarkable; may have positive findings during **micropsychotic episodes**

INSIGHT & JUDGMENT: Variable; depends on severity of disorder and current stressors; generally impaired; do not have the emotional distance to forsee consequences

SUICIDE - HOMICIDE: Suicidal threats, gestures and attempts are a constant concern especially when faced with losses, stress or intoxication; can also be a factor in transference reactions and at times of therapist's vacation; violence towards others occurs frequently

Psychodynamic Aspects

Developmental fixation at the **rapprochement phase of separation-individuation** leaves patients overwhelmed with anxiety about abandonment and separation. Because of this, **object constancy** is not achieved. This leaves children feeling that because caregivers are not in sight, they cease to exist. Without object constancy, ambivalence cannot develop, as this requires simultaneously experiencing opposite feelings toward a constant object.

This facilitates an all-or-nothing reaction in children. When a parent is present, all is well with the world. When absent, the child feels abandoned. This develops into a dichotomous thought process, where things are either all good or all bad, and facilitates **splitting** as an ego defense to help organize these experiences. Factors pertinent to children (temperamental aggression or cognitive difficulties) or caregivers (overinvolvement, neglect or abuse), cause a pattern of increasingly negative interactions. Such children develop predominantly negative "introjects" of themselves and others. That is, they feel they are bad, the people around them are bad, and the world is bad.

This explanation does not encompass all of the difficulties that borderline patients manifest. It is too broad a simplification to pinpoint one area of development as contributing to this complex disorder. Difficulties with other developmental stages are readily seen in BPD. Additionally, parenting usually does not deteriorate for one developmental stage; it is more likely to remain uniform throughout. Nevertheless, this explanation facilitates an understanding of some of the symptoms seen in BPD.

Oral issues persist, typified by a longing for caregivers (as per Attachment Theory), or substitutes (**transitional objects**) on whom complete dependence can be assured. Failing this, borderline patients reenact their primitive rage over abandonment. **Splitting** continues to be used as a defense to lessen the overwhelming anxiety felt with confusing or threatening experiences. In order to maintain this split view, patients **distort** their perception of events (sometimes profoundly) to restore equilibrium. Borderline patients continue their quest for attachment, and anyone who can provide a semblance of gratification is viewed with **primitive idealization**, which enhances splitting. Because such expectations are doomed to disappointment, **primitive devaluation** inevitably results.

Developmental fixation at early stages and the use of primitive defenses engender behaviors related to ego weakness - another cardinal feature of borderline patients. Normally, the ego delays the discharge of impulses and/or directs them towards a healthy, or socially appropriate, outlet. However, borderline patients have difficulty sublimating powerful drives and modulating strong affects.

This process is generally referred to as **acting out**. This term was originally used to describe behavior fueled by an unconscious need to master the anxiety accompanying forbidden wishes and feelings. By enacting such scenarios, a sense of power replaced helplessness. Currently, acting out is used to refer to behaviors that are transference manifestations that have not reached awareness, or are too anxiety-provoking (e.g. abandonment) to discuss. Examples of acting out include exhibitionism, voyeurism, **counterphobia**, etc.

Borderline patients have a low threshold for delaying action. Their primitive feelings are expressed in a venomous rage, and impulses as destructive acts. Acting out implies a transference reaction. What also happens frequently in BPD is **acting up**. This is a conscious attempt to get attention, nurturing or other amenities. Borderline patients have poorly developed superegos and do not typically use their conscience to guide their actions.

Borderline patients have poorly developed sense of ego boundaries, known as **identity diffusion**. They experience themselves as discontinuous, and have trouble knowing where they end and another person begins. This makes them especially impressionable and vulnerable to influences around them. Helen Deutsch coined the term **"as if" personality** to refer to this observation. This is reflected in the DSM-IV criteria *three* and *seven*. Patients live their lives "as if" they were someone else. This is frequently seen in the area of sexual identity. Borderline patients may manifest "pansexuality" by defining themselves according those around them. This can result in bisexual promiscuity, fetishism, sado-masochism, etc. Despite this, reality testing on psychological tests remains largely intact.

Kernberg introduced the concept of a **borderline personality organization** to encompasses characteristic patterns of ego deficits. Use of primitive defenses and long-standing difficulties in close relationships are two key features. Several different personality styles can manifest from this "borderline" level of organization (e.g. histrionic, narcissistic and antisocial all can share this etiology).

What Happens in Psychodynamic Therapy?

There are an increasing number of complete books devoted to the therapy of borderline patients. This has been an increasingly popular focus for research, which now yields new approaches and new combinations of therapy. The psychotherapeutic treatment of BPD can be a most difficult, challenging and ambitious task. It is a long and arduous process with no shortcuts.

Psychotherapy seeks to instill what temperament, upbringing and numerous disappointing relationships have left patients without. The goal is to help patients emerge as integrated and dependable, with enough self-esteem to value themselves and others.

Initially, patients are seen as requiring more "support" if they are lower functioning, and a more "interpretive" type of psychotherapy if they are stable and psychologically minded. This supposition has aroused controversy, though there is no particular "formula" or approach that works best with all borderline patients. What appears to be most helpful is a therapist who is flexible enough to employ techniques of both approaches at appropriate times.

Given the identity diffusion and instability characteristic of BPD, it is crucial to establish a contract for therapy that is consistently reinforced. Borderline patients have a poorly developed sense of self, and will, over time, benefit from this external structure. The details of the various parameters (fees, frequency of sessions, provision for emergency sessions, penalties for lateness, after-hour telephone calls, etc.) are less important than their consistent reinforcement. Additionally, these limits should be enforced with sanctions, should they not be respected. Therapists can choose limits according to their level of comfort, but two maxims in the treatment of BPD are that:

• boundary issues will be continually tested
• no amount of gratification will be sufficient; the more patients receive, the more they desire

Some patients react harshly to this structure and complain that they "came for help and all they got were rules." Working within rules is an important aspect of the therapy. Reinforcing boundary issues begins the process of dealing with BPD patients as responsible adults. The therapist must demonstrate a model of a self-respecting person who refuses to be exploited, corrupted, or manipulated into gratifying patients' every whim.

As therapy progresses, therapists are required to act as a "container" for strong affects, particularly anger. Caregivers are powerful transference figures for patients. Verbal barrages, tirades and seething venom will pervade sessions. At these times, patients are not in a frame of mind to consider interpretations. These episodes must be endured and recalled in a way that will benefit patients at a later time. Two gains can be made during sessions such as these:

• by empathizing with the need to split, patients can become aware that they see themselves and others only in polarized terms
• patients incorporate the experience that expressing their "badness" does not destroy themselves, others, or the therapeutic relationship

What makes this such a difficult part of therapy is the use of **projective identification**. Patients outwardly project a part of themselves that is unacceptable, while maintaining a link with it. The projected material is made to "fit" by unconscious pressures, inducing the projected emotional state in the therapist. For example, a borderline patient who is angry with the limits of therapy, regardless of the degree to which their requests have been indulged, may make statements such as:

"How is this therapy supposed to be useful? I come here each week and all I get is psychobabble. I don't want to talk about my parents. They're in the past and I have bigger problems right now. When are you going to earn your money and do something?"

or

"I've been coming here for four months and nothing has changed. I tell you everything that goes on in my life. You've given me a pile of useless pills, admitted me to hospital twice, and had me off work for two weeks. All this and I'm no better. You're useless!"

Patients will insist that they are angry because the therapist is angry, but statements like these *make* therapists angry. Borderline patients are exceedingly good at manipulating (unconsciously) their projections to make them realistic or fit the person on whom they are projected. This process can be very difficult to endure, and can cause marked countertransference reactions in therapists. Interpretations in such instances need to be made with the understanding that borderline patients do not have an observing ego. Simply telling patients that they are projecting their own anger seems to them like an attack. It may be more profitable to demonstrate a less confrontative approach that incorporates an element of observation:

DISORDERED PERSONALITIES

"I can see that you feel angry at what goes on here. Perhaps you think I have given up on you, and treat you like a hopeless case, much as others have."

This interpretation maintains a "here and now" focus, validating the person's feelings, but offering an alternative for further exploration. Such an approach is necessary, because confrontation, and failure to achieve or maintain a therapeutic alliance, encompass the two most common reasons patients terminate therapy.

Borderline patients are best suited for face-to-face therapy. This requires activity on the therapist's part, as long periods of silence foster regression and are countertherapeutic.

The other major difficulty in dealing with borderline patients is the propensity for **acting out** behaviors, particularly in the area of self-damage. They often demonstrate a level of denial (bordering on **magical thinking**) regarding the consequences of their acts. Possible sequelae should be examined in detail with patients, and risks repeatedly emphasized. As part of this process, patients should be prompted to look for precipitants to their actions or mood states. This helps establish the connection between feelings, thoughts and actions that can help decrease impulsivity. Because most of the impulsive behavior in BPD is egosyntonic, patients may be quite unaware of what causes them to act at certain times. It is most often worthwhile to look at the details of their current relationships as a starting point for this examination.

SUMMARY OF THERAPEUTIC TECHNIQUES

• Consistency helps foster a stable image of the therapist, the therapy and ultimately the patient
• Maintain a "here and now focus;" transference provides critical information, and if dealt with in the session, may decrease acting out
• Ask for patients' help in resolving dilemmas
• Be active; engage patients; do not let silences continue for too long; discuss strong affects and splits as they are expressed
• Reward assertiveness, not regression
• Be flexible; there is no cookbook treatment for BPD; try different approaches to find effective interventions
• Patients need to experience therapists as empathic, supportive and interested before they need interpretations about their lives
• **Strike when the iron is cold** (PINE, 1986)

Transference and Countertransference Reactions

Transference manifestations with borderline patients can be rough, rougher than even Rodney Dangerfield has it. Patients live out the unsolved dilemmas from their early development. Intimacy evokes fears of being engulfed or controlled by another person. Separateness from others is experienced as abandonment. These oscillations become the central dynamic in the therapeutic relationship. Patients can tolerate neither closeness nor distance. They have been aptly referred to as **help-rejecting complainers** for frantically seeking and then discounting the attempts of others to help.

This upheaval manifests itself in therapy early on. Therapists represent parent substitutes in terms of authority, knowledge, power, etc. Some patients initially idealize their therapists as rescuers and make their affections readily known, "You are the best doctor in this hospital . . . You are the only one who understands me . . . I want you to be my doctor." Patients begin to seduce idealized caregivers in a number of ways: emotionally, morally, sexually, etc. They give lavish presents, always seem to be stopping by, etc. Soon they start to develop unrealistic notions and make unreasonable demands. A person who was once trustworthy is seen as completely so, until he or she disappoints the patient. At this point, this person is then viewed as completely untrustworthy, with an accompanying extreme emotional response. Thus begins the devaluation, which is inevitable because no person can possibly meet the escalating demands. At this time, the devalued person is not treated just *like* someone who disappointed the patient, but **"as if"** he or she *had* ruined the patient's life.

Countertransference reactions can be just as strong. Borderline patients can exert irresistible pull on therapists, who respond by dissolving boundaries. Intimate relationships are started, sessions are extended and given more frequently, extended absences from work are permitted, prescriptions are given for addictive medication, etc. Alternatively, therapists can respond by being unnecessarily punitive or sadistic towards patients. Sarcasm, teasing or hurtful interpretations dominate sessions. An awareness of these feelings is essential in dealing with borderline patients. Because of the uncanny fit of **projective identification**, therapists may have a difficult time sorting out where the patient's pathology ends and their own psychology begins. It is never helpful to act on countertransference feelings; it only serves to repeat the trauma that patients have endured. Transfer of care, consultation, supervision, personal therapy and a review of ethical standards can help clear up difficulties in this area.

Inpatient Management

Though this section is included in this chapter, these principles are applicable to all hospitalized patients with personality disorders. The majority of patients who need admission have a **borderline personality organization**, regardless of diagnosis. In practice, it is Cluster B patients that are hospitalized most frequently.

Hospitalization can have different meanings in the context of treatment. For many, it is seen as a setback and failure of outpatient treatment. Patients are derided for not managing on their own and therapists feel as if their efforts are in vain. However, it may also indicate increasingly adaptive behavior. Patients who feel overwhelmed and ask for hospitalization demonstrate good judgment, especially compared to patients who act out their feelings by abusing substances, harming themselves or being sexually promiscuous.

Regardless of how admission is arranged, patients arrive in a state of crisis. The inpatient unit becomes a holding environment, providing an external structure for internal deficiencies. Patients can easily regress because they feel they will be cared for. Other people are now responsible for them. Additionally, their maladaptive style of relating to others is heightened due to their emotional stress, with **splitting** and **projective identification** being the predominant defenses patients deploy to gratify their needs. Under the conditions of admission, these defenses appear sooner and more dramatically than in individual outpatient therapy.

Splitting in an inpatient setting involves the entire multidisciplinary team. Staff members may find themselves defending and supporting certain patients in increasing opposition to their colleagues. Patients may go about this overtly by idealizing certain individuals and complaining to them about others, or more covertly, with **projective identification** working on different members simultaneously.

Patients have a knack for detecting and reactivating preexisting conflicts in their caregivers (the *fit* of **projective identification**; this phenomenon is also seen in manic patients). Conflict among staff members can become quite heated and cause devastating long-term results. The chaotic internal world of borderline patients becomes reenacted in their external world. For example, some staff members may focus on preserving the patient's autonomy, and recommend privileges that conflict with the safety concerns of the other members.

In order to minimize this, the following steps can be taken:

• educating the staff about the dynamics of these defenses
• regular meetings to discuss progress and setbacks
• sharing the content of all contact with the patient
• special meetings to discuss countertransference feelings when the staff is becoming noticeably split

The last step can be particularly difficult. Often a team will notice that one member feels uniquely able to understand a patient and is uncharacteristically permissive, or alternatively, is denigrating and harsh. It is very difficult to bring such an observation to attention. Therapists experience numerous reactions, but not every nuance is due to the patient. When members of a treatment team are familiar with each other, and can accept that they have countertransference reactions, identifying them will help present a unified front to patients. Repeated failures to provoke expected reactions in people (caregivers) helps patients internalize new objects and increase their stability.

The goals of an inpatient stay are to provide support, curb the direct expression of impulses and strengthen ego function. Interventions may be required to prevent harmful **acting out** or acting up, including medication, restraints or seclusion. Additionally, superego function may need to be strengthened in ways that further the best interests of patients, such as giving reality-based advice.

With the demands of their daily routine temporarily removed, patients have a tendency to regress in hospital. This is seen in various ways: wearing pyjamas all day, chatting with other patients all night, sleeping until late morning hours, asking staff or patients to make phone calls or run errands, finding ways to prolong hospital stay, etc. This can be limited by short admissions, adherence to ward routines as a condition of admission, and setting firm limits on behavior.

The majority of patients can be managed with brief (three to four day) stays. Indications for longer term treatment are:

• repeated failure of brief hospitalizations and outpatient treatment
• an associated Axis I condition
• escalating and intervention-resistant violent, or self-destructive behavior
• severe or psychotic symptomatology
• a choatic environment that provides no social support

PHARMACOTHERAPY

Though there is no definitive drug treatment for personality disorders, over ninety percent of borderline patients still receive prescriptions. This finding illustrates the widespread overlap of borderline symptomatology with Axis I disorders, and the possibility of multiple diagnoses. However, there are other parameters that need to be considered. Doctors may prescribe medication when feeling pessimistic about psychotherapy. Patients in crisis may see a prescription as tangible proof (**transitional object**) that a doctor cares about them. Exaggeration of symptoms or seeing multiple doctors ensures that a prescription is eventually given. For this reason, it is prudent to prescribe medication for clearly-defined target symptoms for a specific time period. Because of the risk of overdose, small amounts of medication should be given and, where faced with an option, the least toxic drug should be used.

Every major group may have a use in ameliorating target symptoms:

Antidepressants: Patients frequently receive antidepressants, though studies have shown an unpredictable response.

• Serotonin Selective Reuptake Inhibitors (SSRIs) have been found to decrease impulsivity and the frequency of self-harm. Some SSRIs have been indicated for control of bulimia. Additionally, they have a large margin of safety in overdose.

• Monoamine Oxidase Inhibitors (MAOIs) have been shown to be more effective than tricyclic antidepressants (TCAs).

Mood Stabilizers: Lithium, Valproic Acid and Carbamazepine have been used primarily for behavioral dyscontrol.

Anxiolytics: These medications are frequently sought by borderline patients to "take the edge off" their mood. Benzodiazepines pose considerable addiction risks as well as potentially worsening impulse control through disinhibition.

Antipsychotics: Use of these medications for short-term control of psychosis and persecutory delusions is warranted. Additional benefit may be derived the sedative effects. Tardive dyskinesia is a risk with long-term administration, particularly in females.

GROUP THERAPY

Group therapy can be a useful form of treatment with borderline patients, either alone or combined with individual psychotherapy.

Groups allow borderline patients to diffuse their intense affects and direct them at more than one member. A group can provide a safe holding environment. It can offer, in a sense, a new family or a benevolent **transitional object**, where **identification** and **introjection** can take place. This fosters increasing maturity and a diminution of the use of primitive defenses. Interpretations made on a group level may be better tolerated than those given in individual therapy. A group setting also allows patients to explore new ways of dealing with people in a protected environment.

Because borderline patients lack a stable self-image, it is ideal to have group members who can provide positive role models. Such a group would contain a number of higher-functioning members with heterogeneous disorders. Short-term inpatient groups can be successful when a "here and now" focus is maintained to work on practical goals such as support, stabilization and limiting regression. A group consisting of recently discharged moderate-to-low functioning borderline patients is not likely to provide a therapeutic milieu.

Simultaneous participation in individual and group therapy, while not standard practice, supports patients through difficulties brought on by the group process. For example, confrontation or scapegoating by the group can be very anxiety-provoking. A stable therapeutic figure may help contain the emotions that might otherwise cause patients to leave the group (e.g. feelings of deprivation or competition). This arrangement can benefit therapists if transference manifestations can be diluted between the group and individual sessions.

Alternatively, group therapy can be difficult with borderline patients. Their direct expression of anger can cause others to see them as unpredictable, offensive and disloyal. This can effectively divide the members and this "split" can dominate the group. When this occurs, borderline patients are capable of **acting out** on this sense of rejection. Suicide attempts, personal attacks and other forms of interpersonal sabotage may result and destabilize the group.

COGNITIVE THERAPY

Basic Cognitive Distortions:
- Mistrust and suspiciousness - "The world is against me."
- Distorted perceptions - "People are deceptive and manipulative."
- Vulnerability - "I am powerless to control my life."
- Worthlessness - "I am unlovable."

ADAPTED FROM BECK, FREEMAN & ASSOCIATES, 1990

The automatic thoughts in BPD create a vicious cycle for patients. Seeing the world as a malevolent place, they feel powerless to get by on their own strengths. They feel inherently unlovable and cannot turn to others. Convinced the world is out to get them, they have no sense of security and cannot tolerate autonomy or dependence.

In a key cognitive feature of BPD is called **dichotomous thinking**. Events and people are distorted into only two categories: *good or evil; love or hate*. Dichotomous thinking perpetuates their internal and external conflicts, magnifying their already low sense of self-efficacy and further decreasing motivation. Borderline patients can be difficult to engage. They lack the introspection and patience to participate in the "collaborative empiricism" needed for cognitive therapy.

Cognitive approaches begin with modification of dichotomous thinking. This can be done by hypothetically assigning characteristics to people at both ends of the spectrum of a given quality, for example, reliability. A borderline patient will then go on to list impossibly high expectations for a reliable person and the embodiment of evil for a unreliable person. By then looking at real people in their lives, patients can begin to see that others can be *mainly, mostly* or *usually* reliable. As these dichotomous thoughts decrease, impulse control becomes possible:

Recognition of dichotomous thinking and the impulse to act on it
↓
Listing of alternatives and their pros and cons in achieving a goal
↓
Implementing the response that yields the greatest benefit

Working towards a goal provides a structure that develops a clearer sense of identity. This gives patients the confidence to experiment by expressing themselves in a proactive and assertive manner, instead of being victims of fate who have neither strengths nor supports.

Course of BPD

BPD manifests itself prior to the demonstration of diagnostic criteria. As children, borderline patients frequently had difficulties in school, particularly with concentration, and possibly had learning disabilities. Friendships may have been jeopardized or terminated because of behavioral dyscontrol, bringing about early social alienation.

In adolescence and early adulthood, the symptoms of the disorder flourish. Patients often do not complete their education or vocational training. With dissolution of their family of origin, or upon leaving home, they become involved in relationships that perpetuate and worsen their difficulties. Substance abuse is common, perhaps as a means of calming their intense feelings. The vast majority of patients diagnosed with BPD manifest consistent symptomatology over time. Few patients are re-diagnosed with other disorders, though other conditions can develop in addition to this personality disorder.

It is in late adolescence or early adulthood that patients usually come to medical attention. First visits are frequently precipitated by DIRs. From this point on, BPD usually runs a rocky course punctuated with attempts at self-harm, hospital admissions, difficulties in relationships and emotional instability. The consumption of health care resources can be enormous. Emergency room visits, with resuscitation and detoxification, in addition to hospitalization, demands for outpatient therapy and multiple prescription medications, all add to the cost. This is in addition to the lost productivity caused by sick days and other absences from work. The treatment of BPD is a long process that often requires hospital admission and crisis intervention.

Despite this pessimistic picture, BPD appears to lessen in severity within a decade of the first hospitalization. Several studies have documented higher levels of functioning and stability in jobs and relationships over this time. Despite the wear and tear on therapists in this first decade, it may be that patients incorporate something from each caregiver or hospital stay and integrate this over time.

Suicidal attempts and gestures are the most worrisome complication. Though this is often a primitive method of securing treatment and attention, repeated attempts are a risk factor for completing suicide, which happens in up to a tenth of borderline patients. Additionally, morbidity is increased by failed attempts that leave patients with lifelong disfigurement due to scars or burns, and handicaps such as brain damage or paralysis.

References

American Psychiatric Association
DIAGNOSTIC AND STATISTICAL MANUAL OF MENTAL DISORDERS, FOURTH EDITION
American Psychiatric Press; Washington, D.C., 1994

N. Andreason, D. Black
INTRODUCTORY TEXTBOOK OF PSYCHIATRY
American Psychiatric Press; Washington, D.C., 1991

A. Beck, A. Freeman & Associates
COGNITIVE THERAPY OF PERSONALITY DISORDERS
The Guildford Press; New York, 1990

G. Gabbard
PSYCHODYNAMIC PSYCHIATRY IN CLINICAL PRACTICE, THE DSM-IV EDITION
American Psychiatric Press; Washington, D.C., 1994

H. Kaplan, B. Sadock (editors)
COMPREHENSIVE GROUP PSYCHOTHERAPY, THIRD EDITION
Williams & Wilkins; Baltimore, 1993

H. Kaplan, B. Sadock (editors)
COMPREHENSIVE TEXTBOOK OF PSYCHIATRY, SIXTH EDITION
Williams & Wilkins; Baltimore, 1995

N. McWilliams
PSYCHOANALYTIC DIAGNOSIS
The Guildford Press; New York, 1994

E. Othmer & S. Othmer
THE CLINICAL INTERVIEW USING DSM-IV
American Psychiatric Press; Washington, D.C., 1994

R. Pies
CLINICAL MANUAL OF PSYCHIATRIC DIAGNOSIS AND TREATMENT
American Psychiatric Press; Washington, D.C., 1994

F. Pine
Supportive Psychotherapy: A Psychoanalytic Perspective
PSYCHIATRIC ANNALS, 16, p. 526-529, 1986

Unpredictable.

¶I met her downtown at a Vorpel Gallery opening. (I was invited, she crashed.) Dressed in red—the color of a fire truck—she was meant to start fires, not to put them out. I could hear her laughter from across the room. Everyone could. Her presence drew me to her. Like a moth to a

Intense.

fatal flame. Enticing. Consuming. She left soon after arriving, quickly bored and I by her side. We escaped into the darkness of her loft. We drank. We danced. We thrilled to the night until Dawn—her former bisexual lover and current roommate—objected to the noise. Passionate and reckless, she threatened to punch out

Reckless.

Dawn's lights. ¶It was a stormy relationship. She was a rollercoaster of emotion. Quick to tears. Then to laughter. I was the best thing in her life. I was the worst. It was hard to keep up with her. She was a whirlwind of activity. Shopping. Drinking. Partying. More shopping. The sex

Provocative.

was good. Actually, it was great. Until I found her in bed with another man and a woman. She was just having fun, she said. She told me she loved me so much she would kill herself (after killing me) if I ever tried to leave her. She was so emotional, so provocative. Never dull.

Passionate.

¶I guess you could say she was a BORDERLINE™ woman.

BORDERLINE

Calvin Kline

©1990 Wry-Bred Press, Inc.

Concept, design, & advertising copy: Glenn C. Ellenbogen, Ph.D.

Photography: Donna Lynn Brophy

Copyright 1990 by Wry-Bred Press, Inc. Reprinted from the Journal of Polymorphous Perversity by permission of the copyright holder.

FILL-IN-THE-BLANK PERSONALITIES:
FATAL PERSONALITIES INSTINCTIVELY ATTRACT

ACT I
Seemingly out of nowhere, a talented, attractive and highly available underline=borderline drops into the plot. A glimpse of her tortured past is given, but through a series of clever and evasive maneuvers in script writing, the details are concealed. She quickly gets the attention of a roving narcissist, and lavishes on him the attention that his dependent wife and schizoid child are not supplying in sufficient quantities for his hypertrophied ego.

ACT II
Idealization runs rampant. They live. They love. They frolic. They Cluster B all over each other. They do things even a paranoid couldn't imagine, or a schizotypal wouldn't even predict.

ACT III
Eventually things get a little rough. He needs to get back to reality, she just needs more of him. He levels with his obsessive-compulsive friend, who draws up a twelve-step plan for her emotional independence, but it is of no avail. Erratic job performance eventually comes to the attention of his avoidant boss, who after empathically hearing all the details, is forced to hand out a suspension.

ACT IV - OPTION 1
Admitting his stupidity to his wife causes a re-emergence of her histrionic side, the very qualities that drew them together in the first place. They pool their antisocial qualities and devise a plan to rid themselves of his borderline lover.

ACT IV - OPTION 2
Events escalate to histrionic pitch. He realizes life without his borderline lover would be dull, if she allowed him to have any. Together, they make a pact not to exploit each others' antisocial qualities, and live happily after, at least until next time.

From the *PsychoIllogical Bulletin*.

THE ANTISOCIAL PERSONALITY

Biographical Information

Name:	Vinny Scumbagglia
Occupation:	Had "career" since childhood
Appearance:	Sibeburns, muscle shirt, tattoos
Relationship with animals:	Trained dog to snatch purses
Favorite Song:	*Criminal Mind*

At the Therapist's Office

Before Session:	Robs pharmacy in the lobby
Waiting Room Reading:	Steals magazines; leaves copies of *Playboy*, sans centerfold
During Session:	Starts sentences with, "!@#$%^&*"
Fantasies Involve:	Seducing probation officer
Relationship with Therapist:	Picks pocket, uses long distance phone card
Behavior During Session:	Carves up armrest, finds *Histrionic's* phone number
Takes to Therapy:	Brochure for a car alarm (that he can dismantle)

Diagnostic Shorthand

Mnemonic - "Callous Man"

Conduct disorder before age 15; current age at least 18

Antisocial acts; commits acts that are grounds for arrest

Lies frequently

Lacks remorse

Obligations not honored (financial, work, etc.)

Unstable; can't plan ahead

Support lacking for children or spouse

Makes no provisions for the safety of self or others

Aggressive/assaultive

Not occurring during schizophrenia or mania

INTRODUCTION

The antisocial personality disorder (ASPD) is the oldest and best validated of the personality disorders.

Some of the key names associated with the ASPD are:
- **Pinel** (France, 19th Century) described this condition as "moral insanity" in that there was a circumscribed deficiency of morality without other signs of mental illness
- **Cleckley** (1941) published THE MASK OF SANITY, a seminal publication in the description of this disorder; he distinguished the *psychopathic personality* from criminal acts and social deviance; these views influenced the DSM I & II and reappear in the DSM-IV
- **Lee Robbins** (1960's) classic study called, "Deviant Children Grown Up" specified the antisocial acts in the criteria of the DSM III & III-R
- **Maudsley, Meyer, Kraeplin, Schneider, Alexander** and **Rush** all made contributions to the description of ASPD

The antisocial personality disorder (ASPD) is characterized by guiltless, exploitative and irresponsible behavior with the hallmark being conscious deceit of others. ASPDs have a lifelong pattern (defined as being present prior to age fifteen) of disregard for the rights of others. This disorder has also been called **psychopathic, sociopathic** and **dyssocial** (ICD-10). The DSM-III/III-R diagnostic criteria for ASPD involved a checklist of specific criminal acts. The term **psychopathy** is defined as, "a cluster of both personality traits and socially deviant behaviors." The DSM-IV incorporates this expanded definition, instead of providing a list of behaviors.

Criminal activity, itself, does not necessarily imply the presence of ASPD. Those who run afoul of the law may do so for reasons other than having this personality disorder. Similarly, not all ASPDs have criminal records. Some carry on lengthy sprees of emotional and financial destruction without getting caught.

Because ASPD is egosyntonic, these patients virtually never come to attention because they are distressed by their actions. The most common reasons for contact involve: alcohol or drug detoxification, prescriptions for drugs with a street value, a note or medical reason for missing work, a forensic assessment to relieve them of criminal responsibility, and avoiding military service or other work they consider undesirable.

MEDIA EXAMPLES

TV shows, movies and fictional bestsellers are teeming with antisocial characters. They fulfill the requirements of the media "id" - sex and violence - and, as such, are pivotal characters in any kind of human drama. ASPDs make for fascinating entertainment because they commit acts at the very depths of morality: murder, sexual assault, blackmail, kidnapping, extortion, torture, theft and vandalism. They carry out common fantasies of such behavior, satisfying the audience's voyeuristic interests and advancing the plot.

A vast array of antisocial characters exist in the popular media. Bad guys, Mafioso, con men, murderers, "psycho-killers," forgers, adulterers, terrorists, drug lords, and James Bond villains are just a few. The number of films and novels with these characters would constitute a book on its own. Some notable examples are seen in:

• **SILENCE OF THE LAMBS** - contained a brilliant portrayal of a sociopath by Anthony Hopkins. He easily exploited the vulnerable Agent Starling (Jodie Foster), and gave a very good feel for the remorselessness of this disorder. The transvestite in this film demonstrated a good example of the antisocial detachment by seeing people only as objects (this is **not** object relations). He used the word "it" to refer to the woman he'd kidnapped. Also, the manipulative qualities of the FBI supervisor were noteworthy.

• **THE DIRTY DOZEN** - a number of stars portrayed ASPDs who were sent on a suicide mission during W.W. II. This movie tried to demonstrate that the "talents" possessed by these characters would be useful during war. However, actual experience in the armed forces is quite unlike the movie version. It is a long-standing Hollywood myth that turning a sociopath inside out creates a hero.

• **WALL STREET** - Michael Douglas played the part of a ruthless tycoon who cared nothing for the companies he liquidated, or the lives disrupted in the process. He gave an excellent example of a mind operating without a superego with his "Greed is Good" speech.

• **WHISPERS IN THE DARK** - included a compelling performance by Alan Alda (Hawkeye from M*A*S*H) as a psychopathic psychiatrist who has an erotomanic attachment to a former student.

INTERVIEW CONSIDERATIONS

Antisocial patients can be easy or quite difficult to interview. They have what Kernberg has termed a **malignant grandiosity** - a *deliberate* attempt to use others (as opposed to the more unconscious kind of manipulation seen in other personality disorders). They openly brag about con jobs, conquests and scams to impress others. Shamelessly, they will try to pull one over on you, just as they tell you how successful they've been in deceiving others.

As long as there is interest in hearing about these exploits, along with free rein to speak, rapport is easily established. This can be subtly, or even overtly encouraged, and needs to be developed before looking at more sensitive areas. For example, statements such as the ones below will have ASPDs eagerly awaiting to tell more.

- "You really seem to have a way with people."
- "You're a pretty smart guy."
- "You must have a lot of respect out on the street."

Once they realize that condemnation is not forthcoming, it is not difficult to maintain a positive atmosphere. It is important to remain morally neutral, and not do anything that could be misconstrued as approval for the antisocial acts mentioned. To ASPDs, this will seem like collusion. Difficulties begin when patients' manipulations are resisted, or their requests are refused. Once started, they can become hostile, critical, derogatory, intimidating and even violent. A gentle segue can be helpful in refocussing attention to clinical matters:

- "How could someone so clever end up in so much trouble?"
- "How come nothing seems to be going right for you?"
- "Where did things go wrong for you this time?"

If rapport is lost or difficult to initiate, appeal to patients' sense of grandiosity. They strive to be the center of attention and may respond to an air of indifference from interviewers. By demonstrating that this interview is not of the highest priority, and being vague about rescheduling, cooperation can be obtained. Also, if someone of "lesser" clinical rank is suggested as an alternative interviewer, patients may not be able to bear the insult to their self-importance. ASPDs desire immediate gratification, and seize opportunities when they are available.

As with other personality disorders, ASPDs do exist at higher levels of functioning. Such patients can be quite sophisticated, and may be able deceive with rehearsed lines and convincing explanations for their "dilemmas." This will be especially evident with remorse. Most will relate feeling "bad" about something, but this has more to do with being caught than genuine regret.

Another interview consideration is that ASPDs tend to minimize their involvement, or the outcome of their actions. Words are twisted to achieve this effect (for example "skirmish" or "spat" instead of fight). Language is used to manipulate, an important clue in interviews.

ANTISOCIAL THEMES

In addition to the diagnostic criteria and Cleckley's sixteen descriptive elements (both are listed later in this chapter), the following features become evident in the interview and history:

- Glibness, shallow emotion
- Requires constant stimulation
- Criminal versatility
- Parole/probation violations
- Promiscuity
- Juvenile delinquency
- Grandiosity
- Poor impulse control
- Avoids responsibility for actions
- Abuse of substances
- Superior physical prowess
- Behavioral problems as a child
- Social "parasites;" may have several sources of financial assistance, "under the table" cash, or profit from stolen property or drugs

PRESUMED ETIOLOGY

BIOLOGICAL: The antisocial personality disorder has some of the strongest evidence for the heritability of personality disorders. Chess and Thomas found that as children, antisocial patients were innately aggressive, with higher activity and reactivity levels and lowered consolability. This may indicate an inborn tendency toward aggression and a higher than average need for excitement.

Twin studies also indicate a genetic factor. Studies have shown a higher than (societal) average incidence of ASPD in the adopted away children of antisocial biological parents. The studies screened for the presence of ASPD in adoptive parents.

If there is a genetic component, physical aberrations may serve as a marker, with a number being reported:

- "Soft" or non-localizing neurological signs, especially in childhood:
  - Persistence of primitive reflexes: palmar-mental, grasp, snout
  - Impaired coordination, gait, balance and motor performance
  - Graphesthesia, Positive Romberg Sign, Dysdiadochokinesis

- Lower reactivity of the autonomic nervous system (also, a reported inability to learn from experience)
- Low cortical arousal and reduced level of inhibitory anxiety
- Lowered levels of 5-HIAA (a metabolite of serotonin) have been found in impulsive/aggressive patients, indicating lowered metabolism
- Changes in skin electrical conductivity and EEG abnormalities
- **Attention-Deficit/Hyperactivity Disorder** is a risk factor
- ASPD appears to be genetically related to alcoholism and is frequently complicated by alcohol abuse

PSYCHOSOCIAL: Several factors in childhood are thought to be etiologically significant in the development of ASPD:

- Frequent moves, losses, family break-ups; large families
- Poverty, urban setting, poorly regulated schooling
- Little emphasis on communication; instead, language was used as a tool with which to manipulate, not express feelings
- Indulged materially, but deprived emotionally
- **Enuresis, firesetting** and **cruelty to animals** may be particularly strong indicators of future ASPD

Parents that are neglectful, harsh, physically abusive or substance abusers have a large impact on the development of this disorder. Often, patients with ASPD were victims themselves. A family history readily reveals physical/sexual/emotional abuse, often with a substance abusing caregiver. Frequent parental characteristics are:
Mother: weak, depressive, masochistic, somatizing
Father: explosive, inconsistent, sadistic, alcoholic, criminal history

Blending genetic and psychosocial factors, etiologic factors involve children, with a high degree of aggression, that are difficult to calm down, comfort and love. Other factors such as a hyperactivity, or a demanding nature require an active, energetic parent. Recalling the *goodness of fit* between child and parent, these children may be at the extreme where a poor fit has disastrous long-term consequences. Children need a benevolent authority figure to check aggression and balance crime with punishment. Attachment to only one caregiver may not be sufficient for some children.

Some studies indicate the increase in single parent families may be a cause for higher numbers of sociopaths. Without a father figure, there may be a lack of effective limits set on behavior, with no, or insufficient, consequences for impulsivity. Children learn that in an environment lacking consistent discipline, consequences can be avoided by seducing or bullying others.

EPIDEMIOLOGY

Estimates of the prevalence of ASPD are in the range of 3% for men and 1% for women. The prevalence can be up to 75% for incarcerated individuals. There is a sex difference in that men are more frequently diagnosed with ASPD, and women with Borderline Personality Disorder.

EGO DEFENSES

ASPD is characterized by use of primitive defenses to exert power, for the purpose of defending against shame. The primary defenses are:

- **Controlling** (need omnipotent control over others and their situation)
- **Projective Identification** (described in the PARANOID CHAPTER)
- **Acting Out** (described in the BORDERLINE CHAPTER)
- **Dissociation** (see also OTHER PERSONALITY TOPICS)

Controlling is an excessive attempt to manage or regulate events, objects, or people, in order to minimize anxiety and resolve inner conflicts (**primary gain**).

ASPDs are very prone to action. They gain no increased self-esteem from controlling an impulse. Many lack even social anxiety, though it has been suggested that this has to do with the speed with which they act. Feelings are not well-tolerated (especially "weak" ones), and action is imparted quickly enough to prevent anxiety from being felt.

Dissociation is a temporary, but drastic, modification of one's sense of identity or character in order to avoid emotional distress. Dissociative phenomena range from minimizing one's role to total amnesia for a violent crime. Indeed, the majority of murderers claim to be amnestic for the event. This poses the question whether emotional dissociation is related to abuse. There is growing evidence for such an association in other disorders, and because of the high incidence of abuse in ASPD, there may be a relationship between abuse and dissociation.

Diagnostic Criteria

A. There is a pervasive pattern of disregard for and violation of the rights of others occurring since age 15 years, as indicated by three (or more) of the following:

(1) failure to conform to social norms with respect to lawful behaviors as indicated by repeatedly performing acts that are grounds for arrest
(2) deceitfulness, as indicated by repeated lying, use of aliases, or conning others for personal profit or pleasure
(3) impulsivity or failure to plan ahead
(4) irritability and aggressiveness, as indicated by repeated physical fights or assaults
(5) reckless disregard for safety of self or others
(6) consistent irresponsibility, as indicated by repeated failure to sustain consistent work behavior or honor financial obligations
(7) lack of remorse, as indicated by being indifferent to or rationalizing having hurt, mistreated, or stolen from another

B. The individual is at least age 18 years.
C. There is evidence of Conduct Disorder with onset before age 15y.
D. The occurrence of antisocial behavior is not exclusively during the course of Schizophrenia or a Manic Episode

Diagnostic Criteria for Conduct Disorder

A. A repetitive and persistent pattern of behavior in which the basic rights of others or major age-appropriate societal norms or rules are violated as manifested by the presence of three (or more) of the following criteria in the past 12 months, with at least one criterion present in the past 6 months.

Aggression to people and animals
(1) often bullies, threatens, or intimidates others
(2) often initiates physical fights
(3) has used a weapon that can cause serious physical harm to others
(4) has been physically cruel to people
(5) has been physically cruel to animals
(6) has stolen while confronting a victim
(7) has forced someone into sexual activity

Destruction of Property
(8) has deliberately engaged in fire setting with the intention of causing serious damage
(9) has deliberately destroyed others' property (other than by fire setting)

Deceitfulness or Theft
(10) has broken into someone else's house, building, or car
(11) often lies to obtain goods or favors or to avoid obligations
(12) has stolen items of nontrivial value without confronting a victim

Serious Violations of Rules
(13) often stays out at night despite parental prohibitions, beginning before age 13 years
(14) has run away from home overnight at least twice while living in parental or parental surrogate home (or once without returning for a lengthy period)
(15) is often truant from school, beginning before age 13 years

B. The disturbance in behavior causes clinically significant impairment in social, academic, or occupational functioning

C. If the individual is age 18 years or older, criteria are not met for Antisocial Personality Disorder
REPRINTED WITH PERMISSION FROM THE DSM-IV.
COPYRIGHT, AMERICAN PSYCHIATRIC ASSOCIATION, 1994

DIFFERENTIAL DIAGNOSIS

ASPD is not diagnosed if the antisocial acts occur during a **Manic Episode**, or during the course of **Schizophrenia**. While suffering from a manic episode, there is an inflated amount of energy and enthusiasm, and a sense of grandiosity (entitlement, privilege, etc.). These factors, combined with serious impairments in insight and judgment, can result in criminal behavior.

Similarly, delusions or psychosis in schizophrenia or severe mania can fuel the commission of offenses. Mania, schizophrenia and ASPD can share features such as: willful destruction of property, financial irresponsibility (evasion of debts, spending sprees, etc.), theft, vandalism, physical intimidation and violence. Additionally, general medical conditions such as **Dementia**, **Delirium** and **Epilepsy** can lead patients to commit violent acts on an infrequent basis.

Substance abuse is a key factor to consider in ASPD. Many individuals commit crimes to obtain drugs, or while intoxicated, but not at other times. Males with ASPD may have a distinct type of alcoholism, associated with: an early age on onset, a high degree of novelty seeking and criminality in their fathers, but with only an average prevalence of alcoholism in the extended family.

A key diagnostic point is that not all criminal behavior is due to the presence of an ASPD, and not all ASPDs commit actual offenses. Proper evaluation of this diagnosis requires a longitudinal history, with an understanding of patients' interpersonal behavior. The diagnosis of ASPD represents a pervasive and long-standing disregard for the rights of others. While unlawful behaviors are the usual manifestation, other acts can be motivated by cruelty, sadism and profit, regardless of the effects on others. ASPDs are supportive of criminal activity, and are shallow, proud or remorseless when confronted. This is a different response than one would see in a patient after a mood disorder or psychotic episode motivated an antisocial act - unless they have ASPD in addition to their Axis I disorder!

OTHER DIAGNOSTIC CONSIDERATIONS

The overlap of ASPD with substance abuse (especially alcoholism) has already been mentioned. Separating the effects of one diagnosis on the other can be quite difficult.

First-degree female relatives of ASPD males have been described as having a higher incidence of **Briquet's Syndrome** (essentially **Somatization Disorder**).

ASPDs are also prone to **Malingering**, which is feigning mental illness for an obvious secondary gain. **Ganser's Syndrome** is a related syndrome of *approximate, but not correct answers* thought to be more due to conscious malingering than dissociative or hysterical causes.

MENTAL STATUS EXAMINATION

APPEARANCE: Stereotypically have long hair, open shirt, excessive jewelry, scars, tattoos, tight-fitting pants with large belt buckles, boots, knives in sheaths; mesomorphic build (bodybuilder); Females may have heavy make-up; tight-fitting or revealing clothing

Behavior:	Strutting walk and erect posture; use space around them if trying to impress; move closer when trying to manipulate; move forcefully; strong handshake; often casually slump down in chair with knees apart
Cooperation:	Varies with degree of interviewer's interest - ranges from highly engaging to quite hostile
Affect	Expansive, cocky, hostile, irritable, shallow
Speech:	Exaggerated, vague, grammatical errors; glib, foul language; malapropisms; "pseudo"sophisticated
Content of Thought:	Grandiosity quite evident; past exploits are repeatedly emphasized; eventually get around to their agenda; blame environment exclusively
Thought Form:	No characteristic abnormality
Perception:	No characteristic abnormality, if present, consider malignering
Insight & Judgment:	Impaired, but can give "lip service" to what sounds morally decent; have great difficulty in seeing their deficits or contributions to problems
Suicide - Homicide:	More likely to be dangerous to others than to themselves, but may emphasize suicide to manipulate for their agenda

CLECKLEY'S PSYCHOPATHIC PERSONALITY FEATURES

- Superficial charm and good "intelligence"
- Absence of delusions and other signs of irrational thinking
- Absence of "nervousness" or psychoneurotic manifestations
- Unreliability
- Untruthfulness and insincerity
- Lack of remorse or shame
- Inadequately motivated antisocial behavior
- Poor judgment and failure to learn by experience
- Pathologic egocentricity and incapacity for love
- General poverty in major affective reactions
- Specific loss of insight
- Unresponsiveness in general interpersonal relations
- Fantastic and inviting behavior with drink and sometimes without
- Suicide rarely carried out
- Sex life impersonal, trivial and poorly integrated
- Failure to follow any life plan

SOURCE: CLECKLEY, 1988. REPRINTED WITH PERMISSION OF MRS. E. CLECKLEY

Psychodynamic Aspects

Sociopaths primarily need to exert power over others to defend against an awareness of shame. The central dynamic is an absence of conscience or a defective superego (Cleckley, 1988). Meaningful attachments to others are conspicuously lacking. Other people are seen only as objects over which to exert control. The harsh inner world of the antisocial is one of chaos, insecurity and intolerance. Expressing ordinary emotions reveals weakness and vulnerability; only the extremes - blind rage or manic exhilaration - are experienced. Tender or softer emotions expressed by others are actively devalued.

They exhibit a *primitive envy* and may seek to destroy what they most desire. The victims of many serial killers were attractive women or happy, stable families. It may be that aggressive and sadistic acts stabilize their sense of self, and boost self-esteem.

These patients have profound deficits in internalization. They do not attach to others, have not experienced a *good object*, and do not identify with a caregiver. They have never received love, do not love others, and have no sense of society or culture.

Modeling parental psychopathy is another dynamic aspect. Parents may encourage a demonstration of power with repeated messages that life should pose no limits, leaving their children feeling entitled to exert dominance. An example would be be parents who act with outrage at teachers, police, or counselors who try to set limits. The term **superego lacunae** is used to describe the process where parents who have their own problems with authority, encourage this in their children. It is "inherited" in terms of imitating parental behavior.

Lacking a sense of omnipotence and power at developmentally important phases leaves patients spending their lives seeking to confirm their power. If they are temperamentally more difficult to love, the lack of attachment leaves them more focused on themselves, and they make up and follow their own rules.

A common denominator may be that after such continual blows to their self-esteem, they view the external world as barren and self-serving. They become predators, exerting power, and remorselessly justify their disregard for the rights of others and the rules of society.

What Happens in Psychodynamic Therapy?

It is frequently stated that antisocial personalities are not treatable. At this time, there is no consistently successful form of psychotherapy or pharmacotherapy available.

"Why should I treat this lowlife?" This question crosses the minds of all therapists, who need to make personal decisions about investing their time and talents in attempting to help sociopathic personalities. A proper assessment is critical. Some may be so damaged, dangerous and determined to destroy the therapist or therapy that help is not possible. It may well be that these patients should not be accepted for treatment. Reasons for such a decision may be as follows:

- A history of serious assault (sexual/weapon), murder, sexual sadism
- Lack of remorse for a crime committed against an individual
- Obvious secondary gain for "being in treatment"
- Long periods of time spent in institutions or prison
- Extremes of intelligence
- An inability to develop any emotional attachment
- Threats to you (overt or implied)
- Arousal of strong countertransference reactions

SOURCE: ADAPTED FROM GABBARD, 1994

Within the diagnosis of ASPD, there exists a range of sociopathy. On one extreme is the predatory serial killer. On the other are moderately sociopathic professionals who cheat on their spouses, steal office supplies from work, have unpaid debts, and smuggle undeclared goods from abroad. Factors such as: ego strength, an ability to express remorse, evidence of compassionate feelings, and at least one enduring attachment need to present to have some success.

If a sufficient number of positive factors are present to start therapy, the most important feature is *incorruptibility* of the therapist and the therapy. Convey this almost to the point of being inflexible. Sociopaths don't understand empathy; they see people only as exchangeable objects. Any deviation will be seen as a sadistic triumph, not gratitude for wavering from the boundaries of therapy. Anything that can be interpreted as a weakness will be seen as such.

Use unwavering honesty in outlining a therapeutic contract. Use straight talk, keep promises, make good on threats and address reality.

Antisocial patients project their cold and self-serving nature onto others. They will try to discern what gain there is in being a therapist. You may have to admit to "selfishness" regarding fees.

Gratitude is not likely, but respect may be forthcoming for being scrupulous, tough-minded and exacting. Do not bend to their "special needs," regardless of the reasonableness of the explanation.

There is power inherent in confession; most patients *want* to talk about themselves. The first step in "acquiring" a conscience is caring enough about someone that that person's opinion matters. This can be developed by being a consistent, nonpunitive and nonexploitable person. Power is all that ASPDs respect. They can inflict extreme violence on someone seen as "disrespecting" them (treating them as powerless or worthless). Some demonstration of power may be helpful by "out-conning" or "out-psyching" them as a means of getting respect, or at least attention. We can use our own antisocial reactions in a way that allows a connection with their emotional world.

At least initially, empathy can't be used therapeutically. Also, inviting the expression of feelings is not likely to be useful because of their deficient superego. Because of this, they are committed to *act* in order to feel strong and omnipotent. Restrict discussion to the possible outcomes of antisocial behavior, and focus interventions on confronting denial and minimalization. Try using a sense of humor when making this point. While the penalties of breaking the law may be severe, the discussion doesn't have to be sterile.

Avoid emotional investment in patients or the progress of therapy. Show an independent strength verging on indifference. As a demonstration of power, therapy is likely to be sabotaged as soon as patients sense there is an investment in the outcome. However, it is important to be respectful, and to weather their continual grandiosity. Callousness is their response to an incomprehensible or abusive environment, which becomes generalized from early relationships.

Progress is being made when words change from being used as manipulative tools to expressing feelings. Another positive indication is feeling pride at suppressing impulses. A profound, or even psychotic depression, may develop in a successful therapy. This depression may herald extreme remorse and the onset of feelings for others.

Despite the summary provided here, psychotherapy with ASPDs is fraught with difficulty and unlikely to be successful.

Transference and Countertransference Reactions

Basic transference is the projection of predation; patients view the therapist as using them for selfish purposes. Patients will not be convinced of genuine motives and will try to figure out the "angle."

ASPDs will be preoccupied with using the therapist, and trying to outsmart the therapist's (perceived) exploitative agenda. Countertransference is felt as resistance to the extent that an identity as a helper becomes eroded. A common reaction is to try to prove good intentions and helpfulness. When this fails, hostility, contempt, moral outrage, and even outright hatred are generated. Here, the patient doesn't care about the therapist, and the therapist finds it difficult to care about the patient. This gives a glimpse of what it is like to have a sociopathic personality.

Countertransference frequently involves an ominous fear, often described as an eerie feeling of being under patients' influence. Commonly, the particularly cold, remorseless eyes of the sociopath contribute to the feeling of being their "prey."

It is very difficult to be actively or sadistically devalued. This produces a sense of hostility, or hopeless resignation. Tolerate, but don't deny or minimize these feelings. **Do not** disclose feelings of countertransference. This will be seen as frailty, and may cause patients to exercise their power. Privately admit countertransference; otherwise, hostility and dangerousness may be ignored and acted on, causing a potentially dangerous situation. Strike a balance between being confrontational and non-judgmental, but rigorously avoid any collusion with antisocial acts.

Summary of Therapeutic Techniques

• Don't moralize
• Invest in increasing understanding of the "here and now," particularly with transference reactions and devaluation of therapy
• Set a tone of doing the job competently; be stable and persistent
• Communicate that it is up to the patient to take advantage of therapy (or not); progress is slow; be attuned to control issues
• Firmness of purpose and rock-bottom respect seem to be a winning combination

DISORDERED PERSONALITIES

GROUP THERAPY

Some institutions have reported gains via group therapy with inmates or inpatients. A frequent observation is that group members develop remarkable insight into the problems of others, but have a striking lack of insight into their own. A homogeneous group of ASPDs is the only indication for group therapy (hilariously demonstrated in the movie RAISING ARIZONA).

Even in inpatient educational groups, ASPDs mock authority, cause disturbances among other patients, and often try to lead a "rebellion" of other patients. They act as catalysts for disruptive, acting out behavior among impressionable and fragile co-patients.

PHARMACOTHERAPY

Antisocial patients can have rage attacks or uncontrollable outbursts of anger that may be responsive to **mood stabilizers** like lithium, clonazepam, carbamazepine, propranolol or L-tryptophan. Impulsivity may respond to **pericyazine** (a neuroleptic), and **serotonin selective reuptake inhibitors** (fluoxetine, fluvoxamine, paroxetine and sertraline) may be useful for aggression and impulsive behavior. None of these drugs is "officially" approved for use in antisocial or aggressive behavior.

COGNITIVE THERAPY

BASIC COGNITIVE ASSUMPTIONS:
- Justification - "The end result justifies the means."
- Thinking is believing - "I say it or feel it and it has to be right."
- Infallibility - "I always do the right thing."
- Devaluation of others - "Other people do not matter."
- Denial of consequences - "I won't get caught."
ADAPTED FROM BECK, FREEMAN & ASSOCIATES, 1990

Cognitive therapy involves a series of guided discussions, structured exercises and behavioral experiments designed to give patients a broader, more *prosocial* way of interacting with others. For example, in the following exercise, patients determine the advantages *for them* in following a certain course of action after being demoted at work:

CHOICE	ADVANTAGE	DISADVANTAGE
Tell boss to shove it & quit	Immediate revenge, "Don't mess with me"	Need to find another job; looks bad on resume
Find a way to make boss look stupid at work	Feel better about what he did to me	Boss may find out I did it and get me back later
Meet minimum expectations	Keep job; get some satisfaction	Won't get old job back as soon; may be boring
Show a positive attitude; work hard	May get job back sooner, not boring	Company demoted me; now get more work out of me

ADAPTED FROM BECK, FREEMAN & ASSOCIATES, 1990

From this exercise, patients learn that their actions have an effect on others, and have long-term outcomes that are important.

COURSE

By the time patients qualify for the diagnosis of ASPD, they have had many years of turbulent behavior. As children, they were often eneuretic, hyperactive, sadistic and disruptive. With growth in size and strength, more damaging acts became possible, especially aggressive and sexual ones. As young adults, they exploited others financially and emotionally. The inability to live up to the demands of society are quite obvious by the time the diagnosis is made. Antisocial activity appears to peak in early adulthood and then diminish slowly with age. However, there is conflict over the degree to which it disappears. Some authors report that antisocial behavior dramatically reduces over age forty-five, others feel it can continue well beyond this age. Sociopathic behavior can be attenuated by the social, economic, legal, medical and interpersonal consequences. Long prison terms, physical injuries, and financial and emotional bankruptcy later in life can make an impact. Other factors may be the loss of speed and strength, substance abuse or positive life events (marriage, employment, etc.). Evaluation of these factors gives a more accurate prediction than expecting the disorder to "burn out." The most reliable indicator of future antisocial behavior is the degree to which it has been present in the past.

References

American Psychiatric Association
DIAGNOSTIC AND STATISTICAL MANUAL OF MENTAL DISORDERS, FOURTH EDITION
American Psychiatric Press; Washington, D.C., 1994

N. Andreason, D. Black
INTRODUCTORY TEXTBOOK OF PSYCHIATRY
American Psychiatric Press; Washington, D.C., 1991

A. Beck, A. Freeman & Associates
COGNITIVE THERAPY OF PERSONALITY DISORDERS
The Guildford Press; New York, 1990

K. Z. Bezchlibnyk-Butler, J. Joel Jeffries & B. A. Martin
CLINICAL HANDBOOK OF PSYCHOTROPIC DRUGS, FOURTH REVISED EDITION
Hogrete & Huber Publishers; Toronto, 1994

H. Cleckley
THE MASK OF SANITY, FIFTH EDITION
Emily S. Cleckley, Publisher; Augusta, Georgia, 1988*

G. Gabbard
PSYCHODYNAMIC PSYCHIATRY IN CLINICAL PRACTICE, THE DSM-IV EDITION
American Psychiatric Press; Washington, D.C., 1994

H. Kaplan, B. Sadock (editors)
COMPREHENSIVE TEXTBOOK OF PSYCHIATRY, SIXTH EDITION
Williams & Wilkins; Baltimore, 1995

N. McWilliams
PSYCHOANALYTIC DIAGNOSIS
The Guildford Press; New York, 1994

E. Othmer & S. Othmer
THE CLINICAL INTERVIEW USING DSM-IV
American Psychiatric Press; Washington, D.C., 1994

> *THE MASK OF SANITY, FIFTH EDITION is available from:
> Emily S. Cleckley, Publisher
> 3024 Fox Spring Road
> Augusta, Georgia
> U.S.A. 30909
> The cost is $25 plus $4 shipping and handling (US dollars).

SOCIOPATHY 101 *

INTRODUCTION:

Erik Erikson developed the now familiar stages of his *Life Cycle Theory*. In one of his first applications, he compared the anomalous development of the Singleton twins, one of whom called in a bomb threat the very night his brother was to receive the Nobel Peace Prize.

NORMAL (Nobel Prize)	ANTISOCIAL (No Prize)
STAGE 1	
Trust vs.	Lust vs.
Mistrust	Misogyny
STAGE 2	
Autonomy vs.	Auto Theft vs.
Shame & Doubt	Doubtful Shame
STAGE 3	
Initiative vs.	Insanity Defense vs.
Guilt	Guilty Plea
STAGE 4	
Industry vs.	Repeat Offender vs.
Inferiority	Reform School
STAGE 5	
Identity vs.	Narcissism vs.
Identity Confusion	Base Sincerity
STAGE 6	
Intimacy vs.	Gang Allegiance vs.
Isolation	Solitary Confinement
STAGE 7	
Generativity vs.	Crime Spree vs.
Stagnation	Collecting Pogey
STAGE 8	
Integrity vs.	Most Wanted List vs.
Despair	Two-Bit Reputation

* FROM THE *PsychoIllogical Bulletin*, VOLUME 1, SUMMER 1994, P. 18

AGGRESSIVE

We met in the Uomo Menswear store; he had to steal a tie for his probation hearing. Blunt and direct, he was a man of few words, most of them with four letters.

SLICK

He said I could call him Ted, Billy Ray, or Freddy - he had i.d. for each name. The sex was fast, furious and always in a public place. He missed his other girlfriend, and got her to join us after threatening to turn in her dealer.

PREDATORY

He wanted to commemorate the occasion with matching tattoos - black scorpions. It complemented the ones he already had - **NFA** on his left arm and **NRA** on the right. He promised the artist payment next week, but ended up ripping him off anyway.

DANGEROUS

We skipped his AA meeting; it only drove him to drink, and drive. So we did, racing another stolen car into the sunset. He handled it all like a pro - and said so.

Truly an **8 BALL** man.

The cologne for real men.

* FROM THE *PsychoIllogical Bulletin*, VOLUME 1, SUMMER 1994, P. 24

FILL IN THE BLANK SUSPENSE:
ANATOMY OF A JAMES BOND ADVENTURE

ACT I

Bond, a government contracted <u>antisocial</u>, is summoned from some exotic locale where he is risking his life recreationally, instead of in the line of duty. His sadistic, <u>schizoid</u> boss, who has never even set foot outside the building to serve England, briefs him on an impossibly dangerous mission.

Bond picks up a great new gadget from the <u>schizotypal</u> in the research department. Though it seems cumbersome and the instructions tedious, it inevitably saves his life - only after he tries it out on a lowly <u>obsessive</u> sap from elsewhere in the department.

ACT II

Bond quickly dumps his <u>dependent</u> girlfriend, who actually portrayed the <u>histrionic</u> in the last adventure. His itinerary is abruptly changed when his boss's <u>passive-aggressive</u> secretary uses his plane tickets for her own vacation.

ACT III

After arriving first class at an even more interesting destination than originally planned, he is enamored by the charms of the <u>borderline</u> sent by his nemesis. Although she plans to kill him, Bond's superficial charm persuades her to switch allegiances. In doing so, she pays with her life but not before revealing the identity of a gorgeous <u>avoidant</u> who is the right-hand assistant to the bad guy.

ACT IV

Bond enlists the help of the local <u>paranoid</u> FBI/CIA/IRA/IBM/IRS agent with a soft spot for assisting the British. Though Bond prefers to work alone, the assistance he is invariably forced to accept enables him to defeat the evil empire built by the megalomaniac <u>narcissist</u>, and return the world to safety.

* FROM THE *PsychoIllogical Bulletin*, VOLUME 4, WINTER 1996, P. 19

THE FRACTIONATED PERSONALITY DISORDER*

BY MORTON RAPP M.D.

The Multiple Personality Disorder (MPD), a malady in which, "The essential feature . . . is the existence within the person of two or more distinct personalities or personality states" [1] has gained much popularity in usage among members of the clinical community. This relatively new diagnostic entity has only been in vogue during the second half of this century. It remained rare until the 1950's, when scientific advances in the area were bolstered by two critical discoveries: (1) there's a sucker born every minute, and (2) books describing MPD were ultimately highly lucrative for the authors.

Controversy has always surrounded MPD as a diagnosis. Its supporters claim that many patients who were subjected to severe child abuse early in their lives tend to evidence MPD later on, and further, that those who would challenge the validity of this may themselves suffer from MPD. The author feels that this diagnosis has heuristic value and presents here a related and ancillary disorder - the **Fractionated Personality Disorder (FPD)**.

RATIONALE:
In mathematics, every number has a reciprocal; for example, the reciprocal of 2 is 1/2. It follows logically that if individuals exist who have more than one personality, then there must be others with only a fraction of a personality in order that the fundamental equilibrium of the universe be maintained.

EMPIRICAL BASE:
No studies have been performed to test the hypothesis of FPD. It was felt that the intrusion of coarse methods such as standardized interviews, or the intervention of psychiatric epidemiologists would cheapen the area of study - and possibly ruin the author's chances of success in launching his forthcoming book(s) on this exciting new diagnostic entity.

ETIOLOGY:
The specter of child abuse underlies much of the FPD, as illustrated in the following case:

M.R., a 16 year old teenager of Yuppie background, had been enjoying a successful career as a malingerer until his 16th birthday. On that date, his father refused to buy him a Jaguar Sovereign, stating that the family's second car, a 5.0 litre Mustang, would have to do. The patient had a history of abuse at the hands of his father, namely being forced to study and refrain from using LSD. M.R., upon hearing the Jaguar was a no go, immediately stopped speaking, and became a "1/3" personality, characterized by sleeping 14 hours per day and attending school one day out of three.

CLINICAL FEATURES:
Despite a lack of systematic study, workers in the field of FPD have identified a number of characteristic epidemiological features:

1. It afflicts all sexes.
2. It is more common in right-handed people.
3. In South-East Asia, it is more common in Asians, whereas in Europe, it is more common in whites.
4. Its highest incidence is between ages two to ninety-four.
5. It is surprisingly common among people who are in need of a clinical diagnosis to excuse some otherwise maladaptive behavior.
6. It has a high incidence among certain occupational groups (e.g. hospital administrators). However, it is conspicuously absent in lawyers, suggesting that these professionals may have no personality whatsoever.

QUANTITATIVE ECOLOGY:
The diagnosis of FPD lends itself to easy quantification. For example:

$$p(FPD) = N + B^{(L/D)}$$

where:
- p(FPD) is the probability of a clinical case suffering from FPD
- N is the number of current believers in the diagnostic entity
- B is the number of financially successful books on the topic to date
- L is the lurid nature of the FPD patient's history, in luridity units
- D is the number of detractors of the diagnostic entity (IQ > ninety)

One fruitful avenue for investigation might be determining the smallest fraction of a personality to be found in an individual (e.g. from a clinician's perspective, a one-eighth personality would be four times more interesting than a one-half personality). As yet, there is no evidence to support the existence of an Exponential Personality (where the personality would be represented mathematically by two to the nth degree), or even a square root personality.

The author has described the presence of a diagnostic entity that supplements the Multiple Personality Disorder - the Fractionated Personality Disorder. The manuscripts for six books have already been completed and copyrighted by the author. A major motion picture loosely based on one of these volumes is slated for release next summer at a theatre near you. Diane Keaton will star.

[1] American Psychiatric Association, 1987, Diagnostic and Statistical Manual of Mental Disorders, Third Edition Revised, Washington, D.C.

THE NARCISSISTIC PERSONALITY

BIOGRAPHICAL INFORMATION

Name:	James Pond
Occupation:	Window dresser for a fashion store
Appearance:	Silk suit, cubic zirconium cufflinks & tie pin, alligator shoes
Relationship with animals:	Walks friend's Afghan in order to meet women
Favourite Song:	*King of the Road*

AT THE THERAPIST'S OFFICE

Before Session:	Preens with a portable mirror
Waiting Room Reading:	*GQ*; tells others he will appear in the next issue
During Session:	Starts each sentence with, "I . . . "
Fantasies Involve:	Wonders what he's like in bed
Relationship with Therapist:	Self-appointed fashion consultant
Behavior During Session:	Acts as if session is being filmed
Takes to Therapy:	A discount coupon for his store

DIAGNOSTIC SHORTHAND

MNEMONIC - "FEEDS A GAME"

Fantasizes about unlimited success, brilliance, beauty, etc.

Empathy lacking for others

Exploitative

Demands to be treated according to high expectations

Special people are needed to understand him or her

Admiration required in excessive amounts

Grandiose sense of self

Arrogant

Manipulates others to render automatic compliance

Envious of others

INTRODUCTION

Narcissus was a mythological figure who scorned the love of others. One of the many heartbroken maidens had a prayer answered by the goddess Nemesis, "May he who loves not others love himself." Narcissus fell in love with his reflection in a pool. Unable to leave it, he became fixed in a long gaze, pined away and died. The flowers underneath his body were given his name. The narcissistic personality disorder stems from this mythological basis. It is characterized by grandiosity, lack of empathy and a need for admiration.

Some key names associated with development of this disorder are:
- **Freud** (1914) brought the mythological term into common usage, referring to narcissism in two ways: *primary narcissism* - an early stage of self-absorption; and later in life as *secondary narcissism* - an ego-ideal that embodied a person's aspirations
- **Reich** (1930's) through his analysis of resistance, recognized that patients protected themselves with **character armor**; he used the term *phallic-narcissist* to refer to individuals who were self-assured, arrogant and protected themselves by attacking others first
- **Jones** (1913) wrote a book called, "The God Complex" describing patients who were overtly grandiose, judgmental and aloof; they also overestimated their abilities and had fantasies of omnipotence; if such patients decompensated, they commonly expressed the delusion of being God
- **Kohut** (1971) pioneered self-psychology, he saw narcissistic individuals as requiring responses from people in the environment, which maintained their self-esteem and sense of cohesion
- **Kernberg** (1967) conceptualized the narcissistic personality disorder as one outcome a **borderline personality organization** using primitive defense mechanisms, but with a higher level of ego functioning

The narcissistic personality disorder (NPD) was first added to the diagnostic nomenclature in the DSM-III. Though it had long been of interest to psychoanalysts, it was Kernberg's description of the behavioral characteristics that influenced the diagnostic criteria.

NPD is less thoroughly validated as a diagnosis than other personality disorders. The ICD-10 has no corresponding diagnosis. Many of the diagnostic criteria require introspection by patients, as well as significant levels of inference from clinicians. Narcissism, itself, is a trait observable to varying degrees in everyone and is adaptive under many circumstances.

Media Examples

Narcissists are frequently cast as main characters, and especially as leaders in books, movies and plays. They have a "tragic flaw" which is either corrected or punished. In such portrayals, the main character "just doesn't get it" usually due to vanity, despite being surrounded by good friends, abundant opportunities or an unnoticed love interest. Notable examples can be seen in:

• **Groundhog Day** - Bill Murray portrays a weather reporter sent to cover the festivities in a town called Punxsatawney, PA. Snide and conceited, he gives a good demonstration of narcissistic behavior at the beginning of the film. As punishment, he must relive the same day until he mends his self-serving ways.

• **The Fisher King** - Jeff Bridges portrays a disc jockey/radio show host who launches into a vitriolic tirade against yuppies who frequent a particular bar. His final remark about them "having to be stopped" is misinterpreted by an impressionable caller, leading to disastrous results. His self-serving demeanor and use of the program as a vehicle for personal commentary exemplifies narcissistic behavior.

• **Indecent Proposal** - Robert Redford plays the part of a cocky, high-rolling billionaire who satisfies his lust by paying a married woman a million dollars to spend one night with him. Though suave and debonair, he is shallow and cannot hold her interest.

• **Apocalypse Now** - Robert Duvall superbly plays the part of the narcissistic Lt. Col. Kilgore. His erect bearing, strutting walk, and omnipotent presence add to the performance. Kilgore is a surfing fanatic and demands an impromptu demonstration for his enjoyment. Duvall played another narcissistic military officer in **The Great Santini**.

Other narcissistic characters (to varying degrees) are seen in:

• **Star Wars Trilogy** - Han Solo
• **Star Trek (Original Series)** - Captain Kirk
• **Bugs Bunny Cartoons** - Foghorn Leghorn
• **Soap Operas** - Teeming with narcissistic characters
• **Twelfth Night (Shakespearean Comedy)** - Malvolio
• **A Few Good Men** - Marine Colonel played by Jack Nicholson
• **Jurassic Park** - Island owner portrayed by Richard Attenborough
• **Rain Man** - Tom Cruise character, Charlie Babbitt

Interview Considerations

Narcissistic patients, as with other Cluster B personalities, revel in the attention they receive in interview situations. Especially in the opening few minutes, when patients are given free "reign" to speak their mind, interviews go quite smoothly. Narcissistic patients "take the ball" and run with it quite well. Every nuance regarding their presenting complaint is related as essential information.

Narcissistic patients like to surround themselves with "special" people. An interested interviewer paying undivided attention soon becomes the "best in the hospital." The interview is used as an opportunity to reaffirm and enhance an already inflated sense of importance.

Even as the bombardment of information proceeds, there is often a rehearsed or detached quality to the interview. Narcissistic patients talk "at" you instead of "to" you, making little eye contact.

Difficulties arise when the patients' grandiosity is confronted with reality. Patients can become hostile under such conditions and suffer a **narcissistic injury**, leading to a **narcissistic rage**. Responding with heated emotion, patients devalue interviewers for not having sufficient experience or intelligence to understand them. This may pass quickly, with the interview resuming after a brief delay. In other situations, rapport can be re-established with appeals to patients' grandiosity:

- "It seems that others do not appreciate your abilities."
- "Tell me more about your accomplishments in this area."
- "You really seem to be headed somewhere."

Developing rapport with narcissistic patients can be difficult. Collusion with their idealized self-perception prevents a check with reality, impeding an assessment. Empathically addressing reality, or the consequences of narcissism, can detract from the interview by evoking a grandiose repair of threatened self-esteem.

Narcissistic Themes

- Condescending attitude
- Dwells on observable assets
- Hypersensitive to criticism
- Difficulty maintaining a sense of self-esteem
- Many fantasies, but few accomplishments
- Readily blames others
- Conspicuous lack of empathy
- Highly self-referential

Presumed Etiology

BIOLOGICAL: NPD does not appear to be genetically linked to other disorders. Temperamental factors may involve high energy, overconscientiousness, increased sensitivity to unverbalized affect, or lacking tolerance for the anxiety caused by aggressive drives.

PSYCHOSOCIAL: NPD has not been as extensively investigated as other personality disorders. Because it lacks a genetic link to Axis I conditions, or a major impact on society, research has not been as abundant. Other factors involved are:

• narcissism is a component of several other personality disorders
• NPD can be difficult to validate due to subjectivity of the criteria

Early theories focussed on erratic, unreliable caretaking that caused an early fixation at a stage where narcissism is a developmental process.

Kernberg views narcissism as a pathological process involving a psychic hunger or **oral rage**, caused by indifferent or spiteful parenting. However, some positive aspect of the child (e.g. a talent) or the environment may allow an escape from parental threats or indifference. This "specialness" facilitates a sense of grandiosity that blankets and splits off the real self, which contains envy, fear and deprivation.

Kohut conceptualized narcissism not as a pathological deviation, but as an arrest in development. The seeds of NPD are sown when caretakers do not validate a child's responses. This empathic failure causes the child to develop an idealized image (**imago**) of the parents, and not one based on real limits.

Many theories have postulated some form of parental deprivation, although empirical evidence is lacking for this view. For example, the experiments where the poor little monkeys were taken away from their mothers did not produce narcissistic monkeys, but ones that were sad and withdrawn, with poor physical and social development. Reports are consistent for children similarly deprived.

Other theories posit that children who are treated specially, or at least differently, than others may develop NPD. Such children may be **narcissistic extensions** of their parents, and function to maintain parental self-esteem, or as a replacement for a significant other.

EPIDEMIOLOGY

Accurate estimates are lacking, with prevalence estimated to be less than 1% of the population. In clinical populations, prevalence may be as high as 3%. There is a sex difference, with men being diagnosed almost three times as often as women. Apparently this diagnosis is uncommon in Europe.

EGO DEFENSES

Major ego defences in NPD are **idealization** and **devaluation**. Defenses used to a lesser extent are **projection** and **identification**.

Narcissistic patients demonstrate **idealization** as opposed to **primitive idealization**, which is seen in other disorders. The distinction is a matter of degree. Narcissistic patients generally idealize to the limits of human capabilities, but do not endow people or objects with supernatural powers. Kohut used the term **grandiose self** to refer to the superiority that characterizes the inner world of the narcissist. While ego defenses are unconscious processes, the grandiose self may be outwardly projected. Narcissistic patients are consciously preoccupied with issues of rank. They are constantly attuned to what is considered "the best" or "Number One."

Similarly, devaluation does **not** occur to the extent that people or objects are considered "all bad," or as having powers that are magically destructive. Narcissists strive for perfection, and are critical of themselves if it is not achieved. If the devalued self is **projected** onto others, they are seen as inadequate, incompetent or unworthy.

These defenses operate differently than in the process of splitting. The idealization in NPD has more stability than in BPD, for example. People and objects may be idealized for a lengthy period of time. However, since perfection is the desired goal, disappointment and devaluation are inevitable. This, too, has a greater longevity than with the defense of splitting. Devalued objects are usually discarded in the search for a more suitable replacement. Splitting involves a more rapid oscillation between these extremes.

Narcissistic patients increase their self-esteem by **identification** with idealized organizations or people. With the process of identification, the aura of perfection is seen as extending to include patients.

Diagnostic Criteria

A pervasive pattern of grandiosity (in fantasy or behavior), need for admiration, and lack of empathy, beginning by early adulthood and present in a variety of contexts, as indicated by five (or more) of the following:
(1) has a grandiose sense of self-importance (e.g. exaggerates achievements and talents, expects to be recognized as superior without commensurate achievements)
(2) is preoccupied with fantasies of unlimited success, power, brilliance, beauty, or ideal love
(3) believes that he or she is "special" and unique and can only be understood by, or should associate with, other special or high-status people (or institutions)
(4) requires excessive admiration
(5) has a sense of entitlement, i.e., unreasonable expectations of especially favorable treatment or automatic compliance with his or her expectations
(6) is interpersonally exploitative, i.e., takes advantage of others to achieve his or her own ends
(7) lacks empathy: is unwilling to recognize or identify with the feelings and needs of others
(8) is often envious of others or believes that others are envious of him or her
(9) shows arrogant, haughty behaviors or attitudes

REPRINTED WITH PERMISSION FROM THE DSM-IV.
COPYRIGHT, AMERICAN PSYCHIATRIC ASSOCIATION, 1994

Differential Diagnosis

Narcissism can be an associated feature of several other conditions. Some of the features of **Hypomania** overlap with NPD. These include: grandiosity, a sense of entitlement, increased goal-directed activity, and involvement in risky, yet pleasurable activities. The distinction can be made on the basis of NPD lacking the mood symptoms, and having a long-standing, rather than episodic course. The grief, shame and withdrawal after a narcissistic injury share some of the criteria with a **Major Depressive Episode**, or if of longer duration, a **Dysthymic Disorder**. In NPD, there is an obvious precipitant, and the lack of severity and duration seen in mood disorders.

Substance abuse, especially with stimulants (cocaine, amphetamines), can produce a clinical picture resembling NPD.

NPD can also closely resemble **Delusional Disorder, Grandiose Type**. Delusional disorders tend to have a circumscribed focus, without obvious impairments in behavior or ability to function. NPD is a life-long condition with several other interpersonal manifestations.

OTHER DIAGNOSTIC CONSIDERATIONS

Narcissism, itself, is a normal feature in human development. Infants are **egocentric** in that they see the world as revolving around them. As development proceeds, children discover there are other people in the world, and priorities other than their own gratification. Children and adolescents often have narcissistic traits that do not necessarily lead to NPD. GABBARD (1994, p. 498-9) gives an excellent synopsis of how narcissism is viewed differently depending on life cycle stage. He makes the cogent point that our culture is, itself, narcissistic. He illustrates this point with examples of our obsession with glamour, competitive sports, and how "winning forgives everything."

MENTAL STATUS EXAMINATION

APPEARANCE:	Often immaculately groomed; may have expensive (or expensive looking) jewelry and accessories
BEHAVIOR:	Often assume a rigid or authoritative posture; may caress their belongings or parts of their body
COOPERATION:	Cooperative as long as interview proceeds according to their wishes or expectations
AFFECT:	Can range from withdrawn to animated; tend to be readily expressed and varied; may seem "put on"
SPEECH:	Often well-modulated and articulate
CONTENT OF THOUGHT:	Related to grandiose sense of achievement, power, aspirations, connections and knowledge; can be plaintive and derogatory towards others
THOUGHT FORM:	No characteristic abnormality; tend to overelaborate; may be tangential or circumstantial
PERCEPTION:	No characteristic abnormality
INSIGHT & JUDGMENT:	Impaired; are aware of others' poor treatment and difficulties in relationships; react strongly when confronted with their own (realistic) contribution
SUICIDE - HOMICIDE:	Need to consider this in conjunction with any Axis I disorder; not generally dangerous to others or themselves; risk increases with a **narcissistic injury**

PSYCHODYNAMIC ASPECTS

Before exploring the inner world of narcissistic patients, it is important to be aware that there are descriptions of distinct types of narcissistic characters. The two poles from the continuum of interpersonal behaviors regarded as narcissistic have received various labels:

TYPE 1	TYPE 2
Oblivious, Thick-Skinned	Hypervigilant, Thin-Skinned
Overt, Egotistical, Grandiose	Covert, Dissociative, Vulnerable
• Arrogant	• Self-effacing
• Craves attention	• Diverts attention
• Disregards the feelings and reactions of others	• Highly sensitive to the signals from others; easily hurt

SOURCE: ADAPTED FROM GABBARD, 1994

The DSM-IV criteria describe the more flagrant behaviors and characteristics from the TYPE 1 category. This distinction is useful to help integrate the disparate understanding provided by the two main contributors to NPD, Kohut and Kernberg. Additionally, this helps with conceptualizing the range of outcomes from the various etiologic factors mentioned previously.

Parental deprivation and erratic caretaking are no doubt important in the development of NPD. These factors, however, are non-specific and could be etiologically significant in any personality disorder. For this reason, exploration of some other explanations and theories will be presented.

Kohut was a major contributor to self psychology. The term **selfobject** is used to refer to people, who, while remaining external and separate (object), provide a source of gratification for the person (self). The soothing, affirming and approving function of the selfobject remains, though in mature relationships, other people provide more than just gratification.

In NPD, patients have a pathological need for selfobjects, requiring them to help maintain a cohesive sense of self. This need is so great that everything other people offer is "consumed" (orality or **oral rage**). This leaves narcissistic patients unable to develop relationships with others beyond this need. There is no capacity for empathy, sharing, or loving others.

Narcissistic people function this way because they were treated in a similar manner by their caregivers. To a certain extent, all children become a **narcissistic extension** of their parents. This helps facilitate development through processes like **introjection** and **identification**.

Object relations theory postulates a tripartite self in NPD:
· the true self, which is deprived and hungry
· the false self, being loved for special accomplishments
· the idealized self, living up to the expectations of caregivers

Parents who are too invested in using children as **narcissistic extensions** transmit that love is given for playing this role. Under such circumstances, children learn that gratification comes from others, and comes from being "perfect" or fulfilling their role perfectly. Emotional reactions are not considered or reinforced as important. This facilitates a **false self** as the predominant manifestation in NPD. The evaluative process by which behavior is judged becomes **introjected**, and is experienced as criticism. Narcissistic patients are inwardly critical and constantly strive to be perfect. Perfection is also **projected** onto others, who then are admonished for not living up to patients' own standards. The internal world of NPD is also made up of a **real self**, which contains unconscious feelings that were denied expression. Patients feel empty, inferior and fragile. Being a   narcissistic extension invokes feelings of deprivation and falseness.

Patients strive to be perfect in all aspects of their lives, trying to aspire to the idealized image (Kohut's **imago**) of their parents, who did not encourage a more realistic sense of self. Regardless of the degree to which there is a conscious awareness, narcissistic patients protect their fragile self-esteem by avoiding situations in which they may be vulnerable. Grandiosity guards against feeling painful affects, making it difficult to point out as a defense.

Narcissists envy the successes of others, and are particularly attuned to whether something can be obtained to further their own cause. Innate aggression may explain why some narcissistic patients destroy the work, or good things, of others.

Behavior in NPD is a defensive compensation for fragility. While dependent on others for their self-esteem, narcissists are vain, contemptuous and *pseudo* self-sufficient. Expressions of gratitude are avoided to prevent an awareness of needing others. There is an overall numbness towards the feelings of others, and a lack of awareness that things can be just "good enough" instead of perfect.

WHAT HAPPENS IN PSYCHODYNAMIC THERAPY?

Unlike several other personality disorders, narcissistic patients do present for help. They are aware that something goes awry in their relationships, but rarely see themselves as the common denominator. A typical situation involves a patient presenting in a dysphoric state, usually after a narcissistic injury or a DIR.

Therapy is often sought as a boost to re-establish their self-esteem. Several themes may be present in the initial meeting, with patients looking for a "qualified professional" (or the "department head") to:

- carefully listen to the minute details of the presenting complaint
- collude with the devaluation of the other party
- reinforce that the right thing was done in the situation
- assuage whatever guilt might be present
- help patients to perfect themselves, rather than gaining an understanding of who they are, and how they interact with others

Therapy with narcissistic patients presents difficulties. NPD involves a particularly defensive character structure that is reinforced by the way in which society views success. The traditional benchmarks of psychological health - being able to work and to love - may be difficult to set as therapeutic goals. Highly narcissistic individuals can do extremely well in certain occupations. Additionally, they can find partners with personality structures that complement their own, and enjoy comfortable, but emotionally compromised relationships.

A stereotypic difficult case would involve a bloated, recently fired CEO who wants "some kind of therapy" because he isn't sleeping well, and can't seem to get over his dismissal. His company was part of a recent merger, and the new CEO was someone he bulldozed over on his way to the top many years ago. His marriage ended one year ago, and he is currently involved with his secretary. He drinks excessively, but does not see this as a problem. In the past, he picked up a lot of important business tips in bars, and hopes to find out something he can use to take revenge for his "predicament."

The goal in NPD is to help patients accept themselves without grandiosity or devaluing others, which may take several years. One of the difficulties encountered is that psychotherapy is a learning situation. Narcissistic patients often avoid novel situations that highlight their ignorance or deficiencies.

Kohut and Kernberg are the major contributors to the contemporary understanding of the etiology and treatment of NPD. Their complex theories diverge in many areas, possibly because they developed their approach with different types of narcissistic patients. Since each approach has its own merits, an awareness of both enhances the flexibility with which NPD can be handled. McWilliams (1994, p. 181) uses a plant analogy. Kohut's concept is a *developmental* one, in which a normally growing plant is deprived of sunlight and water. Kernberg's concept is a *structural* one, in which the plant sprouted an aberrant part.

Kohut theorized that parental empathic failures were the main cause of narcissism. Therapy centers on the repetition of this failed relationship in transference reactions such as the need for affirmation (mirror transference), idealization (idealizing transference), and imitating the therapist (twinship transference). Kohut emphasized the fragility of narcissistic patients and advocated a gentle approach:
· take therapeutic material at face value, preventing the message that what patients actually feel is different than what they express
· therapists should take responsibility when patients are upset
· avoid what may be seen as criticism, stressing the positive aspect of experiences; highlight progress when it is made

Kohut accepted the patient's need for idealization as normal, and, returning to the plant analogy, sought to provide sunlight and water.

Kernberg views greed, and the devaluation of others, as defensive operations that require tactful confrontation and interpretation. Both positive and negative transference reactions are considered early on, with envy being a particular focus. A cognitive understanding is sought to show patients how their defenses prevent them from receiving help. Kernberg's plant requires a pruning of its mutant parts.

Kohut's approach may work best with the Type 2 or hypervigilant narcissist, with Kernberg's being more suitable for Type 1. These two approaches to therapy are not mutually exclusive. One approach may benefit certain patients at a given time, and with progress, the other becomes more valuable. Attention to transference, countertransference and the effectiveness of trial interpretations, will indicate which approach is more useful.

Combining these approaches yields useful therapeutic guidelines. Narcissistic patients are exquisitely sensitive to shame. A remark considered critical in early sessions (or at any point) can lead to termination. The gentle, accepting approach advocated by Kohut fosters a therapeutic alliance. Recognizing and admitting to imperfections not only avoids an empathic failure, but the patient internalizes a more realistic and humane attitude.

TRANSFERENCE AND COUNTERTRANSFERENCE REACTIONS

Transference reactions in NPD are strong. The therapist is either idealized as wonderful, or devalued as incompetent. These reactions are like those seen in BPD, but have more stability. A frequent pattern involves idealization of the current therapist, with devaluation of those from the past. Patients experience these perceptions as if they were based on objective evidence. What sets the transference manifestations in NPD apart from other personality disorders, is that patients show little interest in *why* they have these reactions. Attempting to explore these issues is seen as indulging the therapist's needs, and superfluous to the therapy. Narcissistic patients "ventilate" in sessions, using the therapist as an audience. Kernberg used the term **satellite existence** to refer to the oblivious reaction to the therapist.

Transference reactions in NPD specifically undermine therapy and arouse strong countertransference reactions. Therapists who identify with the idealized transference can be seduced into a "mutual admiration society." This arrangement is short-lived because narcissistic patients need others only for their gratification. Inevitably, devaluation results. The subsequent barrages evoke feelings of irritability and hostility. It can be difficult to resist taking punitive action against patients. With the lack of interpersonal involvement, boredom is a common countertransference reaction.

SUMMARY OF THERAPEUTIC TECHNIQUES

• Find out what the agenda is in seeking therapy
• Be cautious about making remarks that may be seen as critical; frame or "couch" questions and statements to sound benign
• Acknowledge errors, but do not be overly self-critical, as this reinforces what exists within patients' internal existence (superego)
• Encourage patients to openly express their needs, and to ask others what their needs are
• Monitor countertransference; avoid gratification or punishment

Pharmacotherapy

Narcissistic patients can experience mood swings that correspond to their defensive structure. While the effusiveness accompanying idealization rarely seems to need medication, the dysphoria of a **narcissistic injury** frequently brings about treatment with an antidepressant. If a major depressive episode develops, the focus in prescribing should be to treat target symptoms. Narcissistic patients are adept at persuading doctors to give them medications that may be ill-advised, especially benzodiazepines and opioids. They are vulnerable to hypochondriacal preoccupation; pain (psychic or physical) is poorly tolerated, and impels patients to seek medication.

Group Therapy

Convincing patients to participate is the main obstacle in group therapy for NPD. Often, the suggestion is seen as a rejection, or projected as the therapist being incapable of treating the patient. This process can be facilitated by beginning individual therapy first, and when the alliance is strong enough, continuing in a group format. Another recommendation involves simultaneous participation in both types, ideally with the same therapist. Each mode of therapy can complement the other, as narcissistic patients tend to run from their mistakes and hide from those who are aware of them. However, this practice may be seen as an affirmation of specialness, and make group members not afforded this arrangement feel left out.

Narcissistic patients often dominate group settings, and take up a disproportionate amount of time airing their concerns. While they may enjoy the larger audience, the other members are soon resented for taking any of the group's attention. Narcissists rapidly seem to forget that they have any difficulties, and often take up the role of cotherapist. Their sense of entitlement makes them prone to transgress group rules, especially contact with members outside of sessions. Limiting the group membership to one NPD can help minimize this.

Narcissistic patients stir powerful transference feelings in group settings, and instigate considerable interaction. This can facilitate an active "here and now" confrontation, visible to group members. An additional benefit to group therapy is the dilution of transference and countertransference. Feedback on a group level can be a powerful learning experience, and lessen the desire to terminate therapy when confronted.

COGNITIVE THERAPY

Basic Cognitive Distortions:

- Self-Righteousness - "I did it correctly. I always do."
- Grandiosity - "Can you meet my standards?"
- Exploitation - "I'll find someone with better skills next time."

Cognitive therapy can be used to address three major features of NPD: grandiosity, hypersensitivity to criticism and lack of empathy.

The all-or-nothing aspect of grandiosity is examined. Patients are encouraged to limit their comparisons to within themselves, not against others. Enjoying activities is stressed, instead of focusing only on attaining goals, i.e. "I can enjoy ordinary things."

Systematic desensitization can help lessen hypersensitivity to criticism. Patients can learn to be more discriminating when receiving feedback. They can learn to control their emotional responses and look for positive elements, i.e. "Other people can have helpful ideas."

The failure to develop empathy may need to be overtly pointed out by asking about an awareness of the feelings of others. With role-playing exercises, emphasis can be placed on how someone else might *feel*, not just *react* in a situation. Alternative ways of treating others is examined, i.e. "Other people have feelings that are important."

COURSE OF NPD

NPD has often run a lengthy course by the time patients seek help. Narcissism may have certain advantages in early adulthood, and combined with the tendency to leave therapy, patients often do not seriously engage in treatment until later in life. By this time, they have firmly established a pattern of using and discarding other people.

NPD is frequently disguised under other complaints, usually physical or marital. Narcissistic patients have difficulty surrendering their physical assets to time. They resist aging, in some cases by putting themselves in jeopardy with extramarital affairs or strenuous activities to "stay young." They do not easily forgive others, nor celebrate the successes of those around them, particularly if surpassed in some manner. When motivation is sufficient, therapy can bring about modifications that enhance personal acceptance and relationships.

REFERENCES

American Psychiatric Association
DIAGNOSTIC AND STATISTICAL MANUAL OF MENTAL DISORDERS, FOURTH EDITION
American Psychiatric Press; Washington, D.C., 1994

A. Beck, A. Freeman & Associates
COGNITIVE THERAPY OF PERSONALITY DISORDERS
The Guildford Press; New York, 1990

G. Gabbard
PSYCHODYNAMIC PSYCHIATRY IN CLINICAL PRACTICE, THE DSM-IV EDITION
American Psychiatric Press; Washington, D.C., 1994

H. Kaplan, B. Sadock (editors)
COMPREHENSIVE GROUP PSYCHOTHERAPY, THIRD EDITION
Williams & Wilkins; Baltimore, 1993

H. Kaplan, B. Sadock (editors)
COMPREHENSIVE TEXTBOOK OF PSYCHIATRY, SIXTH EDITION
Williams & Wilkins; Baltimore, 1995

O. Kernberg
SEVERE PERSONALITY DISORDER: PSYCHOTHERAPEUTIC STRATEGIES
Yale University Press; New Haven, 1984

H. Kohut
THE ANALYSIS OF SELF. . . THE PSYCHOANALYTIC TREATMENT OF NPD
International Universities Press; New York, 1971

N. McWilliams
PSYCHOANALYTIC DIAGNOSIS
The Guildford Press; New York, 1994

E. Othmer & S. Othmer
THE CLINICAL INTERVIEW USING DSM-IV
American Psychiatric Press; Washington, D.C., 1994

R. Pies
CLINICAL MANUAL OF PSYCHIATRIC DIAGNOSIS AND TREATMENT
American Psychiatric Press; Washington, D.C., 1994

INNERSPACE
THE INTERPERSONAL FRONTIER . . .

THIS IS THE SAGA OF THE VOYAGER NARCISSUS,
ON A FIVE YEAR JOURNEY TO SEEK A WAY OUT OF THE

EGOCENTRIC UNIVERSE

EPISODE 1
Narcissus has a rendezvous with Comet
Kohutek, encountering an empathic
betazoid species who
mirror the prime directive.

EPISODE 2
Full battle stations as Narcissus grapples
with Darth Kernberg, and must make use
of the ship's defensive capabilities to
avoid a photon interpretation.

ENTERPRISING PERSONALITIES

CAPTAIN
NARCISSIST

MR.
OBSESSIVE

DOCTOR
HISTRIONIC

THE AVOIDANT PERSONALITY

Biographical Information

Name:	Tim I. Ditty
Occupation:	Model for "before" picture in weightlifting ads
Appearance:	Matches clothes to office wallpaper
Relationship with animals:	Dog introduces him to others
Favourite Song:	***Born to be Mild***

At the Therapist's Office

Before Session:	Followed *Schizoid's* path; hoped they might meet
Waiting Room Reading:	Reads nothing so as not to disappoint others
During Session:	Discusses detours, off-ramps & exits
Fantasies Involve:	Reincarnating Dale Carnegie as his uncle
Relationship with Therapist:	Protects car from *Antisocial*
Behavior During Session:	Spends time with head in lampshade
Takes to Therapy:	**Invisible Man** comic book

Diagnostic Shorthand

Mnemonic - "A Circus"

Avoids activities

Certainty of being liked required before involvement

Inhibited when meeting people

Restrained within relationships

Criticism or rejection is a preoccupation

Unusually reluctant to take risks

Self-deprecating

INTRODUCTION

The avoidant personality disorder is characterized by inhibition, introversion and anxiety in social situations.

Some key names associated with developing the concepts of this disorder are:

- **Kretschmer** (1925) described a "hyperaesthetic shut-in" character type, which resembles the current concept of the avoidant personality
- **Fenichel** (1945) described the phobic personality, a conceptual forerunner to the avoidant personality disorder
- **Horney** (1945) wrote about "interpersonally avoidant" personalities who withdrew into solitude due to the strain of relating to others
- **Millon** (1969) first used the term avoidant to refer to an *active-detached* pattern of interaction in which individuals desired relationships, but withdrew to avoid the possibility of being hurt
- **Burnham, Gladstone & Gibson** (1969) described a "need-fear dilemma," whereby avoidant personalities felt a strong need for people, but feared being destroyed through abandonment

Avoidant personality disorder (APD) was first included in the DSM-III from Millon's description. The DSM-III-R criteria were changed to correspond to the concept of the phobic character disorder. The DSM-IV emphasizes hypersensitivity, fear of rejection and feelings of inadequacy, in addition to the avoidant behavior.

The concept of APD has been criticized for having too much overlap with the schizoid personality disorder, despite their assignment to different clusters. The main distinction is that schizoid personalities do not desire close relationships; avoidant personalities do, but fear rejection. Other studies have found considerable overlap between APD and the Dependent Personality Disorder. APD has been previously described as the **inadequate personality disorder** (p. 275).

APD shares considerable overlap with **Social Phobia, Generalized Type**. Patients have an increased incidence of other anxiety disorders, including **Panic Disorder With Agoraphobia**. APD is often diagnosed in conjunction with other Axis I and II conditions.

The psychoanalytic concept of schizoid encompasses avoidant, schizoid and schizotypal personality disorders. The ICD-10 contains a related diagnosis called the Anxious (Avoidant) Personality Disorder.

Media Examples

Avoidant characters are often cast as latent heroes. They long for love and acceptance and, upon receiving it, develop their potential like Popeye eating a can of spinach. Plots frequently involve an extroverted character coaxing out an introverted, or avoidant one. The extrovert is subsequently rewarded with a loyal friend or lover who often has some special ability or hidden talent.

Examples can be seen in the following films:

• **Superman** (comic series, movies in 1978, 1980, 1983, 1987) Clark Kent, the dual identity of Superman, is a mild-mannered newspaper reporter. His self-effacing manner, bumbling antics and love of Lois Lane at a distance are good examples of avoidant behavior.

• **Always** - Brad Johnson plays the role of a junior pilot who aspires to become a waterbomber. He slowly develops a relationship with the girlfriend of a deceased pilot. His "Aw, shucks, ma'am" approach and reticent manner demonstrate avoidant qualities.

• **The Mask** - Jim Carrey portrays an "Everyday Joe" banker who can't set aside his inhibitions to live out his romantic fantasies.

• **Four Weddings and a Funeral** - Hugh Grant portrays Charles, a clearly avoidant fellow, who is strongly attracted to a woman he meets at a series of weddings. He cannot tell her he has feelings for her, as amply demonstrated in a scene where she announces her intention to marry another (clearly narcissistic) man. He is equally inept at telling another woman he dislikes her and, through his ineffectual style, becomes engaged to her.

• **The Wizard of Oz** (1939) - The cowardly lion, lacking the courage to become the King of Beasts, sums up his dilemma with, "If I only had the nerve."

• **Threesome** - Eddy, the shy, sensitive roommate, exhibits some avoidant behaviors in the process of sorting out his sexuality.

• **The Accidental Tourist** - William Hurt portrays a travel writer who displays a mixed bag of personality traits, some of them avoidant.

Interview Considerations

Avoidant patients may or may not pose difficulties in interview situations. When some notion of a "guarantee" of acceptance is given, they become more amenable to sharing information and their emotional experiences. This acceptance is usually present to a greater degree in clinical situations than social situations. Patients may well be quite open in interviews, making it difficult to gauge the degree to which avoidant behavior is present under more normal circumstances.

Empathic acceptance of patients' sensitivity and past suffering generates rapport. Once a sense of trust and a protective atmosphere are established, the interview will readily proceed. A detailed history of various emotional trauma often ensues. Another major component patients express is feeling ashamed about many aspects of their lives. In order to maintain the interview, it is important not to criticize these concerns as silly or trivial, even if the patients identify them as such. Confrontation will result in a retreat that reduces the effectiveness of the interview, though the usual avoidant behaviors will become more apparent.

Some patients are extremely sensitive and anxious when interviewed. Unfamiliarity with clinical situations or past upsetting experiences may provoke reticent behavior. Again, while the **content** of the interview suffers, the **process** provides valuable information. Under such circumstances, it may be possible to gather only essential information, deferring the details until rapport has been established.

Avoidant Themes

- Feelings of being defective
- Low tolerance for dysphoria
- Self-criticism
- Exaggeration of risks
- Shyness
- Fear of rejection
- Hypersensitivity to criticism
- "Love at a distance"
- Abrupt topic changes away from personal matters

Epidemiology

Prevalence is estimated to be less than 1% of the general population. In clinical settings the diagnosis may be applied to as many as 10% of patients, with an equal frequency in men and women.

PRESUMED ETIOLOGY

BIOLOGICAL: APD does not have a clear genetic etiology. Studies of temperament have found a predisposition to social avoidance when faced with unfamiliar people or situations. Introversion also has been found to be a hereditary factor.

Anxious and inhibited patients share some of the biological features of **Generalized Anxiety Disorder**, particularly hyperarousal of the sympathetic nervous system. Tachycardia, pupillary dilation and laryngeal tightness are common physical signs. Baseline levels of cortisol may also be abnormally high.

The hippocampus and limbic system may be involved in inhibiting behavioral responses. Cognitive processing abnormalities may be present, as evidenced by both decreased habituation and decreased flexibility when presented with novel situations.

PSYCHOSOCIAL: While shyness may have a genetic or constitutional origin, psychosocial factors mediate the extent to which it is expressed. Intuitively, it would seem that children who were belittled, criticized and rejected by parents have decreased self-esteem, resulting in social avoidance. As children grow, these experiences are be reinforced by their peers, perpetuating self-criticism and avoidant behavior. Through the cognitive process of generalization, patients come to expect similar treatment from everyone. Millon's developmental perspective of APD is in accordance with this scheme.

Alternatively, children may find that timidity helps cope with raging impulses. Fears that expression of their anger can have destructive consequences leads to a pattern of avoidance. An awareness of situations where guilt, anger or embarrassment may be provoked, along with a strong and unpleasant emotional response, can promote avoidant behavior.

As with the paranoid personality, avoidant traits can develop in response to having developmental handicaps such as sensory impairments or a disfiguring illness. There is a common thread between paranoid and avoidant reactions in that they share an alertness to external threats. An equal emphasis on, or awareness of, personal limitations may modify emotional expression in these circumstances to produce avoidant, rather than paranoid traits. An example of this can be seen in the movie, THE MAN WITHOUT A FACE.

Ego Defenses

Ego defenses in APD are generally higher-level or more mature defenses (see **neurotic** defenses on p. 38). Chief among avoidant defenses is **repression**, which prevents ideas and feelings from reaching consciousness. Other defenses used are:

• **Inhibition** - an evasion of conflict, either among internal agencies (e.g. id versus superego) or externally with other people
• **Isolation** - separating an idea from the emotion that accompanies it

The psychological processes and defenses used in **Phobic Disorders** are similar to APD. When a forbidden wish or impulse threatens to emerge, bring on real or imagined punishment, three mechanisms of defense are recruited:

• **Displacement** - shifting anxiety from an unconscious idea or object to an external one (which often bears some resemblance)
• **Projection** - externalizing the source of harm or punishment
• **Avoidance** - consciously attempting to control anxiety

Diagnostic Criteria

A pervasive pattern of social inhibition, feelings of inadequacy, and hypersensitivity to negative evaluation, beginning by early adulthood and present in a variety of contexts, as indicated by four (or more) of the following:

(1) avoids occupational activities that involve significant interpersonal contact, because of fears of criticism, disapproval, or rejection
(2) is unwilling to get involved with people unless certain of being liked
(3) shows restraint within intimate relationships because of the fear of being shamed or ridiculed
(4) is preoccupied with being criticized or rejected in social situations
(5) is inhibited in new interpersonal situations because of feelings of inadequacy
(6) views self as socially inept, personally unappealing, or inferior to others
(7) is unusually reluctant to take personal risks or to engage in any new activities because they may prove embarrassing

Differential Diagnosis

APD has considerable overlap with **Social Phobia, Generalized Type**. APD involves a wider range of situations that cause anxiety, a pervasive difficulty in relationships, and is egosyntonic. **Generalized Anxiety Disorder** is distinguished in that APD patients lack overt anxiety when not in social situations. **Agoraphobia** has a more direct focus on the fear that an escape or help from others may not easily be available. Extreme anxiety may result in occasional **panic attacks** or the development of **Panic Disorder**.

Avoidant behavior can be seen in **Mood Disorders, Schizophrenia** and **Other Psychotic Disorders**. Disorders with real or perceived changes in appearance (e.g. **Anorexia Nervosa** and **Body Dysmorphic Disorder**), often cause patients to restrict social contact.

Substance-Related Disorders, particularly use of sedative-hypnotics, alcohol, or cannabis can lead to introversion and avoidant behavior. **General Medical Conditions** (e.g. hypothyroidism) also need to be considered.

Mental Status Examination

APPEARANCE:	None characteristic; not concerned with latest fashions
BEHAVIOR:	May be anxious initially, with hand-wringing and agitation; may appear hypervigilant
COOPERATION:	Cooperative, especially in a receptive atmosphere
AFFECT:	Restricted/flat initially; wider range and animation seen as comfort increases
SPEECH:	No characteristic abnormality; restricted by anxiety
CONTENT OF THOUGHT:	Hypersensitive to surroundings; express anxiousness about relationships; may have ideas of reference
THOUGHT FORM:	No characteristic abnormality; may be tangential, circumstantial, vague
PERCEPTION:	No characteristic abnormality
INSIGHT & JUDGMENT:	Partial; are aware of anxiety and hypersensitivity; may have limited insight into avoidant behavior
SUICIDE - HOMICIDE:	Increases in conjunction with an Axis I disorder; not generally dangerous to themselves or others

Psychodynamic Aspects

The central dynamic in APD is that of **shame**. Shame involves the sense of not living up to an internal standard or ego ideal. It carries the connotation of *being seen* as bad, leaving feelings of impotence or helplessness. Guilt is the conviction of violating an internal rule (superego) and the concern with punishment.

While a constitutional predisposition to feel shame may exist, it is reinforced and perpetuated through environmental experiences. Shame becomes a reaction within the first year of life and is especially evident during toilet training. Internalizing a variety of shameful experiences (e.g. emotionally expressive caregivers who are hostile or intolerant) leads to a diminished sense of self-esteem and a conviction of being "defective." Accompanying the low self-esteem is a painful sense of dysphoria, which develops, not only from feeling rejected, but also because of their sense of being defective.

Patients generalize the experience with critical and rejecting caretakers, and assume other people will react similarly. To avoidant patients, revealing anything of themselves leaves them vulnerable. They fear that should someone get to know them, their deficiencies will become obvious, bringing on criticism, and ultimately, rejection. The resulting dysphoria is especially hard to bear because, to an avoidant person, the rejection appears justified.

Avoiding potential harm from others becomes the central behavior in APD. Though patients have an awareness that relationships can be satisfying, they engage in social, emotional and behavioral strategies to protect themselves. Patients even avoid thinking about things that may bring on dysphoria. They frequently find diversions to occupy their time. Television, movies and theater offer a semblance of human interaction, while remaining at emotionally safe distances. These outlets facilitate another form of escape: wishful thinking and an active fantasy life. Avoidant people do not have enough faith in their own abilities to bring about change, and hope that some event or relationship will appear as magically as it does in fictional works.

Another method of coping is to adopt a façade to attract others and camouflage weakness. One of the most popular ways this is achieved is through substance abuse, particularly alcohol. A common description of an alcoholic personality is a person who is, "shy, isolated, irritable, anxious, hypersensitive and sexually repressed." (Source: Synopsis of Psychiatry, p. 399)

What Happens in Psychodynamic Therapy?

Avoidant patients are generally well-suited to the process of psychotherapy with a **supportive-expressive** approach. Initially, a supportive approach may encourage patients to take a closer look at the multitude of "escapes" they have developed over time. This is facilitated by empathizing with their sensitivity to social situations and their quick sense of rejection. With time, expressive approaches become possible when connections can be made between developmental experiences and their impact on current functioning.

As rapport develops, patients can be asked about the specifics of their reactions. This is especially helpful when done in a "here and now" manner with transference reactions. Patients can be encouraged to verbalize their feelings instead of avoiding them.

Two types of avoidant personalities have been described and may indicate differing treatment approaches:

TYPE A - constitutionally or temperamentally overanxious; more likely to have had a varied (and potentially normal) attachment history; may benefit from behavioral interventions, social skills training and **exposure therapy**

TYPE B - narcissistically vulnerable; more likely to have had shaming or intolerant parents with negative attachment experiences; may benefit from more traditional psychotherapy (see NPD).

Transference and Countertransference Reactions

Avoidant patients enter therapy with the same trepidation as other relationships. To whatever extent they are concerned that others will see through them, they are especially anxious about being transparent to a "professional." They may expect to be magically helped, or try even harder to deflect attention away from their perceived defects. Patients may go overboard and ingratiate themselves with their therapist, doing anything to please and avoid confrontation. Avoidant patients desperately evaluate social interactions for a hint of acceptance or rejection. Since an "expert" is involved, an undue amount of weight may be put on any aspect of the patient-therapist interaction. The major countertransference reaction involves collusion with the guarantee of acceptance patients seek. Therapists may find themselves stifled in not wanting to hurt or offend patients.

Summary of Therapeutic Techniques

• A good deal of effort may be required to interest patients in therapy; empathy and a supportive approach increase comfort
• Don't make promises or overtures that are unrealistic or not likely to be found elsewhere; avoid becoming overprotective
• Be attuned to the possibility of substance abuse
• Encourage patients to take a more active role in relationships

Pharmacotherapy

Because of the overlap with anxiety disorders, and the continual exposure to social situations, avoidant patients may require anxiolytics. Benzodiazepines are often sought because of their effectiveness and quick onset of action. However, their addiction potential, and the chronicity of the difficulties encountered due to personality variables, make these medications advisable for only short-term crises. Other medications are efficacious in alleviating anxiety:

• MAOIs have been used in anxiety disorders, with phenelzine being the best studied of this group.

• Tricyclic antidepressants, buspirone and β blockers may be useful.

It should be kept in mind that medication is not going to significantly change personality characteristics. Medications are best used as one component of a comprehensive treatment approach.

Group Therapy

Avoidant patients can be ideal group members and benefit considerably from this type of therapy. Much as in individual therapy, supportive approaches are necessary in the early stages. Therapists may need to be protective and see that patients are not pushed by the rest of the group. Overt encouragement will often be beneficial.

Avoidant patients have difficulty speaking in public. When doing so, they are self-effacing and reluctant to involve others. These features can be directly addressed in a group setting. Secondary benefits, such as developing a more appropriate style of dress and an awareness of social trends, can help patients fit in more smoothly outside the group.

Cognitive Therapy

Basic Cognitive Distortions:
- Avoidance - "I am defective. How could anyone like me?"
- Rejection - "If someone rejects me, I must be inadequate."
- Criticism - "I'll never amount to anything."
- Misinterpretation - "If people think I'm useless, it must be true."
- Discounting praise - "Someone who likes me must not know me."
- Catastrophizing dysphoria - "If I feel down, it will overwhelm me."
- Giving Up - "I'm going to lose anyway. Why should I bother?"

Adapted from Beck, Freeman & Associates, 1990

The effectiveness of any form of psychotherapy increases appreciably for avoidant patients if they confront the actual situations causing them anxiety. This makes a combination of cognitive and behavioral therapy an ideal form of treatment for APD.

Patients demonstrate the same cognitive, emotional and behavioral patterns towards the therapist as they do towards others. Transference manifestations can be dealt with in a "here and now" manner in order to develop a working alliance. This can be done as soon as an emotional change is observed during a session. It takes considerable effort and perseverance to encourage avoidant patients to open up. They fear that when their reactions and behaviors are revealed, the therapist will no longer be interested in treating them. Only when patients feel comfortable enough to discuss their reactions to the therapist, can the cognitions that pervade their relationships be explored.

Cognitive therapy requires the recording of dysphoric thoughts and feelings. Patients actively avoid such experiences both between and during sessions. For this reason, an early intervention is to focus on the elements involved in the avoidant process. In order to do this, "Socratic" questioning (guided discovery) can be used to have patients accede that, in general, avoidance will not help achieve their goals.

Situation where potential for rejection exists
↓
Automatic negative thought/distorted cognition about self
↓
Dysphoric emotion
↓
Avoidant behavior reduces dysphoria

As patients become familiar with this scheme, they can start to look at their reactions in therapy, instead of discussing something that happened recently. When this happens in a "here and now" manner, patients are prompted to share their feelings ("I'll have a mental breakdown"). As they develop a tolerance for dysphoria, they can test out their predictions and dysfunctional beliefs.

Some of the behavioral techniques used in the treatment of anxiety disorders can be useful in APD, especially **exposure therapy.** Patients first develop a hierarchy of threatening situations. This can be done either by using imagination (**systematic desensitization**) or real situations (**in vivo** or **role playing**). A list of predictions of the feared consequences is constructed for each situation. Generally, patients catastrophize the outcome, and observations made during the exposure supply evidence to contradict their predictions. In the treatment of phobias, **relaxation training** occurs prior to contact with the feared object. This may be beneficial for use in APD as well.

A lifetime of avoiding relationships and social situations can leave patients lacking certain skills. Formal instruction can be given in areas such as assertiveness training, personal management, sexuality and grooming. Other pointers can be given informally, such as paying attention to non-verbal cues, making conversation and increasing awareness of current trends.

COURSE OF APD

Avoidant patients can also be conceptualized as being observers of life instead of participants. They lead their lives hoping and wishing for better, yet are harshly self-critical when they make a move to achieve their goals. While shyness can be adorable and even adaptive early in life, it becomes a serious impediment later in life, when competition and assertiveness are rewarded. Avoidant patients often work below their level of ability. They have difficulty speaking in public, exercising authority and delegating tasks - all qualities required for professional advancement. Additionally, a self-effacing demeanor and hypersensitivity to criticism do not generally bode well as leadership qualities.

APD is one of the character structures most amenable to therapeutic intervention. If patients can endure the initial difficulties in relating in therapeutic situations, they can integrate their tolerance for dysphoria into a more assertive approach to relationships.

References

American Psychiatric Association
DIAGNOSTIC AND STATISTICAL MANUAL OF MENTAL DISORDERS, FOURTH EDITION
American Psychiatric Press; Washington D.C., 1994

N. Andreason, D. Black
INTRODUCTORY TEXTBOOK OF PSYCHIATRY
American Psychiatric Press; Washington, D.C., 1991

A. Beck, A. Freeman & Associates
COGNITIVE THERAPY OF PERSONALITY DISORDERS
The Guildford Press; New York, 1990

G. Gabbard
PSYCHODYNAMIC PSYCHIATRY IN CLINICAL PRACTICE, THE DSM-IV EDITION
American Psychiatric Press; Washington, D.C., 1994

H. Kaplan, B. Sadock (editors)
COMPREHENSIVE GROUP PSYCHOTHERAPY, THIRD EDITION
Williams & Wilkins; Baltimore, 1993

H. Kaplan, B. Sadock (editors)
COMPREHENSIVE TEXTBOOK OF PSYCHIATRY, SIXTH EDITION
Williams & Wilkins; Baltimore, 1995

H. Kaplan, B. Sadock, J. Grebb (editors)
SYNOPSIS OF PSYCHIATRY, SEVENTH EDITION
Williams & Wilkins; Baltimore, 1994

N. McWilliams
PSYCHOANALYTIC DIAGNOSIS
The Guildford Press; New York, 1994

E. Othmer & S. Othmer
THE CLINICAL INTERVIEW USING DSM-IV
American Psychiatric Press; Washington, D.C., 1994

P. Pilkonis, in
THE DSM-IV PERSONALITY DISORDERS; J. LIVESLEY, EDITOR
The Guildford Press; New York, 1995

First date checklist

- ☐ 5 packages of breath mints
- ☐ Flowers
- ☐ Bone for dog
- ☐ Odor eaters
- ☐ Chocolates
- ☐ Cab fare home

- ☐ Engagement ring
- ☐ Triple-checked address
- ☐ Food critic's review of restaurant
- ☐ Conversation piece
- ☐ Two watches to avoid being late
- ☐ Picture of someone's baby

THE DEPENDENT PERSONALITY

Biographical Information

Name:	Anita Lott
Occupation:	Food Banker & Pet Hotelier
Appearance:	**Just Take Me** t-shirt under a big fuzzy sweater
Relationship with animals:	Confines dog to prevent elopement
Favourite Song:	*Stand By Me*

At the Therapist's Office

Before Session:	Sees another therapist
Waiting Room Reading:	Autographed self-help book from yet another therapist
During Session:	Describes nightmares after seeing *Home Alone*
Fantasies Involve:	Confining therapist to her home
Relationship with Therapist:	Sits in car when *Avoidant* not there
Behavior During Session:	Sits next to therapist; records session
Takes to Therapy:	Nightly dinner invitation

Diagnostic Shorthand

Mnemonic - "NEEDS PUSH"

Needy - other people assume responsibility for major areas of life

Expression of disagreement with others is limited

Excessive lengths are gone to for nurturance and support

Decision-making is difficult

Starting projects independently is difficult

Preoccupied with fears of being left to care for self

Urgently seeks another relationship when a close one ends

Self-confidence lacking

Helpless when alone

Introduction

The dependent personality disorder is characterized by submissive behavior and excessive needs for emotional support.

Some key names associated with development of this disorder are:
- **Freud** (1923) thought that excessive dependency was caused by a fixation at the oral stage of psychosexual development
- **Abraham** (1924) described "oral-receptive" characters, who believed that a mother-substitute would care and provide for them, thereby reinforcing inactivity and an aversion to meaningful work
- **Fenichel** (1945) observed that dependent patients consistently found a "nursing mother" in their relationships
- **Horney** (1950's) described a "compliant type" of character
- **Millon** (1969) described a submissive type of personality, later reclassified as passive-dependent, in which the person remained passive and looked to others to provide pleasure
- **Bowlby** (1969, 1977) saw the dependent character arising from experiences that caused doubt about availability of the attachment figure, causing an *anxious* or *clinging attachment* secondary to fears of losing this person

Dependent traits have long been described in a denigrating manner. As phenomenology and classification systems developed, dependent characters were seen as having a moral defect, typified by being weak-willed, ineffectual and docile.

The dependent personality disorder (DPD) was first categorized during World War II as an immature reaction to military stress, manifested by helplessness, passivity or obstructionism. This description was carried over into the DSM-I, where it was classified as the passive-dependent subtype of the passive-aggressive disorder. In the DSM-II, DPD was covered under the **inadequate personality disorder** (P. 275).

Millon's description formed the basis for the first distinct inclusion of DPD, which appeared in the DSM-III. There were only three criteria in this initial description, which grew to nine in the DSM-III-R.

Dependent behavior is particularly evident in borderline, avoidant and histrionic personalities, as well as, in mood and anxiety disorders. For this reason, DPD is often diagnosed in conjunction with other disorders. The ICD-10 contains a category also called the dependent personality disorder sharing considerable overlap with the DSM-IV.

Media Examples

Dependent characters are natural sidekicks. Their loyalty and devotion to the main character often add an endearing touch to stories. Occasionally, they rescue those who have gone out on a limb to take a chance that they were not willing or able to take themselves. In other instances, they become empowered, and take control over their abusive/controlling/repressing spouses/bosses/friends.

Examples can be seen in the following films:

• **What About Bob?** - Bill Murray portrays a highly dependent patient who cannot bear the feeling of abandonment as his therapist leaves for a vacation. He tracks down the location of the cottage and ingratiates himself with his therapist's family to avoid having to leave. He won't even leave his goldfish behind!

• **Dr. Watson** - In many aspects, Watson remains dependent on Sherlock Holmes. Though a physician, he automatically subjugates his practice to join in on anything that arises in Holmes' detective work.

• **Rocky** - The role of Rocky's wife, Adrian, played by Talia Shire, is a dependent character. Mousy and shy, she seems like an incomplete person without him.

• **Death Becomes Her** - Bruce Willis plays a hapless pawn tied to two narcissistic women. He starts out as a plastic surgeon, but stays in a destructive relationship too long, loses his license to practice, and ends up as a cosmetician for a funeral home. He barely saves himself from an eternally subservient fate.

• **Forrest Gump** - Forrest maintains a dependent relationship with his childhood friend, Jenny. He remains resolutely faithful to her and is forever hopeful that they will be together. His tolerance of her long absences, promiscuity and poor treatment of him demonstrate some of the dependent personality characteristics.

• **All in the Family** (1970's television) Jean Stapleton portrays an excellent dependent personality as Edith "Dingbat" Bunker. She tolerates an incredibly chauvinistic husband who uses her as a stepping stone for his own diminished self-esteem. The mindlessness of this character and her willingness to allow her husband to think for her embody other aspects of DPD.

Interview Considerations

Dependent patients usually are quite easy to interview. They readily respond when given attention, and are cooperative. While anxiety may be a complicating factor initially, this can be assuaged through gentle persistence. Rapport is developed by showing empathy for their needs, and in understanding how they have put their faith in others.

Open-ended questions are often answered appropriately, with elaboration on their close relationships. Dependent patients are overtly concerned with pleasing people. They are very attuned to the expressions and gestures of others. Because of this, they are quite malleable in interview situations. They can readily detect impatience if their answers to open-ended questions do not appear to satisfy the interviewer. They respond equally well to closed-ended questions and do not usually object to an interruption or segue.

Difficulties can develop if patients get the sense they are not doing what is expected of them. Under such circumstances, they may give complete control to the "authority" of the interviewer. They resign themselves to answering questions, but may not contribute spontaneously. It is common for patients to form an immediate attachment with interviewers, and to ask for advice and follow-up sessions. They openly lament having to start over with someone new.

Dependent patients are very sensitive about their submissiveness. They readily misconstrue exploration as criticism and will frequently become tearful. Confrontation of any type frequently brings on tears and a plea for help. For this reason, initial interviews can be more successful by looking for, rather than pointing out, dependent themes.

Dependent Themes

- Neediness
- Rarely live alone
- Subordinate themselves
- Work below level of ability
- Continually seek advice
- Volunteer for unpleasant tasks
- At risk for substance abuse, overmedication, abusive relationships
- Continual involvement in relationships; may endure a difficult one or quickly find another upon dissolution
- May have a "somatic orientation" by expressing their difficulties in terms of physical complaints

Presumed Etiology

BIOLOGICAL: Temperamental features consistent with DPD are submissiveness and low activity levels. There may be a stronger tendency for monozygotic twins to display dependent behavior than dizygotic twins.

Biological factors play a role in DPD. Children who are born with, or develop serious illnesses, can regress and become overly dependent on caretakers. If the illness is of sufficient duration or severity, normal individuation may not occur. Because of the illness, autonomy is not encouraged, which becomes **egosyntonic** for everyone involved in the process.

Some studies have demonstrated an association between medical illness and premorbid dependent traits. Other findings have postulated a relationship between dependency and a general predisposition to disease. Dependent traits become more pronounced after the onset of serious illnesses and may be particularly common after head injuries.

PSYCHOSOCIAL: There are studies to support experiences of both over and under-indulgence in the upbringing of dependent patients.

With respect to under-indulgence, prospective studies have found a higher incidence of dependent traits among children who come from impoverished backgrounds. Overcontrolling caretakers and inhibition of emotional expression are also features of this model.

Children who are indulged by overbearing and overprotective parents can clearly develop dependency needs. Another feature of these families is criticism or punishment following attempts at autonomy. Children may fear their burgeoning independence will mean a loss of love from attachment figures. In this way, dependent parents who are overinvested in their children perpetuate dependency.

Although the **oral phase** of development is considered the fixation point of dependent patients, it is more likely that the above patterns persisted throughout development. The concept of orality is used to refer to the "hunger" for attachment, rather than any reference to feeding habits. Social and cultural factors also require consideration. Additionally, DPD may be more common in the youngest child in a line of siblings.

Ego Defenses

Various ego defenses are used in DPD:

• **idealization** - other people, particularly partners, are seen as all-powerful rescuers who provide protection and make decisions

• **reaction formation** - dependent behavior may be the transformation of aggressive or hostile feelings (see OBSESSIVE CHAPTER for more detail, pun intended)

• **projective identification** - patients induce feelings of guilt and indebtedness for their services to perpetuate relationships

• **inhibition, somatization** and **regression** are also used

Diagnostic Criteria

A pervasive and excessive need to be taken care of that leads to submissive and clinging behavior and fears of separation, beginning by early adulthood and present in a variety of contexts, as indicated by five (or more) of the following:

(1) has difficulty making everyday decisions without an excessive amount of advice and reassurance from others
(2) needs others to assume responsibility for most major areas of his or her life
(3) has difficulty expressing disagreement with others because of fear of loss of support or approval
Note: Do not include realistic fears of retribution.
(4) has difficulty initiating projects or doing things on his or her own (because of a lack of self-confidence in judgment or abilities rather than a lack of motivation or energy)
(5) goes to excessive lengths to obtain nurturance and support from others, to the point of volunteering to do things that are unpleasant
(6) feels uncomfortable or helpless when alone because of exaggerated fears of being unable to care for himself or herself
(7) urgently seeks another relationship as a source of care and support when a close relationship ends
(8) is unrealistically preoccupied with fears of being left to take care of himself or herself
REPRINTED WITH PERMISSION FROM THE DSM-IV.
COPYRIGHT, AMERICAN PSYCHIATRIC ASSOCIATION, 1994

EPIDEMIOLOGY

Estimates of the prevalence of DPD vary considerably among studies. In clinical populations, it is diagnosed in approximately 3% of patients, and may be seen in up to 10% of the general population. There is a sex difference, with women being diagnosed three times as often as men, though this may be a cultural artifact.

DIFFERENTIAL DIAGNOSIS

Dependent traits can be seen in several Axis I conditions, as well as in other personality disorders. A **Major Depressive Episode** may cause a patient to fear being alone and have an exaggerated need for others. Dependent behavior may also be present in **Dysthymic Disorder**, with the presence of a relationship modulating the dysphoria of this disorder. In both these disorders, mood symptoms are prominent and episodic. In DPD, patients are generally content when in a relationship, and exhibit mood symptoms with the loss or threatened loss of attachment.

Anxiety is also a prominent feature in DPD. Patients with **Phobias** often exhibit dependent behavior by needing a certain person around to help calm them. **Agoraphobia**, in particular has an overlap with DPD. The distinction can be made by the generalized fear of being alone in DPD; it is not limited to certain situations such as finding an escape or getting help. Agoraphobic patients can happily lead an independent existence apart from their specific fears. Similarly, patients with **Panic Disorder** can become frantic without someone around them for reassurance and comfort. Sometimes other people can be seen as a "good luck charm" who reduce the frequency or severity of attacks. Patients with panic disorder often have elevated dependency needs. The episodic nature of panic disorder and level of functioning between attacks helps separate these conditions.

Dependent patients are vulnerable to somatize their complaints, particularly in families or cultures where attention is not given to emotions. **Somatization Disorder** and **Hypochondriasis** in particular may perpetuate relationships and ensure a passive, dependent role for patients. Dependent patients usually do not have complaints as widespread, or a focus as far developed, as those seen in **Somatoform Disorders**.

The "orality" of DPD can manifest itself in **Substance Abuse**. While any drug can potentially be involved, alcohol and benzodiazepines in particular can provide a soothing, anxiety-dissolving substitute for attachment. Dependent patients may also turn to food as a substitute for love and develop **Bulimia Nervosa** or obesity.

Commonly, in a **Shared Psychotic Disorder (Folie à Deux)**, the person in whom the delusion is induced or transmitted has a dependent relationship with the "primary case." Occasionally, in **Delusional Disorder, Erotomanic Type**, the lives of patients can be tied to those on whom they are fixated.

MENTAL STATUS EXAMINATION

APPEARANCE:	May be less than stylish; often low esteem is reflected in dowdy or frumpy clothing; often baggy, neutral or bland colors; favor cozy or soft-feeling apparel
BEHAVIOR:	May be anxious towards a new or skeptical interviewer; behavior may include hand-wringing or tremor, holding own hand or an object for comfort
COOPERATION:	Cooperative, especially in a receptive atmosphere
AFFECT:	Usually demonstrate an appropriate range; a genuine sense of despair is conveyed with their fears
SPEECH:	No characteristic finding; may reflect anxiety
CONTENT OF THOUGHT:	Passivity, letting others make decisions; express few opinions; egosyntonic reliance on others
THOUGHT FORM:	No characteristic abnormality; may be circumstantial, vague, or overelaborate
PERCEPTION:	No characteristic abnormality; consider medical cause or substance abuse if findings are present
INSIGHT & JUDGMENT:	Partial; aware of dependence on others, but often do not consider it a problem; often unaware of the extent to which their lives are hampered; do not wish to face or discuss dependency issues
SUICIDE - HOMICIDE:	Need to consider this in conjunction with any Axis I disorder; not generally dangerous to others or themselves; risk increases with the presence of substance abuse or a general medical condition

Psychodynamic Aspects

Psychodynamic theories regarding dependent behavior initially emphasized a disturbance or fixation at the first stage of psychosexual development, the oral phase. Though this is now considered an antiquated concept, it still provides a useful framework.

At the beginning of the oral phase, the infant is in a passive-dependent relationship with the world. Gratification of oral libidinal needs, referred to as **oral erotism**, is achieved by being fed, and upon satiation, falling asleep. Later, when teeth develop, more aggressive features appear. Known as **oral sadism**, this phase is connected with biting, devouring, spitting, etc. The term **oral character** refers to adult analogues of these development stages. Such people depend on others to provide for them (DPD) or give them love and attention (NPD). In a sense, they want to be "fed", but have varying degrees of what they need others for, and what they are willing to give in return. Some psychoanalysts divided the oral character into a passive-dependent type (more consistent with DPD) and an active-dependent type (more consistent with HPD).

Though it may not be intuitively obvious, envy and jealousy are oral traits. Hostility and aggression often occur in dependent behavior:

- "You look after me."
- "You make the decisions."
- "You tell me what to do."
- "You're in charge."

This was recognized in the initial classification of dependent behavior as being a subtype of **passive-aggressive disorder** (p. 262). Dependent behavior may be a compromise or a cover (**reaction formation**) for deeper aggressive impulses. Patients may earn "credits" through their services and use them to induce guilt. Other people are still "controlled," but by a more subtle and acceptable process.

It is also common to find overcontrolling parents in the families of dependent patients. Much as in the development of BPD, attempts at autonomy were not reinforced, and may even have been punished. A less dramatic variant may have involved rewarding dependent behavior. Another consistent feature is a low level of emotional expression in families. This may leave patients seeking overt demonstrations of affection, as verbal ones are not given.

Attachment versus Dependency in DPD

DPD contains concepts and criteria for both pathologic degrees of attachment and dependency behaviors. **Attachment** behavior in DPD achieves and maintains closeness to a person who is seen as more capable. It is usually aimed at a specific person and increases a sense of security. **Dependency** involves reliance on others, diminished self-confidence and a lack of autonomy. It is a diffuse process that involves seeking protection, help and approval.

Attachment dimensions of DPD are:

- Seeking a secure base
- Needing affection
- Desiring closeness with an attachment figure
- Protesting separation from attachment figures
- Fearing the loss of an attachment figure

Dependency dimensions of DPD are:

- Diminished self-esteem
- Submissive behavior
- Need for approval
- Requiring care and support
- Requiring advice and reassurance

What Happens in Psychodynamic Therapy?

Dependent patients are usually eager to get involved in psychotherapy. They ingratiate themselves by taking whatever is offered in terms of appointment times and frequency. They become model patients, rarely canceling appointments or arriving late. Therapists are treated with a sense of admiration bordering on awe. Regardless of the content of sessions, the process of therapy suits dependent patients' needs quite well. Having a strong, competent professional to turn to for understanding and support for an indefinite time period appears to be the answer in itself. **Idealization** in DPD is more subtle and enduring than that seen with in personality disorders, particularly BPD and NPD. Patients are tolerant of the lapses, oversights and mistakes of their therapists. As long as the continuity of therapy is not in question, such occurrences do not bring about the rage or anger that accompanies the **devaluation** seen in Cluster B disorders.

The difficulty in psychotherapy is in conveying to patients that the goal must be to examine and alter dependent behavior, not indulge it to make up for other deficiencies. The therapist, like a catalyst in a chemical reaction, cannot be part of the final solution. In order to be successful, the therapeutic process needs to tactfully and empathically frustrate patients' wishes, and then explore the fantasies and antecedents of dependent behavior. This often takes place by denying requests for advice, extra sessions or overt help with practical matters. Psychodynamic therapy aims to uncover what is being masked by the continual search for a caretaker, and what frightens patients about independence.

In some cases, acknowledging progress invokes fears of separation and termination of therapy. Patients may begin to emphasize their difficulties, or actually regress in order to prolong the attachment to the therapist. A time-limited approach may help deal with this situation. If a certain number of sessions is agreed upon at the outset, the anxiety of termination can be discussed early in the therapy. This can also be used at a later point if progress is not being made. Some patients may not be able to tolerate breaking the attachment to their therapist and require indefinite, but infrequent sessions.

TRANSFERENCE AND COUNTERTRANSFERENCE REACTIONS

Transference reactions involve **idealization** and the fantasy that the all-knowing therapist has all the answers. Frequently, patients expect to be "spoon-fed" and do not realize that their involvement is necessary for improvement. Patients expect therapists to satisfy their longing for a nurturing figure. They may assist this process by flattery, giving presents and imitating the therapist to achieve solidarity. Countertransference reactions can be quite strong to the clinging and passivity of patients. It may feel as if all that is really needed is a "swift kick" to get things back on track. Subservience and ingratiating behavior may cause an avoidant collusion with patients regarding sensitive areas and issues of termination.

SUMMARY OF THERAPEUTIC TECHNIQUES

- Be tactful and gentle when focusing on dependent behaviors
- Convey that the work of therapy is to identify and explore impediments to a more independent lifestyle
- Advice, favors and gratification of other needs will not be beneficial
- Be an example of independent functioning for patients to model

Pharmacotherapy

Dependent patients invoke a strong "pull" in their physicians to do something to help them. This, combined with a frequent mixture of mood, anxiety and somatic complaints, can result in patients receiving medication for their problems. Dependent patients are eager to please and will do things that may not be in their best interests to comply with the treatment prescribed for them. They may not complain of side-effects, may take medication for longer time periods than is advised, and may become "dependent" either psychologically or physically. A prescription can become a **transitional object**, or have some other significance to the patient.

Because dependent behavior can be a feature of many conditions, a careful diagnostic assessment is essential, when it is the presenting symptom. Axis I disorders have specific pharmacologic treatments; there is no medication to cure dependent personality traits.

Still, dependent patients receive prescriptions either as a result of their own initiative, or their physician's. It is important to consider the risks of certain medications when they are used:

• Benzodiazepines - addiction, memory impairment, disinhibition
• Antidepressants - impaired sexual function, risk in overdose
• Antipsychotics - tardive dyskinesia, dystonic reactions

Overall, dependent patients may benefit from a trial of medication if they are particularly symptomatic, or develop an Axis I condition that is a clear departure from their personality traits.

Group Therapy

Groups can be an excellent therapeutic modality for dependent patients. Some group members may gratify the wish for advice, sympathy and enduring attachment. Other members will confront such yearnings and behaviors. This facilitates learning and gives patients encouragement to attempt more independent solutions. The group is also an ideal place to experiment by trying new ways of interacting. Group therapy can also be a place for dependent patients to hide. By **idealizing** other members (and the therapist), they may be perennial favorites and remain in groups far longer than is necessary, or even advisable. Group membership is also not the ultimate solution for their interpersonal deficiencies.

Cognitive Therapy

Basic Cognitive Distortions:
- "I am inadequate and helpless. I can't handle things on my own."
- "I must find someone to care for me and protect me"

ADAPTED FROM BECK, FREEMAN & ASSOCIATES, 1990

The structure and time-limited approach in cognitive therapy can be very helpful in DPD. A frequent misconception is that therapy tries to bring about a completely independent existence. Patients are prone to dichotomous thinking; either they are entirely dependent, or entirely on their own. Autonomy, with enduring emotional connections to others, is a more encouraging goal for patients. Often direct examination of dependent behaviors and attitudes overwhelms patients, who may be unaware that this is their main issue. By use of **guided discovery** and **Socratic questioning**, patients become aware that assertiveness, problem solving and effective decision-making could benefit their lives.

The practical, directive approach in cognitive therapy may foster an early reliance on the therapist. Once committed to therapy, setting limits is useful in helping patients discover their desire to be looked after. For example, if the homework assignment is not done, or patients have nothing to contribute to the agenda, they should not be allowed to deflect the responsibility for what is done in that session onto the therapist. The standard cognitive approach is to provide an agenda if the patient does not. But in DPD, identifying to patients that submissiveness is part of their problem may generate active involvement on their part. Setting goals with an increasing gradient of independence is an important intervention. In behavior therapy, these goals are addressed by using graded exposure, possibly with the direct involvement of the therapist.

Course of DPD

Dependent behaviors, while adaptive early in life, can cause serious limitations for adults. In some situations, dependent patients exist happily in a symbiotic relationship with someone who "needs to be needed." Psychotherapies can be quite effective, once patients understand that the therapist is not there to solve their problems for them. When patients develop an awareness of the limitations caused by their dependence, and see that autonomy holds advantages for them, they can work successfully towards this goal.

References

American Psychiatric Association
DIAGNOSTIC AND STATISTICAL MANUAL OF MENTAL DISORDERS, FOURTH EDITION
American Psychiatric Press; Washington D.C., 1994

N. Andreason, D. Black
INTRODUCTORY TEXTBOOK OF PSYCHIATRY
American Psychiatric Press; Washington, D.C., 1991

A. Beck, A. Freeman & Associates
COGNITIVE THERAPY OF PERSONALITY DISORDERS
The Guildford Press; New York, 1990

G. Gabbard
PSYCHODYNAMIC PSYCHIATRY IN CLINICAL PRACTICE, THE DSM-IV EDITION
American Psychiatric Press; Washington, D.C., 1994

R. Hirschfeld, M. Shea, R. Weise & J. Livesley, in
THE DSM-IV PERSONALITY DISORDERS, J. LIVESLEY, EDITOR
The Guildford Press; New York, 1995

H. Kaplan, B. Sadock (editors)
COMPREHENSIVE GROUP PSYCHOTHERAPY, THIRD EDITION
Williams & Wilkins; Baltimore, 1993

H. Kaplan, B. Sadock (editors)
COMPREHENSIVE TEXTBOOK OF PSYCHIATRY, SIXTH EDITION
Williams & Wilkins; Baltimore, 1995

N. McWilliams
PSYCHOANALYTIC DIAGNOSIS
The Guildford Press; New York, 1994

E. Othmer & S. Othmer
THE CLINICAL INTERVIEW USING DSM-IV
American Psychiatric Press; Washington, D.C., 1994

R. Pies
CLINICAL MANUAL OF PSYCHIATRIC DIAGNOSIS AND TREATMENT
American Psychiatric Press; Washington, D.C., 1994

Key:

1. Paranoid — Uses periscope to scan parking lot
2. Narcissist — Introduces himself as "Wal" from Wal-Mart
3. Dependent — Buys an industrial-sized pudding machine
4. Passive-Aggressive — Writes a check in CASH ONLY line
5. Borderline — Buys analgesics in economy-size
6. Antisocial — Uses cashier closest to exit for fast getaway
7. Histrionic — Frequent flyer card for lingerie section
8. Obsessive — Uses EXACT CHANGE cashier
9. Avoidant — Visits only on "Customer Appreciation Day"
10. Schizoid — Has merchandise delivered to car
11. Schizotypal — Buys high colonic six-pack

THE OBSESSIVE-COMPULSIVE PERSONALITY

Biographical Information

Name:	R. Lloyd Micron
Occupation:	Molecule counter for a chemical co.
Appearance:	Starched underwear and socks
Relationship with animals:	Has sent dog to obedience school every year for 8 years
Favourite Song:	*You'll Do It My Way*

At the Therapist's Office

Before Session:	Washes hands before and after using restroom
Waiting Room Reading:	Rearranges magazines alphabetically
During Session:	Quotes an etiquette book
Fantasies Involve:	Not flushing the toilet
Relationship with Therapist:	Repairs hole in chair with pocket-sewing kit
Behavior During Session:	Demands watches be synchronized
Takes to Therapy:	A bottle of *Obsession*

Diagnostic Shorthand

Mnemonic - "PERFECTION"

Preoccupied with details, rules, plans, organization

Expression of affect is restricted

Reluctant to delegate tasks

Frugal

Excessively devoted to work

Controls others

Task completion interfered with by perfectionism

Inflexible

Overconscientious about morals, ethics, values, etc.

Not able to discard belongings; hoards objects

INTRODUCTION

Hallmarks of the obsessive-compulsive personality disorder are rigidity, perfectionism, orderliness, indecisiveness, interpersonal control and emotional constriction.

Some key names associated with development of this disorder are:
• **Esquirol** (early 19th century) wrote about this personality type
• **Freud** (1908) Linked obsessive behaviors to difficulties during the anal stage of development, and defined the **anal triad**, consisting of orderliness, parsimoniousness and obstinancy
• **Jones** (1919) described a sense of time pressure, frugality with money and preoccupation with cleanliness
• **Abraham** (1921) elaborated on Freud's view and added several features to the list of typical behaviors
• **Schneider** (1923) described the **anankastic personality** as kempt, pedantic, proper, constrained and insecure
• **Reich** (1933) described obsessive characters as "living machines" and also noted them to be indecisive and plagued with doubt.
• **Lazare** (1966) conducted studies contributing to the DSM criteria; in addition to supporting Freud's triad, other defining characteristics were: emotional constriction, perseverance (in the face of undue obstacles), rejection of others, rigidity and a strong superego
• **Janet, Rado, Erik Erikson, Salzman** and **Shapiro** all made contributions to the understanding of this disorder

The obsessive-compulsive personality disorder (OCPD) is named similarly to the Obsessive Compulsive Disorder (OCD), which is classified on Axis I as an Anxiety Disorder. Though some of the early theories did not distinguish a personality style from a clinical disorder, they are phenomenologically distinct (P. 251). An obsession is defined as, "a recurrent thought, impulse or image." A compulsion is defined as, "a repetitive behavior or mental act." Patients with OCPD do not experience distinct obsessions or compulsions. Their thoughts and behaviors are egosyntonic, and therefore are not recognized as excessive or unreasonable, as occurs in OCD.

This disorder was initially called the "compulsive personality disorder" in DSM-I and again in DSM-III. For the sake of brevity, the term obsessive is used in this chapter. In the ICD-10, this is called the **anankastic** personality (Greek for "forced"). The description differs from the DSM-IV by removing parsimony, and adding the features of indecisiveness, and the need to plan activities in unalterable detail.

MEDIA EXAMPLES

Obsessive characters are frequently cast as harsh, mean-spirited "control freaks." They, too, have a tragic flaw that the plot sets out to punish or correct. Typical examples include domineering bosses, know-it-alls, workaholic spouses and loners on a mission.

Examples can be seen in the following films:

• TERMS OF ENDEARMENT - Shirley MacLaine won an Oscar for her portrayal of a clearly obsessive woman who channels her libido into gardening, and ends up with a backyard that threatens to overtake the house. She is a repressed busybody who repeatedly tries to dominate her daughter's life.

• DRAGNET (movie version) - Dan Aykroyd plays the nephew of Joe Friday, the character from the original television series. Aykroyd's grim manner, humorlessness and interest in, "Just the facts," are examples of obsessive behavior.

• STAR TREK (original series) - Mr. Spock is the obsessive's obsessive. He is ruled by logic and rarely betrays a glimpse of emotion. Many humorous moments were provided by his perplexity at the range of human emotional responses.

• REMAINS OF THE DAY - Anthony Hopkins turns in a marvelous performance as Stevens, the head butler of an English country estate. He exists only to serve his employer, and remains singularly focussed on his work. In one scene, he refuses to leave his post during a luncheon, while his father passes away in the same house. In another, he seeks out a former housekeeper (who had a romantic interest in him), only to explore the possibility of her returning to his place of employment. His perfect reserve and absence of emotional expression keep him from exploring the possibilities of life and love.

• MOBY DICK - The role of Captain Ahab - maybe the whale too
• THE ODD COUPLE - The role of Felix, played by Tony Randall
• GORKY PARK - Inspector Arkady Renko, played by William Hurt
• THE MOSQUITO COAST - Lead role played by Harrison Ford
• MO' BETTER BLUES - Bleek, played by Denzel Washington
• A CHRISTMAS CAROL - Scrooge, a Dickens classic
• SEVEN - Detective played by Morgan Freeman

Interview Considerations

Obsessive patients can present difficulties in interviews. They usually relate the history in a pedantic, circumstantial manner. In order for the presenting complaint to be understood, a myriad of other details leading up to the current situation are given. Hearing patients out usually will bring them back to the issue at hand, but this can take considerable time. Trying to narrow the focus can bring about a hostile reaction, as patients feel compelled to supply all possible information. Additionally, obsessive patients are very attuned to control issues, and will try to dominate the interview.

A good deal of the history is related in a "news," as opposed to "weather" fashion. Events are explained in a detached, objective manner devoid of any emotional flavor. Pointing this out is a precarious technique. Patients pride themselves on their objectivity; asking about what they are *feeling* may bring about a blank stare. In some situations you may need to suggest or label expectable feelings for the patient to identify. In other instances, a detour such as the following may result:

Q: "What feelings did you have while speaking with your colleague?" A: "It was my feeling that this person was incompetent, I could have done the job in a much more efficient manner."

In a psychotherapy assessment, it may be appropriate to go back over this statement and explain that this was a thought, not a feeling. In other settings, doing this risks that the majority of the affect expressed will just be anger directed back at the interviewer.

It can be difficult to develop rapport with obsessive patients. Showing empathy for their suffering means that they have not solved their problems. It may be more productive to attempt to understand their "dilemma." Try to use patients' exact words when rephrasing and reflecting, or semantics may become the focus. Wait until the issues are clear before summarizing, as patients tolerate interruptions poorly.

Obsessive Themes

- Emotional constriction
- Indecisiveness
- Fixated with details
- "Misses the forest for the trees"
- Cerebral rigidity and inflexibility
- Hoards money, objects, etc.
- Few leisure activities; can't relax
- Humorless; lack of spontaneity

Presumed Etiology

BIOLOGICAL: There is no information available describing possible genetic links or physiologic findings in OCPD. No less a proponent than Freud, however, thought that obsessive individuals had a rectal hypersensitivity. There does not appear to be a genetic link between OCD and OCPD.

PSYCHOSOCIAL: The classic etiology of OCPD stemmed from difficulties arising during the **anal stage** of psychosexual development (roughly ages one to three). As children approach the age of two, toilet training becomes a major focus of the interaction with parents. Here, the "production" part of a natural process is treated as something unpleasant by parents. Children that are indoctrinated into toilet training too early (before the rectal sphincter is physiologically mature), or too harshly, end up in a power struggle with caregivers.

This is often the first intrusion of socialization into the infant's otherwise unrestrained existence. Achieving continence involves submitting to parental expectations on demand, and then being judged on the outcome. When children fail at the task, over-ambitious or demanding parents evoke feelings of being bad and dirty. Issues of cleanliness, timeliness, stubbornness and control can reasonably be seen as linked to this stage of development. Failing to produce on schedule, with an immediate perception of disappointment, arouses feelings of anger and aggression. Censured by a punitive superego, ego defenses are recruited to dissipate these strong affects.

Erikson's **autonomy vs. shame and doubt** stage overlaps Freud's anal stage. Here, in order to gain parental acceptance and avoid disapproval, children may feel the need to renounce their autonomy. In doing so, they focus on the specifics of what pleases their parents.

Parents who are cold, distant or obsessive themselves, may give the impression that their nurturance is contingent on good behavior.

OCPD appears to be more common in the oldest child in a family, who may have had more responsibility than the younger ones. Lastly, cultural influences are etiologically significant. North American society, in particular, rewards independence, hard work, orderliness and punctuality. Particularly in men, the suppression of emotions and typical attitudes of, "Deal with it" and, "Just do it" reinforce that an obsessive style leads to success.

EPIDEMIOLOGY

The prevalence of OCPD is estimated to be 1% of the general population, with a slightly higher figure for patient populations. There is a sex difference, with men being diagnosed at least twice as often as women. This disorder is also found more frequently within professions requiring meticulous attention to detail and strict dedication to duty.

EGO DEFENSES

The ego defenses in OCPD defend against expression of unfulfilled dependency wishes and strong feelings of anger directed at caregivers.

• **Isolation (of affect)** separates or strips an idea from its accompanying feeling or affect. This is the predominant defense contributing to the obsessive component. An idea is made conscious, but the feelings are kept within the unconscious. When this defense is used to a lesser degree, three others mechanisms may be used:
· Intellectualization - excessive use of abstract thinking
· Moralization - adherence to morality to isolate contradictory feelings
· Rationalization - "rational" justification of unacceptable attitudes

• **Undoing** involves an action, either verbalization or behavior, that symbolically repents, or make amends for, conflicts, stresses or unacceptable wishes. This is the predominant defense contributing to the compulsive component.

• **Reaction Formation** transforms an impulse into diametrically opposed thoughts, feelings and behavior. This is frequently seen as a "counterdependent" attitude in which obsessive patients eradicate dependency on anyone. Similarly, maintenance of a calm exterior guards against an awareness of angry feelings. For example, orderliness is a reaction formation against the desire to play with feces or to make a mess.

• **Displacement** redirects feelings from a conflict or stressor onto a symbolically related, but less threatening, person or object. "Kicking the dog" or "shooting the messenger" are examples of this defense. In OCPD, anger or aggression towards parents is unconsciously forbidden, so substitutes (human, canine and otherwise) are targeted for these feelings. This is also the predominant defense involved in the formation of a phobia.

Diagnostic Criteria

A pervasive pattern of preoccupation with orderliness, perfectionism, and mental and interpersonal control, at the expense of flexibility, openness, and efficiency, beginning by early adulthood and present in a variety of contexts, as indicated by four (or more) of the following:

(1) is preoccupied with details, rules, lists, order, organization, or schedules to the extent that the major point of the activity is lost
(2) shows perfectionism that interferes with task completion (e.g., is unable to complete a project because his or her own overly strict standards are not met)
(3) is excessively devoted to work and productivity to the exclusion of leisure activities and friendships (not accounted for by obvious economic necessity)
(4) is overconscientious, scrupulous, and inflexible about matters of morality, ethics, or values (not accounted for by cultural or religious identification)
(5) is unable to discard worn-out or worthless objects even when they have no sentimental value
(6) is reluctant to delegate tasks or to work with others unless they submit to his or her way of doing things
(7) adopts a miserly spending style toward both self and others; money is viewed as something to be hoarded for future catastrophes
(8) shows rigidity and stubbornness
REPRINTED WITH PERMISSION FROM THE DSM-IV.
COPYRIGHT, AMERICAN PSYCHIATRIC ASSOCIATION, 1994

Differential Diagnosis

Features of OCPD, particularly frugality, concern with perfection, and a stilted personality, overlap with several other personality disorders. Affective constriction also can be seen in a **Major Depressive Episode**. Feelings of guilt can also impel patients to try and undo a perceived wrong. The heightened productivity of **Hypomania** can overlap with the drivenness seen in OCPD. In both cases, other features of a mood disorder are conspicuously lacking, as obsessive patients strive to suppress variations in mood and affect. However, especially later in life, obsessive patients are prone to depression.

Some **General Medical Conditions** (especially epilepsy) cause personality changes that resemble OCPD. Substance-induced disorders must always be considered in the differential diagnosis.

OCD VERSUS OCPD

Despite the similarity in names, these are phenomenologically distinct conditions. Key features to distinguish between the two are:

FEATURE	OCD	OCPD
Central Concept	Recurrent, intrusive thoughts and/or behaviors/mental acts	Enduring preoccupation with perfection, orderliness and interpersonal control
Subjective Experience	Egodystonic; recognize irrationality of mental events and behavior	Egosyntonic until close relationships are affected or defenses break down
Impact on daily routine	Time consuming; interferes with ability to function	Defends traits and methods as being effective and justified by productivity
Mentation	Aware of forced nature of thoughts, recognize as a product of own mind; resists compulsions	Thoughts lack quality of intrusiveness; behavior occurs automatically, most processes remain unconscious
Manifestations	Often involves themes	Pervasive throughout
Anxiety	Marked; anxious dread	Not usually evident
Etiology	Growing evidence for genetic factors	Psychosocial influences predominate
Biological Features	Abnormal CT & PET scans; some structural abnormalities found	None consistently present
Treatment	Role of serotonin strongly implicated	Psychotherapy in various forms

OCD and OCPD were initially formulated as one disorder, hence the similarity in name. There are conflicting opinions about the degree to which OCPD exists prior to the onset of OCD. Currently, there is more evidence against this association. OCD is associated with other Cluster C personality disorders more frequently than with OCPD.

MENTAL STATUS EXAMINATION

APPEARANCE:	Traditional clothing; "square" or "nerdish"; prim and proper; colors usually conservative; neatly groomed
BEHAVIOR:	Paucity of movement; body language not expressive; few gestures or facial expressions
COOPERATION:	Often try to control interview; can pose difficulties
AFFECT:	Low degree of variability; if expressed, often show anger or indignation
SPEECH:	Monotonous; lacks prosody and inflection
CONTENT OF THOUGHT:	Detailed description of events; need to tell whole story in logical sequence; lacks emotional content
THOUGHT FORM:	No characteristic abnormality; often circumstantial, overelaborate, or metaphorical
PERCEPTIONS:	No characteristic abnormality; attentive to fine details
INSIGHT & JUDGMENT:	Often limited; have considerable difficulty in seeing the value of emotional life, or changing workaholic attitude
SUICIDE - HOMICIDE:	Usually not a concern; however, breakdown of defenses with Substance Abuse/Axis I disorder/situational crisis can release rage against self or others

PSYCHODYNAMIC ASPECTS

The central dynamic in an obsessive person is that of feeling like an unloved child. This may occur in reality, due to aloof and demanding parents, or can be due to the perception of this experience. Regardless, obsessive patients did not grow up feeling loved or wanted by their caretakers.

While the classical etiologic construct focused on the anal stage, it is highly likely that parents who were, or at least seemed, harsh and controlling, would have been this way during all development stages. Being forced to "perform" during toilet training, and submit to other experiences, engenders feelings of anger and destructive fantasies. Parents who are unreasonably controlling squash unacceptable behavior, as well as the expression of anger and aggression. Attachment to caretakers is sought, though dependency needs remain unfulfilled. A psychodynamic understanding of OCPD involves the defensive handling of anger and dependency needs, both of which are consciously unacceptable to patients.

As children, obsessional patients were often praised for what they did, as opposed to who they were. Behavior is then shaped according to that which receives the reward of parental approval. The notion of "being seen and not heard" is transmitted, with the result that children behave like little robots. Feelings in general get relegated to the realm of weakness, guilt, shame and being "bad." This leads to an overinvestment in thinking, and rational or logical approaches.

Patients are uncertain what will be accepted, since their automatic reactions and behaviors do not seem to be suitable. This leaves a strong sense of self-doubt, expressed later in life as ambivalence. Obsessive patients are notoriously indecisive, ruminating continuously to avoid making a wrong decision.

Fleeting parental approval for "proper" behavior leads to the desire for permanent approval, by being perfect. The demands of parents are incorporated into a punitive and harsh superego. Patients believe that by developing into a seamless, flawless, high-achiever, they finally will be loved and accepted. This leads obsessive patients to a follow a series of hollow pursuits. They are driven beyond their own interests to succeed, but lack a genuine desire for the activity. The fuel for this fire is placation of the superego. There is a double irony in the relentless pursuit of these accomplishments. First, patients only get a transient increase in esteem, since the motivation for their achievements is to please others. Secondly, despite obsessive patients' apparent autonomy, they actually have little freedom from their superego, which is a persistent and harsh critic.

Patients fear "out of control" situations and compulsively seek to maintain control, both over themselves and others. Internally, compulsions undo or repent for an unconscious sense of having committed a crime (e.g. the acts parents disapprove of and the aggressive feelings generated). Externally, obsessive patients control their relationships, because out of their unconscious dependency needs, arises the fear that attachment to others may be tenuous. When patients were not in control of past relationships, painful consequences were the result.

Obsessive patients' libidinal wishes are punished as if they were crimes actually committed. For this reason, they may avoid situations where they might even *think* about life's baser elements. As a result, they may be overly moralistic and lacking in imagination. Rational thought, discipline and orderliness bolster esteem which has been reduced by perpetual self-criticism.

What Happens in Psychodynamic Therapy?

One of the first challenges involved in treating OCPD is interesting the patient in therapy. Frequently, a crisis or loss needs to occur to cause enough emotional pain for patients to seek help. A lesser stress usually brings about their usual coping mechanism of working harder or finding a bigger challenge.

The principle of **psychic determinism** is difficult to convey. Obsessive patients believe they are in complete control of their lives. Even the existence of unconscious or hidden wishes conflicts with their pragmatic approach to life. Conveying an explicit interest in helping obsessive patients can help secure a commitment to therapy. Patients are used to dubious acceptance by authority figures, and a warm and accepting attitude can help develop rapport.

Occasionally, patients will seek therapy to help with a specific choice. An "expert opinion" is sought to give concrete help with the decision, not to explore the underlying ambivalence. If any lasting gains are to be made, requests such as these are best not addressed directly.

Control issues become evident in early sessions. Patients may seek to dominate by talking continuously. They may devalue early observations and comments as being things that they already knew. Other attempts at control may be seen in resistance to schedule appointments, or taking lengthy time periods to settle their account.

An early difficulty involves the rambling, detailed descriptions of events brought to therapy. While frequently articulate, obsessive patients convey little to no feeling with their narrative accounts. This "droning on" actually serves to keep themselves, and others, in the thick of a smoke screen that covers feelings. This may be particularly evident when a strong affect threatens expression. Asking patients to focus on, and describe their feelings, helps tackle intellectualization. This question may need to be repeated regularly. In some cases, patients may need help in labeling emotional states.

There is a strong effort to become a "perfect" patient. Sessions will be attended on time and rarely cancelled. Patients will work very hard at bringing material they think interests the therapist. In some cases, patients go to great lengths to show that they are getting better. It is important to resist mechanistic explanations from patients by pointing out the difference between intellectual insight and emotional insight.

A major therapeutic intervention involves getting patients to discuss their transference reactions. Frequently, these are reported as non-existent. It is crucial to pay attention to the last thing patients say before leaving, especially as they gather their belongings when the session is "off record." This has been referred to as an **exit line** and is brought about by heightened transference feelings. The defense of **reaction formation** is used to turn aggressive thoughts into ones that sound kind. Expression of concern about their therapist's health or wishes for a happy vacation may indeed be the converse.

Exploring a feeling of frustration with the therapist or the therapy becomes a stepping stone to acknowledging and expressing anger. Over time, the goal of therapy is to modify the superego. In doing so, patients can develop an awareness of their feelings, and integrate them without an accompanying sense of shame.

TRANSFERENCE AND COUNTERTRANSFERENCE REACTIONS

Because the defensive structure in OCPD inhibits an awareness of emotions, patients are not conscious of their transference reactions. Unconsciously, they project their superego, experiencing their therapist as a demanding and judgmental parent. While patients reenact the role of the dutiful child, there is an undercurrent of irritability and opposition. Frequently, this becomes obvious with exit lines, and therapist's vacations. Obsessive patients also project their high expectations onto therapists, and then feel ashamed for not living up to their standards of proper conduct.

Countertransference generally consist of two reactions. The first is boredom with the excessive amount of intellectualized, rationalized material. It is a common experience to feel distanced and to have difficulty focusing on obsessional rambling. The second is a temptation to badger or ridicule patients' affective constriction. Feelings of impatience can be brought about by the disparity between conscious cooperation and unconscious opposition.

SUMMARY OF THERAPEUTIC TECHNIQUES

• Expect a considerable amount of intellectualized material
• Aggressively pursue patients' feelings (by interrupting if necessary); encourage discussion of transference reactions
• Clearly destructive compulsive behavior (food, sex, drugs, alcohol, gambling) may need to be treated prior to starting psychotherapy

PHARMACOTHERAPY

OCD has received a good deal of attention in terms of research, effective treatment interventions and public awareness. What was once thought to be a rare disorder has been found to exist in up to 2% of the population. It has been very satisfying for clinicians and patients alike, to see the understanding of this condition advance so rapidly.

Unfortunately, OCPD is not altered by the medications that are effective in OCD. The neurochemical nature of the obsessions and compulsions are quite different in these disorders.

Patients with OCPD do not usually seek medication. Receiving a prescription feels to them like a reminder that they have a problem they couldn't solve, which is a potent deterrent. Obsessive patients may also be very attuned to side-effects. They may be a "hard sell" and request to read a PDR (U.S.) or CPS (Canada) prior to accepting medication. Additionally, should side-effects impair, or give the impression of impairing productivity, medication will be stopped quickly.

Benzodiazepines can cause disinhibition in some patients. In a crisis situation, the controls that usually keep anger in check may be lacking. A combination of alcohol and benzos, while always a bad idea, may be a particularly destructive combination in this situation.

GROUP THERAPY

Obsessive patients can benefit from group therapy and be valuable additions to the group membership. Their work ethic and reliability are qualities for other patients to model. Use of relatively mature ego defenses provokes less of a disturbance in the group process. Confrontation of long, detailed obsessive explanations in a "here and now" fashion may be better tolerated in a group setting. Obsessive patients can be encouraged to take risks and decrease indecision.

Difficulties arise in groups when obsessive patients try to "fix" problems for others. A myriad of advice, suggestions and plans are offered when other patients discuss their difficulties. Initially, little is offered to the group, as they wish to be seen as perfect patients. This is not often resolved until confronted by the group. In order to satisfy their competitive urges, patients will assume the role of co-therapist to try and assume some control in the group.

Cognitive Therapy

Basic Cognitive Distortions:
- "It must be perfect. I'll have to do it myself."
- "There is a right and wrong way to do everything."
- "There are rules to be followed and punishment for breaking them."
- "If I don't control things, chaos will result."
- "I will dwell on this decision until I make the right choice."

Adapted from Beck, Freeman & Associates, 1990

The aim of cognitive therapy in OCPD is to explore the consequences of patients' automatic assumptions, and then alter them to encourage a more realistic, humane lifestyle. Selection of a goal, based on the presenting complaint, will have greater success if it involves the patient directly (for example, "I'm never satisfied with my work" instead of, "People around me don't work hard enough") Examination of the Dysfunctional Thought Record reveals themes involving the cognitive errors of dichotomous thinking, magnification, overgeneralization and "I should" statements (Shapiro, 1965).

"I need to be perfect, or I am not worthy" **(central schema)** →
- I defer tasks to avoid failing
- I should be meticulous
- I must make the right choice

Each of these sequelae result from, and reinforce, the central schema. Another intervention is to construct behavioral experiments to test the validity of the cognitive distortions. A pitfall in this approach is that a cognitive solution is offered for a cognitive problem, in that obsessive patients look for tidy formulas and overly mechanistic explanations. Cognitive therapy alters thinking and behavior; psychodynamic therapies re-awaken emotions to guide thinking and behavior.

Course of OCPD

Obsessive patterns require considerable energy to maintain. It is common for patients to experience a mid-life depression when they become aware that their efforts will not achieve their idealistic dreams. Friedman and Rosenman (two cardiologists!) developed the concept of behavior patterns known as **Type A** and **Type B**. OCPD has considerable overlap with Type A behavior, which is a risk factor for coronary artery disease. Obsessive patients are at risk for developing stress-related medical conditions and, in particular, psychosomatic illnesses because of their workaholic lifestyle.

REFERENCES

American Psychiatric Association
DIAGNOSTIC AND STATISTICAL MANUAL OF MENTAL DISORDERS, FOURTH EDITION
American Psychiatric Press; Washington, D.C., 1994

N. Andreason, D. Black
INTRODUCTORY TEXTBOOK OF PSYCHIATRY
American Psychiatric Press; Washington, D.C., 1991

A. Beck, A. Freeman & Associates
COGNITIVE THERAPY OF PERSONALITY DISORDERS
The Guildford Press; New York, 1990

G. Gabbard
PSYCHODYNAMIC PSYCHIATRY IN CLINICAL PRACTICE, THE DSM-IV EDITION
American Psychiatric Press; Washington, D.C., 1994

H. Kaplan, B. Sadock (editors)
COMPREHENSIVE GROUP PSYCHOTHERAPY, THIRD EDITION
Williams & Wilkins; Baltimore, 1993

H. Kaplan, B. Sadock (editors)
COMPREHENSIVE TEXTBOOK OF PSYCHIATRY, SIXTH EDITION
Williams & Wilkins; Baltimore, 1995

N. McWilliams
PSYCHOANALYTIC DIAGNOSIS
The Guildford Press; New York, 1994

E. Othmer & S. Othmer
THE CLINICAL INTERVIEW USING DSM-IV
American Psychiatric Press; Washington, D.C., 1994

R. Pies
CLINICAL MANUAL OF PSYCHIATRIC DIAGNOSIS AND TREATMENT
American Psychiatric Press; Washington, D.C., 1994

D. Shapiro
NEUROTIC STYLES
Basic Books; New York, 1965

Rules of Order for the Malignant Obsessive-Compulsive Personality

• Being a Type A personality isn't good enough; strive for an A^+.

• If in doubt, THINK, THINK, THINK it out.

• The inkblot test has no time limit. After giving your response, clean up some of the mess.

• The more you do, and the faster you do it, the longer you live.

• If it's worth doing, it's worth over-doing, **right now**!

• The best reward for hard work is more work.

• Encourage others to do it by the book, **your** book.

• Perfection is the lowest acceptable standard.

• You can get all the rest you need when you're dead.

• The words **compromise**, **choice** and **no** are not in your vocabulary.

• If you can't change the rules, change the game.

• There are others like you in every organization; find them!

• Burn the candle at both ends, and in the middle!

OTHER PERSONALITY TOPICS

The Passive-Aggressive Personality

Biographical Information and Visit to the Therapist's Office

Name:	Maxine Sass
Occupation:	Somewhere in government
Appearance:	Wears black and white together
Relationship with animals:	Makes dog carry its food home
Favourite Song:	***By the Time I Get There, You Won't Need Me Anymore***
Before Session:	Arrives late, blames *Obsessive* for changing therapist's watch
Waiting Room Reading:	Tears out interesting articles
During Session:	Repeatedly interrupts therapist
Fantasies Involve:	Being *gruntled*
Relationship with Therapist:	Forgets insurance card # every week
Behavior During Session:	Miss Manners vs. Terminator
Takes to Therapy:	Weekly notice of termination

Diagnostic Shorthand

Introduction

The essential feature of the passive-aggressive personality disorder is resistance to external demands, often with pessimism and moodiness.

Some key names associated with development of this disorder are:

- **U.S. Military Psychiatrists** (W.W. II) developed the term passive-aggressive to describe an "immaturity reaction" to military stress
- **Kraeplin** (1913) and **Bleuler** (1924) described character types who displayed negative attitudes, and were easily frustrated and irritated
- **Reich** (1945) described a character type who complained continuously and exhibited a low tolerance for unpleasant situations
- **Spitzer** (1977) considered this a "state" rather than "trait" condition
- **Millon** (1981) made several revisions to the DSM-III-R criteria

The passive-aggressive personality disorder (PAPD) was first included as a separate category in the DSM-II. The criteria were refined up to the DSM-III-R, but the diagnosis was excluded from the DSM-IV. It is now also referred to as the **Negativistic Personality Disorder** in Appendix B, "Criteria Sets and Axes Provided for Further Study." Prior to this, PAPD was included in Cluster C. There were two main difficulties surrounding inclusion of PAPD as a separate diagnosis. First was the "situational reactivity" aspect, in that passive-aggressive behavior was seen only under certain circumstances, and was not as widespread as other personality disorders. Second, this disorder was organized around the single theme of resistance to external demands.

Media Examples

Passive-aggressive characters are frequently cast as deceptively bumbling anti-heroes bent on revenge or destruction. Common examples are seen in institutions where people do not have a choice about being there, such as army conscripts. Another common portrayal involves a spouse forced to live with an ultimatum.

Examples can be seen in:

- **Columbo** (T.V. detective show, 1971-77) - had the guilty party practically begging to be arrested by wearing him or her down
- **Gandhi** (1982 movie) - the notion of "passive-resistance"
- **The War of the Roses** - a comedy featuring some passive-aggressive action taken out between divorcing spouses

Interview Considerations

Passive-aggressive patients can be difficult to interview. In the process of gathering information, clarification of certain points may trigger resentment and evasiveness. Two areas that are particularly fraught with danger involve asking patients to what degree they consider themselves responsible for their difficulties, and what their motivation was for a particular act. Trying to address the anger in their response only brings about a higher level of hostility.

Patients seek help most frequently because they feel they have bad luck and that others have let them down. They often seek support for their problems, rather than understanding their own contribution. Exploring patients' point of view, and expressing empathy for their presenting complaints helps to develop rapport.

Passive-Aggressive Themes

- Procrastination
- Indecisiveness
- Constant victimization
- Forgetting "accidentally, on purpose"
- Obstructiveness
- Continual conflict with authority
- Says "yes" but acts "no"

Presumed Etiology

BIOLOGICAL: There is no known genetic pattern to PAPD. Children who have mental or physical disadvantages can develop this interpersonal style if consideration is not given to their circumstances.

PSYCHOSOCIAL: Passive-aggressive behavior may become established as a reaction to caretakers who partially, and grudgingly, meet dependency needs. In order to maintain attachment, children learn to appear grateful for what they receive. Parents who are assertive in providing what *they* think their children want can also foster such behaviors. For example, over-zealous parents who provide nutritious, but otherwise unappetizing lunches, may well encourage hidden hostility in their children. Openly confronting the situation risks a withdrawal of support, so covert disposal becomes necessary. Other early situations may involve the threat of harsh punishment, which strongly discourages children from accepting responsibility for their actions. The other major contributor is blocking the expression of anger, which forces children to retroflex their strong feelings and search for less direct means of expression.

Epidemiology

Passive-aggressive behavior itself is quite common, and has some adaptive elements. Estimates of the prevalence of PAPD show a prevalence of less than 1%, with no obvious sex difference.

Ego Defenses

• **Passive-Aggressive Behavior:** An unconscious mechanism whereby aggression is expressed indirectly; the resulting behaviors (illness, procrastination, etc.) affect someone in addition to the patient

• **Hypochondriasis:** Hostile impulses become somatic complaints

• **Denial:** Who me? Never! How dare you even make the suggestion!

• **Rationalization:** Rational explanations are used to justify attitudes

Diagnostic Criteria

A pervasive pattern or resistance to external demands for adequate social and occupational performance, beginning by early adulthood and present in a variety of contexts, as indicated by at least five of the following:

(1) procrastinates, i.e. puts things off that need to be done so that deadlines are not met
(2) becomes sulky, irritable, or argumentative when asked to do something he or she does not want to do
(3) seems to work deliberately slowly or to do a bad job on tasks that he or she really does not want to do
(4) protests, without justification, that others make unreasonable demands on him or her
(5) avoids obligations by claiming to have "forgotten"
(6) believes that he or she is doing a much better job than others think he or she is doing
(7) resents useful suggestions from others concerning how he or she could be more productive
(8) obstructs the efforts of others by failing to do his or her share of the work
(9) unreasonably criticizes or scorns people in positions of authority

Differential Diagnosis

Though patients successfully blame others, and get away with not doing their share of work, they are at risk for developing **Mood Disorders, Anxiety Disorders** and **Substance Use Disorders**. The lack of productivity and pessimism overlaps with **Dysthymic Disorder**. PAPD lacks the vegetative signs and hopelessness, and involves more of a desire to avoid taking action, rather than indecisiveness. Anxiety is a common response when passive-aggressive patients are forced into a situation (e.g. military service, legal proceedings) where they cannot get by with their usual tactics. The distinction is made in that in PAPD, symptoms are time-limited, have a circumscribed focus, and may be more appropriately termed "fearfulness."

Mental Status Examination

The MSE is usually unremarkable. At times, extreme resistance to an interview may be seen as a thought disorder, such as thought blocking or thought withdrawal. When provoked, patients can lash out and appear to be have a Cluster B personality disorder. As in any interview, inquiries about self-harm or harm to others must be made.

Psychodynamic Aspects

Passive-aggressive patients exhibit two main conflicts. The first is a wish to become dependent. This is dealt with passively because they lack the assertiveness to be direct about their needs. When these unexpressed needs are not met (telepathy failure), patients become frustrated and critical of those around them. The second conflict arises when frustration is transformed into resentment. Again, lacking assertiveness, resentment becomes expressed as procrastination, revenge, sarcasm and sabotage.

PAPD is a blend of dependency and entitlement. Patients cannot seem to remove themselves from relationships they find unsatisfying. They live the saying, "I'd rather a light candle than curse the darkness" in reverse. The term **help rejecting complainer** is also an applicable description. Finding an alternate route to express anger can protect relationships deemed too tenuous for direct confrontation. Additionally, passive-aggressive behavior makes possible the expression of hostility and frustration in a way that diminishes or avoids responsibility.

What Happens in Psychodynamic Therapy?

Individual insight-oriented approaches have relatively high failure rates and dropout rates. Patients rarely present themselves for help because their behavior distresses them. They frequently look towards psychotherapy to support their perceived disadvantaged position and coping mechanisms. Obliging the demand for support may reinforce maladaptive behavior. On the other hand, refusing to offer the support of therapy is likely to be seen as a rejection.

Themes of provoking anger in others come up in the session material. When these are reflected or pointed out, patients often respond with resentment. The frustration of dependency needs and the suggestion of personal contribution to relationship difficulties, sets the stage for an ongoing battle. When patients evoke strong countertransference anger in therapists, non-judgmental exploration helps direct the search for similar behavior in other relationships. Another technique is to make a connection with patients' desire for leniency, but that the resentment and disappointment of not receiving it is taken out against that person.

Transference and Countertransference Reactions

Passive-aggressive patients are usually unaware of their behavior. They disavow feeling of anger, and are aware only that others mistreat them. Authority figures are treated with envy and contempt.

Countertransference reactions can be quite strong. Patients have an uncanny knack for being able to hone in on weaknesses and exploit them. Demeaning remarks, lateness and non-payment of fees are all expectable. Denial of any awareness of effects of these behaviors, or the motivation behind them, is also typical.

Summary of Therapeutic Techniques

- Expect a struggle when exploring perceived mistreatment
- Use countertransference as information about how the patients interact with others; identify discrete behaviors and precipitants
- Avoid collusion with passive-aggressive behaviors, regardless of their effectiveness or cleverness
- If sufficient rapport exists, or all else fails, consider being completely frank with patients about their behavior; the awareness may benefit them, and demonstrates a more overt approach to expressing anger

Group Therapy

Group Therapy

Group therapy is an effective modality for PAPD. The desire for dependency and difficulty expressing anger are experiences to which group members can relate. Problems arise when passive-aggressive members contribute little, but sabotage or ridicule the efforts of others. Early expression of feeling, as opposed to a reaction to the feelings of others is encouraged. Confrontation on a group level is a powerful motivation for change.

Pharmacotherapy

Unfortunately, a medication to reduce passive-aggressive behavior has not yet been developed. Antidepressants and anxiolytics may be used.

Cognitive Therapy

Basic Cognitive Distortions:
- "If I don't do what I want, someone will take advantage me."
- "If I get angry at someone, that person will punish me or leave me."
- "People continually mistreat me and devalue my efforts."
- "Nothing I do ever seems to come out right. Why bother?"
- "I shouldn't have to do that. I deserve a break."

ADAPTED FROM BECK, FREEMAN & ASSOCIATES, 1990

To get around obstructiveness, homework assignments can be given in an "either-or" fashion. Either the assignment is completed, or the reasoning that prevented completion is discussed. Once these automatic thoughts are elicited, they can be constructed as hypotheses for testing. This helps involve patients in the process of collaborative empiricism, and helps reduce their perception of therapists as controlling figures. When evidence is lacking to support their cognitions, patients are directed towards more valid explanations. Behaviors directed at "getting even" with others are examined in a cost-benefit manner, with an emphasis on exploring consequences.

Course of PAPD

Passive-aggressive patients generally do not lead happy existences. They have frequent difficulties with anxiety, depression and somatic complaints. Additionally, they have numerous and serious difficulties in long term, intimate relationships. Employment is another problematic area, given the resentment directed at authority figures.

THE U-SCREW-SCREW-U CORKSCREW

LADY MACBETH KNOWS DIRT

Having to worry about everything from delusional blood stains to Arabian perfume, Lady M certainly had her hands full. We obtained her famous DUNSINANE CASTLE formula and are pleased to bring you a new household cleaner, "OUT, DAMNED SPOT!" named in honor of her ladyship.

AVAILABLE
AS YOU
LIKE IT, AS
A SPRAY,
AEROSOL,
OR
LIQUID.

MULTIPLE PERSONALITY DISORDER

INTRODUCTION

Multiple Personality Disorder (MPD) was renamed as **Dissociative Identity Disorder** (DID) in the DSM-IV. The essential feature is the co-existence of two, or more, distinct identities, or personalities that take control of an individual and cause deficits in the recall of information.

Some key names associated with development of this disorder are:

• **Morton Prince** (1906) wrote an account of a patient with several personalities called, "The Dissociation of a Personality"
• **Eugène Azam** (France, 1850's) described the symptoms of multiple personality disorder in a patient named Félida X
• **Pierre Janet** (France, 1880's) conceptualized and investigated the process of dissociation
• **Freud** and **Breuer** (1883-85) proposed a model of mental functioning in which traumatic memories were kept out of conscious awareness by repression, as seen in their famous case, Anna O

MPD is not considered a disorder of personality, but is included for its heuristic value. It is categorized as a Dissociative Disorder and has historically been classified under **Hysterical Neuroses, Dissociative Type.** Renaming this condition re-emphasizes the psychological process producing the different identities, rather than the observable manifestations. Additionally, it implies that a single person manifests different internal and external experiences of themselves.

However, this is not meant to detract from the fascinating variability observed in the "alters" which can be sufficiently well-defined to be considered separate "personalities." The alters can have distinct: names, sexual identities and orientation, voices, facility with foreign languages, handedness and handwriting. Amazingly, each can have distinct illnesses, EEGs, eyeglass prescriptions and even allergies!

The usual arrangement involves a dominant personality that is aware of all of the fragments, though this is not usually the personality that seeks treatment. Alters appear to be variably aware of one another. The total number of personalities has been reported to exceed fifty, with the average being in the range of ten to twelve. Frequently, the personalities have some connection with one another. For example, all of the persons involved in a traumatic episode (victim, perpetrator, witness, etc.) can be embodied by different personality. Also, dichotomous personalities (e.g. a good-evil pairing) are often present.

MEDIA EXAMPLES

Multiple personality themes have often involved the duality of human nature. A classic example is Robert Louis Stevenson's DR. JEKYLL AND MR. HYDE, which has been made into several movie versions. Many other movies and books have been constructed around this theme. Movie versions have been made from real cases, in particular:

• THE THREE FACES OF EVE - a book by Drs. Thigpen and Cleckley (the same Cleckley featured in the Antisocial Personality Chapter). Interestingly, Morton Prince's book recorded the case of a Miss Beauchamp, whose three personalities were referred to as, "the Saint, the Devil, and the Woman." These are the same three manifestations of the character played by Joanne Woodward, who won an Academy Award for her performance.

• SYBIL - Sally Field won an Emmy for her portrayal of the character from Flora Rheta Schreiber's book. As an interesting aside, Joanne Woodward plays the psychiatrist in this film.

ETIOLOGY

BIOLOGICAL:
• Epilepsy or head injuries have been found in up to a quarter of patients.
• Evoked potentials show clear characteristics for each personality.
• Non-dominant temporal lobe dysfunction may be present.
• High frequency of mood symptoms in host personality.
• A genetic component may contribute to higher familial incidence.

PSYCHOSOCIAL:
• Frequent history of **imaginary companions** as children.
• In almost all cases, severe psychological, physical, or sexual abuse, or some other traumatic event occurred.
• Absence of support from significant others is thought to contribute to the extensive use of **dissociation** to cope with trauma.

DIFFERENTIAL DIAGNOSIS

AXIS I:
• Schizophrenia
• Other Dissociative Disorders
• Posttraumatic Stress Disorder
• Mood Disorder (e.g. bipolar - rapid cycling or psychotic features)
• Substance Use Disorders (especially hallucinogens)

AXIS II:
• Borderline Personality Disorder

AXIS III/OTHER
• Brain tumors   • Malingering/Factitious Disorder
• Epilepsy, especially temporal lobe/partial complex seizures

COMMENT ON MPD:
The apparent prevalence of this disorder has increased dramatically in recent years. This may well be due to an increased awareness and sensitivity to dissociative states on the part of therapists. On the other hand, this epidemic has sparked considerable controversy, as well as evidence of improperly made diagnoses (see H. MERSKEY, 1992).
The diagnosis of MPD may well carry reduced expectations for taking responsibility for one's actions. This makes the condition attractive to impulsive characters and malingerers. Regardless of the legitimacy of this diagnosis, "if one of the alters robs a bank, the host personality still goes to jail."

MASOCHISTIC (SELF-DEFEATING) AND SADISTIC PERSONALITIES

THE MASOCHISTIC (SELF-DEFEATING) PERSONALITY

The term masochism derives from the writings of Leopold von Sacher Masoch (1836-1895). He was an Austrian novelist whose works contained characters who derived sexual pleasure from being hurt, abused, or humiliated. When the term is used in a sexual context, it is called **erotogenic** or **primary masochism**. Freud used the term **moral masochism** to refer to behavior that was self-damaging, which is the focus of most most psychiatric literature. Masochistic patients are notable for repeating self-damaging relationships (**repetition-compulsion**).

Many other writers have described this type of personality, including Krafft-Ebing (1908), Reich (1933), and Kernberg (1988).

The DSM-III-R included **Self-Defeating Personality Disorder** in the appendix for disorders requiring further study. It was not validated as a discrete personality disorder and was dropped from the DSM-IV.

Masochistic behavior itself is common, and not necessarily pathological. Suffering for some longer gain, or for the benefit of others has a good deal of overlap with the mature ego defense of **altruism,** or more specifically, **altruistic surrender.** Self-defeating behavior is manifested as being: accident-prone, self-injurious, a silent sufferer, and a moral victor at the expense of self-sacrifice. Masochism may develop as a strategy to secure or perpetuate attachment. Being punished or teased as children may have been the only emotional connection with their caregivers. A common cognition is that, "an abusive relationship is better than no relationship at all."

Masochistic behavior can be conceived as a blend of **depressive** and **paranoid** behavior. While patients may feel worthless, they retain the hope that this quality will bring sympathy and care from others. They share the same perception of threat as paranoid patients, but instead, attack themselves to ward off an attempt by others to do so.

THE SADISTIC PERSONALITY

The term sadism is named after the French writer Marquis de Sade (1740-1814). It was initially used to refer to people who derived erotic pleasure from inflicting cruelty on others. In a global sense, sadistic behavior involves the enjoyment of inflicting physical violence, pain, humiliation and harsh discipline onto others. Frequently, sadistic patients were brutalized as children. This disorder is thought to result from an amalgamation of sexual and aggressive drives.

The **Sadistic Personality Disorder** also appeared in the appendix of DSM-III-R, but was similarly not included in the DSM-IV. Sadistic behavior is a large component of the observed behavior in **antisocial personalities,** and to a lesser extent, **passive-aggressive** personalities. Sexual sadism is diagnosed as a **Paraphilia,** a type of sexual disorder.

Descriptions of a **sadomasochistic personality** disorder exist, reflecting the co-existence of both elements in patients. This is in keeping with the observation that most intrapsychic states exist with their opposite. Many examples of sadomasochism can be seen in the performing arts.

Treatment involves psychotherapy, where patients can become aware of their aggressive impulses and fear of/need for punishment.

The Inadequate Personality

Description on next page →

The Asthenic Personality

Description on next page →

The Inadequate Personality Disorder was included in the DSM-I and DSM-II. The hallmark of this disorder is an ineffectual response to day-to-day demands and the expectations of others. While patients are aware of their shortcomings, they have neither the desire nor the resources to change. They see their low level of achievement as natural, and in this sense, egosyntonic.

Other characteristics include:

• poor social judgment and adjustment
• low level of occupational performance and frequent job changes
• lack of stamina (physical and emotional)
• low level of adaptation to societal demands
• poor ability to plan for the future

This description overlaps with the criteria for **Dependent**, **Avoidant** and **Schizoid** Personalities.

THE ASTHENIC PERSONALITY

The Asthenic Personality Disorder appeared only in the DSM-II. The word *asthenia* derives from the Greek word for weakness. The term is still used to describe someone of slight build or body structure.

The main features of this personality are:

• lassitude, lethargy, lack of will (abulia)
• lack of enthusiasm and the capacity for enjoyment (anhedonia)
• inability to withstand average/expectable stresses

This description shares considerable overlap with the features of **Depression** and the **negative symptoms of Schizophrenia**. A more acute "neurasthenic neurosis" has been described, which may now be considered an **Adjustment Disorder**. This disorder was thought to have a constitutional origin.

An example combining both of these concepts can be seen in the H. T. Webster character called CASPAR MILQUETOAST, from the comic strip called *The Timid Soul*. The word "milquetoast" refers to one who is easily dominated or intimidated.

THE CYCLOTHYMIC PERSONALITY

Description on next page ➔

THE EXPLOSIVE PERSONALITY

Description on next page ➔

THE CYCLOTHYMIC PERSONALITY

The Cyclothymic Personality Disorder was included in the DSM-I and DSM-II. The hallmark of this disorder was a fluctuation in mood that occurred on a regular basis and was serious enough to affect functioning. In the DSM-III, this condition became the cyclothymic disorder, a type of affective disorder. In the DSM-IV, it is still listed under this name; however, the category is now called **Mood Disorders**.

The disorder resembles **Bipolar Mood Disorder** except the mood symptoms occur with a smaller amplitude. The "highs" are hypomanic (not manic), and the "lows" do not meet the criteria for a **Major Depressive Episode**.

THE EXPLOSIVE PERSONALITY

The Explosive Personality Disorder appeared only in the DSM-II, though the DSM-I had a category called the "Emotionally Unstable Personality. This has also been referred to as the **epileptoid personality disorder**. This diagnosis was given to patients who had volatile emotional responses to minor upsets. When incited, patients raged with verbal barrages and physical destructiveness.

This disorder was reclassified in the DSM-III as the **Intermittent Explosive Disorder**. In the DSM-IV, this is classified under this name in the category of Impulse Control Disorders. The DSM-IV criteria emphasize occurrence of physical assault or destruction of property.

This disorder was changed to an Axis I condition because the loss of control was not typical behavior for patients. Additionally, it was egodystonic. However, the inter-episode personality characteristics have been variably described. Some patients were described as well-adjusted, pleasant and calm. Aberrations were only seen upon provocation with seemingly minor events. Other patients appeared to have aggressive, defiant, caustic and provocative features that were consistently seen between explosive episodes. These patients may be better accounted for by the diagnoses of **Antisocial Personality Disorder** or **Narcissistic Personality Disorder** (when experiencing a narcissistic rage), in addition to the Intermittent Explosive Disorder.

REFERENCES

American Psychiatric Association
DIAGNOSTIC AND STATISTICAL MANUAL OF MENTAL DISORDERS,
THIRD EDITION
American Psychiatric Press; Washington, D.C., 1980

American Psychiatric Association
DIAGNOSTIC AND STATISTICAL MANUAL OF MENTAL DISORDERS,
THIRD EDITION REVISED
American Psychiatric Press; Washington, D.C., 1987

A. Beck, A. Freeman & Associates
COGNITIVE THERAPY OF PERSONALITY DISORDERS
The Guildford Press; New York, 1990

A. Freedman, H. Kaplan, B. Sadock (editors)
COMPREHENSIVE TEXTBOOK OF PSYCHIATRY, SECOND EDITION
Williams & Wilkins; Baltimore, 1975

H. Kaplan, B. Sadock (editors)
COMPREHENSIVE TEXTBOOK OF PSYCHIATRY, FIFTH EDITION
Williams & Wilkins; Baltimore, 1989

H. Kaplan, B. Sadock (editors)
SYNOPSIS OF PSYCHOTHERAPY, SEVENTH EDITION
Williams & Wilkins; Baltimore, 1994

N. McWilliams
PSYCHOANALYTIC DIAGNOSIS
The Guildford Press; New York, 1994

H. Merskey
The Manufacture of Personalities, The Production of MPD
BRITISH JOURNAL OF PSYCHIATRY; **160**: 327, 1992

R. Pies
CLINICAL MANUAL OF PSYCHIATRIC DIAGNOSIS AND TREATMENT
American Psychiatric Press; Washington, D.C., 1994

I. Turkat
THE PERSONALITY DISORDERS:
A PSYCHOLOGICAL APPROACH TO CLINICAL MANAGEMENT
Pergamon Press; Elmsford, N.Y., 1990

THE AXIS II GROUP - A FINAL SYNTHESIS

The ideal group may well be composed of one of each of the personality disorders. The following script shows typical, but hypothetical, interactions between the different character types.

CAST OF PERSONALITIES

R. LLOYD MICRON: The Obsessive
VINNY SCUMBAGGLIA: The Antisocial
CINDI VALENTINE: The Histrionic
MAXINE SASS: The Passive-Aggressive
ALDRIN Q. COSMOS: The Schizotypal
WANDA CUTTER: The Borderline

JAMES POND: The Narcissist
I. B. KNEADY: The Dependent
I. M. HOPING: The Avoidant
WESLEY WART: The Schizoid
P. NOYD: The Paranoid

POND: Well, I . . .

MICRON: Nice try, Pond. I have to call the session to order first.

SASS: This is a group therapy session, not a board meeting, dufus.

MICRON: What about circulating the minutes from last week's meeting? I have them right here.

COSMOS: You're such a yin force, Micron. Try some yang foods tonight. I'll make a list for you.

THERAPIST: We were all here. I'm sure we're well acquainted with what went on.

SASS: That's quite an alliteration, sweetie.

MICRON: Well, I still have my agenda to deal with [opens daytimer]. I've been reading a book called ***Thinking About Feelings***.

HOPING: Gee, that sounds *really* interesting. I wonder if it's available through my book club? I could use my bonus points to get everyone a copy, that is, if it's OK with everybody.

SCUMBAGGLIA: [leaning towards Hoping] I thought that, ahem, you know, you promised those bonus points to me in exchange for. . .

THERAPIST: It seems that we're forgetting the policy about contact outside the group. What's going on?

SCUMBAGGLIA: [glaring at Hoping to ensure silence] Well, life goes on. But my time is money, right? Besides, she's the one who needed a date for the Correspondence Course Reunion.

Pond: Liberté, Egalité, mais pas de Fraternité, mes enfants.

Cosmos: I'm sensing some bad karma right now. . .

Noyd: Are we going to be safe here? . . . Duck!!

Cutter: You jerk, Vinny! That's where you were! I waited up all night. I was so mad I got a headache and starting taking some pain killers, and then I overdosed on them. You made me do it!

Pond: He's not worth it. You should look for better men. [preens and then mutters audibly] No one overdosed because of me.

Therapist: I thought it was clear that group rules were meant . . .

Micron: To be obeyed and strictly enforced.

Scumbagglia: To be bent, and if need be, broken. There wouldn't be rules otherwise.

Wart: [freezes, then takes a renewed interest in shoelaces] Uh huh.

Cosmos: Natural laws are too complex for human understanding.

Sass: [shrugs] What*ever*.

Cutter: For others.

Pond: To be open to interpretation.

Valentine: [giggles] I don't know. I can't remember. Can someone remind me? A guy, maybe?

Noyd: To watch out for . . . or else.

Kneady: To get someone to explain them to you. I need help.

Hoping: W. . w. . whatever you say. The thought of all those new people just frightened me, and Vinny can be such a charmer. I just didn't know anyone else.

Sass: So tell us what else happened between you two, or three, I guess it is now.

Valentine: And don't spare any details!

Therapist: We're getting away from what Micron was saying.

Hoping: I'm sorry, Micron. Did that make you feel . . . upset?

Micron: No, actually, I never feel anything.

Cosmos: Do you have a horoscope in that daytimer? What's a *non-sequitur* anyway? I never studied Latin, but they have voodoo in Latin America.

Pond: I don't think that's important right now. What makes Micron and his book so special tonight? I could bring a book next week. I've had a simply *horrific* week, and no time to air my concerns.

Cosmos: I sense a split in the karma right now.

Noyd: Is that good or bad? Both, or neither? Can it be harmful?

Cutter: Men are all the same, always me, Me, ME. What about me? Guys seem *so* supportive at the beginning and then they just don't care. Women are the only truly nurturing beings. I hate you all.

Kneady: You're so right! I can't remember all the times I've been let down. You keep pouring yourself out and when you're in need, there's nobody there. I need some support right now to talk about this.

Cosmos: There is an abrupt positive force descending upon us now.

Noyd: But how long will it last? What's going to come next?

Cutter: I can't believe it . . . you really and truly understand me. Now that I think of it, you've always there for me. How could I have been so blind? Now that we have each other, maybe we don't need anyone else. [gets up and sits next to Kneady]

Valentine: [gushes] I'm glad you're feeling better. I'm sooo happy for you. I'll bring a card next week.

Micron: Is this making sense to anyone? Shouldn't you at least do a feasibility study first?

Noyd: Or at least a blood test or something?

Pond: Why not consider other options . . . I think you might find somebody wonderful very nearby.

Hoping: I wish I had the courage to just reach out like that.

Cosmos: The celestial forces strongly oppose this union. The gravitational pull exerted by Kneady's Moon can only slightly alter the course of Cutter's Comet. If a black hole gets hit by the split of an asteroid, a super nova will result.

Sass: Just as he says, it won't work. What's your opinion, Wart?

Wart: If everyone here pairs up . . . I can be alone again.

THERAPIST: Wasn't our agreement to talk about our feelings, not carry them out?

SCUMBAGGLIA: Really honey, not so fast - just like you heard here. I was planning to surprise you. The books were going to be a gift - you know how you've always wanted to study Psychology. It's just that, uh, uh, what's her name here, really gets going once you give her a chance. I was on the way to the hospital when I met a few old *business partners* and got side-tracked. I was on my way back to you.

HOPING: Well, it's back to fantasizing about the personal ads for me.

THERAPIST: We've got just a short time left. Maybe it's time to check in with Wart. What would you like to share with us today?

WART: Uh . . . . nothing.

POND: What do I have to do to get some air time here? Bring a book? Overdose? Say nothing and play with my laces?

NOYD: You've been dominating this group and my life for too long now, Pond. Watch out!

MICRON: Maybe we could make a schedule for next session. I'll bring my stopwatch.

KNEADY: We could extend the time of the session - an eight hour session would only leave sixteen, and then there's my other groups . .

SCUMBAGGLIA: Couldn't we divide into little groups and change partners each week.

CUTTER: Sounds like you do that anyway.

SASS: Small things amuse small minds . . .

VALENTINE: While the smaller ones take note! I read that in *Cosmo*. You sure do learn a lot in those quizzes. Maybe we can all do one. I'll bring in some old issues next week.

POND: Those quizzes are far too simple for this vapid sophisticate.

MICRON: Sometimes I just think you're so neurotic.

SASS: He sure is.

POND: Well if I am, so are you.

THERAPIST: I see we're out of time. Hold that thought, and we'll start there next week.

INDEX

Rapid Psychler Merchandise

• T-Shirts
Grey, with "Rapid Psychler" & logo embroidered on left chest, royal blue letters, red cyclist, high quality cotton.
Sizes M, L, XL, Huge **$22***

• Baseball Hats
Canvas cap, suede peak, embroidered name and logo, leather strap. Available in: **red, tan, black, navy blue, royal blue, purple, green, burgundy.** **$13***

• Gym Shorts
Grey, with black "Rapid Psychler" & black logo embroidered on left leg, drawstring, pockets high quality cotton, perfect match for t-shirts.
Sizes S, M, L, XL **$16***

• Coffee Mugs
White; blue name/red logo opposite handle **$7***

• Key Chains
Silver colored metal, blue name & red logo on one side **$ 5***

• Memo Pads
Beige colored paper, 50 sheets, extra pen included
Style 1: Informal
Style 2: **Formal** **$ 5***

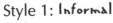

* Free pen with any purchase, postage included

Website: http://www.odyssey.on.ca/psychler

Humor Index